FURTHER SPECULATIONS

Further Speculations

T. E. HULME

Edited by
Sam Hynes

UNIVERSITY OF NEBRASKA PRESS · Lincoln · 1962

LIBRARY

FEB 2 8 1963

UNIVERSITY OF THE PACIFIC

116157

Copyright © 1955 by the University of Minnesota.

All rights reserved. No part of this book may be reproduced in any form without the written permission of the
publisher. Permission is hereby granted to reviewers to
quote brief passages in a review to be printed in a magazine or newspaper.

Manufactured in the United States of America.

Bison Book edition reprinted by arrangement with the
University of Minnesota Press, from whom the clothbound
edition is available.

✓ PREFACE

Although T. E. Hulme's position in the history of twentieth-century thought is now fairly secure, it rests on a relatively small portion of his total work — those essays and notes included in *Speculations*. The present volume makes available a further selection of Hulme's writings, on the theory that the evaluation of a man's work becomes more accurate as the amount of material on which such an evaluation can be made is increased; it contains all of Hulme's work not included in *Speculations* which is likely to be of importance or interest.

This book was prepared in England on a Fulbright Fellowship, and I am indebted to the United States government for that grant. Hulme's friends and relatives have been generous in giving me assistance and information. I am especially grateful to Hulme's sister, Mrs. K. Auchterlonie, for details of Hulme's life and work and for permission to publish the writings contained herein and to quote from unpublished letters. I wish particularly to thank Lord Russell for permission to include the two essays which appear in Appendix A. I have also been helped by conversation and correspondence with Dr. F. S. Adams, Mr. Richard Aldington, Mr. David Bomberg, Mr. Richard Curle, Mr. Ashley Dukes, Mr. T. S. Eliot, Sir Jacob Epstein, Mr. Alfred Haigh, Mr. H. W. Hulme, Professor J. Isaacs, Miss K. Lechmere, Mr. C. K. Ogden, Mr. Ezra Pound, Sir Herbert Read, Mrs. Michael Roberts, Mr. Paul Selver, Dr. Henry Slonimsky, Mr. A. Tattersall, and others.

Most of the essays and poems included here first appeared in the *New Age* (see the Hulme bibliography in Appendix C). The "Essays on War" are from the *Cambridge Magazine*, as are Lord Russell's replies. "Notes on Language and Style" was first published in England in the *Criterion* and in the United States as a

University of Washington Chapbook; the text printed here is a later, fuller version which appeared as an appendix to Michael Roberts' *T. E. Hulme*. Publication here is by kind permission of Mr. Glenn Hughes, holder of the American copyright. The "Diary from the Trenches" has not previously been published. The texts are unchanged from the original sources, with these exceptions: I have silently corrected Hulme's spelling, which was erratic and inconsistent, and I have regularized his rather eccentric punctuation where it seemed necessary in the interests of clarity.

I am indebted to the following copyright holders for permission to quote from the books named: to Sir Jacob Epstein, for *Let There Be Sculpture*; Eyre and Spottiswoode, for Wyndham Lewis' *Blasting and Bombardiering*; Harcourt, Brace & Company, for *The Letters of Ezra Pound* and C. R. W. Nevinson's *Paint and Prejudice*; The McBride Co., for Edwin Muir's *The Present Age*; Ezra Pound, for his "This Hulme Business" and *Polite Essays*; Rinehart and Company, for John Gould Fletcher's *Life Is My Song*; and Sir John Squire, for *The Honeysuckle and the Bee*.

I should also like to thank Mr. Clifford Josephson, of The City College of New York, who has helped me in many ways and to whom for his wide knowledge of the Hulme circle I am considerably indebted.

SAM HYNES

March 1955

For the Bison Book edition I have brought the bibliography of Hulme's writings up to date, and have added a number of recently discovered items, including several essays which Hulme wrote under pseudonyms. In preparing the revision, I have drawn upon recent researches by Mr. Alun Jones, of the University of Hull, and Mr. Wallace Martin, of the University of Toledo.

September 1961 S.H.

INTRODUCTION

I

Intellectual London in the decade before the First World War existed in a curious state of confusion, between two traditions: the moribund Victorian tradition survived feebly in the laureate, Alfred Austin, and in his successor; the new tradition of "modernism," while it was stirring, had not yet found its direction. One might take the year 1909 as symbolic of the situation, for in that year Meredith and Swinburne died, and Ezra Pound published *Personae*, his first important volume. The following year saw the first performance of the Russian Ballet in London, and the first Post-Impressionist exhibition. Subsequent years brought Imagism, Futurism, Vorticism, and all the other manifestations of the general intellectual ferment of the time; it was a time of growing excitement, and of intellectual and artistic anarchy, one of those periods of muddle, as Pound put it, in which "a few of the brightest lads have a vague idea that something is a bit wrong, and no one quite knows the answer."[1]

One of the "brightest lads" was T. E. Hulme. Perhaps more than anyone else at the time, he was aware of the muddle, and he devoted himself to exposing the ideas that he considered responsible — liberalism, romanticism, and soft thinking in general — and to defining the answer as he saw it. Unfortunately, he died before his ideas had gained any currency beyond his own circle, and it is only since his death, or more precisely since the appearance of *Speculations* in 1924, that he has come to be taken seriously. His reputation as a philosopher is almost entirely posthumous, and, like most such posthumous reputations, it is inaccurate enough to merit re-examination.

[1] Ezra Pound, *Polite Essays* (Norfolk, Conn., 1940), p. 9.

FURTHER SPECULATIONS

Hulme first appeared in London in 1904, twenty years old and just sent down from Cambridge. With a small allowance from an aunt to support him, he set about his own education. He took a room in Gower Street, near University College, and enrolled there in classes in botany and physics (he continued the latter study for two years). There is no record of other activities during this period, though presumably he initiated the course of reading in philosophy which he continued for the rest of his life, and he may have begun to write poetry. In 1906 he left London and worked his way to Canada. During his two years in the English capital he had met no one, written nothing, and made no impact whatsoever.

His second visit, however, was more successful. After short stays in Canada and Brussels, he returned to London toward the end of 1907. In 1908 he helped to organize the Poets' Club, and published poems in the club's first annual anthology. In 1909 he began to write for the *New Age*, and in the next seven years published more than forty articles there.

Hulme gained little recognition or influence, however, either through his Poets' Club activities or through his essays. He left the Poets' Club after a year or so; and his essays, while they contain virtually everything he had to say, were not widely read. "London knew little about him," Ashley Dukes recalls, "and his articles on philosophical subjects in the *New Age* and elsewhere made little impression except on students of metaphysics." Pound puts it more succinctly, as one might expect: "Hulme wasn't hated and loathed by the ole bastards, because they didn't know he was there." [2]

Hulme's real influence was direct and personal. Shortly after his withdrawal from the Poets' Club he established his remarkable salon in Frith Street, Soho Square, and it was at these weekly gatherings, which continued until the outbreak of the war, that his position as an intellectual leader was established. "Large numbers of people — writers, painters, philosophers, patrons — used to assemble there and smoke and drink liqueurs; while Hulme, as massive as Johnson, but a non-smoker and a teetotaller, consumed sweets, argued with anybody who was willing to cope with him, or

[2] D. D. Paige, ed., *The Letters of Ezra Pound* (New York, 1950), p. 296.

soliloquized on almost any theme, ancient or modern. Sometimes he talked great sense, sometimes great nonsense: when it was non-sense he was fully aware of the fact, but not all his listeners were. Always his talk was fluent, well-shaped, subtle, various in allusion, full of illuminating simile; he was combative, fiery-tempered, intolerant of those who crossed him, catholic otherwise in his taste in friends, an utter individualist in his habits, and afraid of nobody." This recollection by Sir John Squire [3] is typical of a number of accounts of Hulme's salon. Hulme was a remarkable man, and virtually everyone who has produced memoirs of intellectual life in London during his decade there has included pages on the impact of his personality.[4]

In a circle which included poets, novelists, painters, sculptors, and dramatists, it is curious that Hulme stood at the center, for he was emphatically not an artist by intention. Yet he shared one quality with the artists around him: he was against the conventions and traditions of his time, and in search of new forms, new methods, new attitudes. Hulme's function in his circle was to give this chaotic rebellion direction and purpose, and to make it, in fact, a *reaction*. For Hulme was a reactionary in the most literal sense of the word: he reacted against the values and conventions of his time, and aimed backward, toward values and conventions which he regarded as superior. These included certain conventions which we tend to regard as uniquely modern — geometric art, for example, and irregular, unrhymed verse. Hulme thus helped to produce the odd circumstance in our time of an *avant garde* art at the service of a reactionary philosophy.

Hulme's personality was a curious mixture of intellectual brilliance, aggressiveness, and sheer buffoonery. At school, when he was required to apologize to a mathematics master whom he had

[3] Sir John Squire, *The Honeysuckle and the Bee* (New York, 1938), pp. 155–156.

[4] See, in addition to Squire, Richard Curle, *Caravansary and Conversation* (New York, 1937); Jacob Epstein, *Let There Be Sculpture* (New York, 1940); John Gould Fletcher, *Life Is My Song* (New York, 1937); C. R. W. Nevinson, *Paint and Prejudice* (New York, 1938); Ezra Pound, "This Hulme Business," in Hugh Kenner, *The Poetry of Ezra Pound* (Norfolk, Conn., n.d.); Wyndham Lewis, *Blasting and Bombardiering* (London, 1937).

tormented to tears, he composed the apology in the form of an illuminated manuscript, and *sang* it to the astonished man. Yet he was a brilliant student, and particularly in mathematics; he won two scholarships at his school, and when he was awarded an exhibition at Cambridge, his headmaster wrote: "I feel they have not offered him as much as he deserves." But at Cambridge he took only a third in his first May examinations, and when he was sent down during his second year, for knocking down a policeman, his academic status was apparently almost as low as his disciplinary one.

In London he was equally clownish and bullying. He once held Wyndham Lewis upside down on the railings of Soho Square, and on another occasion, when Henry Simpson, Hulme's principal opponent in the Poets' Club, appeared at one of the Frith Street gatherings, Hulme threatened to knock him down the stairs (which were four flights long). He carried a knuckle-duster with him always, and a lady of whom he was fond recalls that when her conversation became too self-centered he would thump her on the arm with it and exclaim, "Forget you're a personality!"

This last remark is significant, for Hulme's aggressiveness was intimately connected with his theories; he seemed to desire so strenuously that people should see things as he saw them that he would assert his ideas by sheer force if necessary. With Hulme, as with many powerful men, the separation of idea and action was not natural or easy.

But bullying and buffoonery alone could not account for the affection and admiration which Hulme inspired in the people who knew him. He was a good friend — warm, humorous, and loyal. He was open and honest, and a little countrified: Pound has described him as "the outward image of a Yorkshire farmer — the pickwickian Englishman who starts a club." It was this frank, disarming honesty, coupled with a brilliant tough-mindedness which even his enemies admitted, that made him the leader he was.

Hulme's death in 1917 went virtually unnoticed. His friends mourned him, but even the *New Age* did not record the event, nor did the *Cambridge Magazine* include his name in its weekly list of university casualties. Only gradually has Hulme gained general recognition as one of the important figures of his time; now, almost forty years after Hulme's death, Jacob Epstein's valedictory to his friend does not seem hyperbolical: "His death was a loss to England. The fine measuring instrument that was his mind would have . . . shown up many a dark patch of pretence and sham and pomposity, and cleared away many weeds, that have penetrated from being only troublesome undergrowths into the high places in the world of art and literature and philosophy." [5]

II

"I am a heavy philosopher," Hulme was fond of saying (with perhaps an intentional pun, since he weighed two hundred pounds); "I shall write nothing until I am forty." He died before he could fulfill this promise; at thirty-four he had written a great deal *about* philosophy, but nothing that could be called original or "heavy."

In all, Hulme published fourteen essays on philosophers. He had promised Orage, the editor of the *New Age*, an article a week in the "Searchers After Reality" series, but, he wrote to a friend, "I've been too lazy," and he published only three. It was surely this laziness, at least in part, that made him postpone his "heavy philosophy"; he was always confident that he had plenty of time for everything—the philosophy, the ten children he said he wanted, the books and articles. One could make an impressive list from the present volume alone of the works which Hulme announced he would write, but didn't: a series to be called "The Break-Up of the Renaissance," a second essay on de Gaultier, and one on Epstein's drawings, and some further remarks on war. Hulme was inclined to be optimistic about these projected works, and would blandly refer at the end of an article to "next week's" contribution, which he would then not get around to writing.

In addition to the promised articles there were a number of books in various stages of preparation, including a study of Epstein's sculpture and an "Introduction to Bergson." The latter

---

[5] *Let There Be Sculpture*, p. 57.

was apparently offered to at least four publishers; two of them actually advertised it as "in the press," and "ready soon." But it never appeared, I suspect because it was never finished to Hulme's satisfaction. (Herbert Read believes that the core of this book is contained in Hulme's lectures on Bergson, printed in *Speculations* as "The Philosophy of Intensive Manifolds.")

This hand-to-mouth method of writing gives Hulme's philosophical work a fragmentary, repetitious character which is misleading. The critic who comes to Hulme's essays in search of systematic thought is disappointed, and is likely to dismiss him as a plagiarizing pseudo-philosopher. But to do so is to misinterpret his aims, and to misevaluate his achievement.

No one who has read Hulme's complete writings with any objectivity could describe him seriously as a philosopher; to be accurate one should, I think, call him rather a propagandist. This title may be less respectable, but the main point is that it is *different*. Hulme was a man with a mission, but that mission was the publicizing of a philosophical attitude, not the formulation of it. In this respect Hulme is closer to George Bernard Shaw than he is to Karl Marx (to cite two writers whom he considered equally obsolete).

Throughout Hulme's writing life this philosophical attitude remained more or less constant, though it was applied, in turn, to several subjects. Hulme's interests were various, but they tended to be consecutive rather than simultaneous; while he was writing the philosophical essays he wrote nothing else, and the same is true of the essays on art. The literary essays are more difficult to date: the "Lecture" was probably written for delivery in 1908 or 1909, and revised in 1914, when it was again delivered. The Notes seem to be of the same period. The division of essays in this volume by subject is more, therefore, than an editorial convenience: it is roughly chronological, and indicates the way Hulme turned from one subject to another, each of which was, while it interested him, his exclusive concern. This habit of applying a constant system of values to separate subjects in succession accounts in part for the repetitiveness of some of his arguments.

Hulme's propagandizing was at first specifically Bergsonian. Bergson represented to Hulme "a great influence and a great excitement"; he had provided an answer to the nightmare of materialism. To celebrate this achievement, Hulme set about to "execute a war-dance" in the pages of the *New Age*. He reviewed *L'Evolution Créatrice* there in 1909; he wrote the five-part "Notes on Bergson"; and he championed the cause of Bergsonism against all comers in the correspondence columns. In addition he gave public lectures, and he translated (though apparently with considerable help from F. S. Flint) Bergson's *Introduction to Metaphysics*.

In this enthusiasm for Bergson, Hulme was, if only slightly, ahead of his time. ("He had," says Edwin Muir, "in an exaggerated form the snobbery which consists in saying today what a good number of people will be saying tomorrow." [6]) His first article on Bergson appeared in 1909; by 1911 he could refer to a bibliography of two hundred Bergson items. *Creative Evolution* and *Matter and Memory* appeared in English translations in the same year; and by 1914 there were some fifteen books on Bergson in print in English.

Such attention to Bergson by English critics does not, however, imply general approval. Much of the writing about him was antagonistic and derogatory, and Hulme was kept busy defending his master. In 1912, when word got around that Hulme was back at St. John's College, Cambridge, at work on his translation of the *Introduction to Metaphysics*, a correspondent wrote to the *Cambridge Magazine*: "I was somewhat scandalised to learn . . . that the name of this college is to be associated, however remotely, with the translation into English of writings which surely cannot add to its reputation wherever sound philosophy is held in esteem." And this was the general tone of the anti-Bergson letters to the *New Age* as well. Hulme invariably answered these, in his most insulting manner.

Hulme was not, however, the Compleat Bergsonian. As his own ideas developed, he became aware that he was guilty of certain apparent contradictions, particuarly in his simultaneous approval

[6] *The Present Age* (New York, 1940), p. 167.

of Bergson and *L'Action Française* (who were mutually antagonistic), and he paid a special visit to Pierre Lasserre, the philosopher of *L'Action Française*, to discuss the problem. Gradually
the subject of his writing became less Bergson and more the general current of anti-intellectualism developing at the time, of
which Bergson was only one manifestation. This deviation is nowhere more apparent than in the "Notes on Bergson," which stray
from the ostensible subject more than they attend to it, and are, as
Hulme admits, rather a "confession" than an analysis.

In this more general propaganda work, certain central ideas
stand out. They are mostly negative — antirationalism, antiscien-
tism, antiromanticism, and, in a milder way, antihumanism. The
positive side is less developed — it would, no doubt, have appeared
in the promised "heavy philosophy"— though one might mention
his defense of such Christian concepts as Original Sin and the doctrine of the soul.

But it is ridiculous, on the basis of these concepts, to label Hulme
a "neo-scholastic," as Miss Kathleen Nott has done,[7] and to lump
him with Christian apologists like C. S. Lewis and Dorothy Sayers;
for there is nothing formal, nothing deductive in his method, and
there is little enough Christianity in his theories. Hulme regarded
philosophy rather cavalierly as an art, the object of which was "the
drawing of a peculiarly complicated but quite definite line which
will mark you off finally and distinctly from the people you can't
stand." This vigorous taking of sides is Hulme's greatest value — he
spoke out vociferously for the things that he admired, and against
the things he detested, at a time when English thought needed
strong language.

The role of antirational propagandist which Hulme undertook
had certain effects on his writings. He was naturally inclined to
be aggressive, and propagandizing made him more so. He could
be heavily ironic and sarcastic at the expense of his opponents,
particularly in his correspondence, and he argued in a no-holds-
barred fashion that is not always attractive. His treatment of poor
Ludovici (in "Mr. Epstein and the Critics") is appallingly harsh,

[7] In *The Emperor's Clothes* (Bloomington, Ind., 1954).

and his remarks on the characters of Roger Fry and Clive Bell (in the *New Age*, January 13, 1916) seem flatly libellous.

Hulme is also inclined to repeat himself. He once told Pound that all a man's ideas could be written on a half-sheet of note paper, and this does seem true of Hulme, at any rate. The central ideas I have mentioned above appear again and again, with slight variations, throughout these essays. This hammering home of unpopular ideas is the technique of the propagandist, not of the philosopher.

Nevertheless, Hulme's friends agree that he regarded himself as a philosopher. He read philosophy at Cambridge, and even after he was sent down he surreptitiously attended the philosophy lectures of Sorley and McTaggart. He read little but philosophy — "thick German books," Richard Curle recalls — and even had a special case made to carry them with him on trips. Yet he was not, by academic standards, well trained or well read; he remained an amateur, and a number of his contemporaries have recorded his humiliation before the dialectical skill of Henry Slonimsky, a Ph.D. who had been educated in philosophy at Marburg. Dr. Slonimsky recalls that "Hulme was fond of talk and discussion but he was not good at argument, not good at the thrust and parry of debate. He propounded opinion or laid down the law. He was like a boxer who is not very quick in his footwork but packs a powerful punch if and when he can land it."

It is perhaps too severe to dismiss Hulme, as Wyndham Lewis does, as a "mere journalist with a flair for philosophy and art," [8] but one must admit that at his death he was still a philosopher *manqué*. Hulme's contribution to English thought lies in the shape and currency he gave to ideas which were not new, but which needed restatement, rather than in any "new philosophy." He made no claims to original thought: "This, then," he wrote, "is the only originality left to a philosopher — the invention of a new dialect in which to restate an old attitude." Measured by this standard, Hulme stands up well, for the essays in this book do speak in a "new dialect."

[8] *Blasting and Bombardiering*, p. 106.

III

Hulme first appeared to the public, however, not as a philosopher, but as a poet. He was a founder of the Poets' Club (in the club's 1908 prospectus he is listed as the "Honorable Secretary"), and his first published writings were two poems in the club's first annual collection, *For Christmas MDCCCCVIII*. When F. S. Flint criticized this volume in a review in the *New Age*, it was Hulme who replied for the club.

Flint had compared the Poets' Club to recent French poets: "I think of this club and its after-dinner ratiocinations, its tea parties, in 'suave South Audley Street'; and then of Verlaine at the Hotel de ville, with his hat on the peg, as a proof of his presence, but he himself in a cafe hard by with other poets, conning feverishly and excitedly the mysteries of their craft — and I laugh. Those discussions in obscure cafes regenerated, remade French poetry; but the Poets' Club — ! . . . the Poets' Club is death." [9] Hulme replied, in the following issue of the *New Age*, that Flint was a "belated romantic . . . obsessed by the illusion that poets must be addicted to Circean excess and discoloured linen."

From this somewhat unfortunate beginning, a firm friendship developed. Hulme apparently came to share Flint's opinion of the Poets' Club; at any rate by March, 1909 he had resigned his membership, and was meeting each week in a Soho Restaurant with Flint, Francis Tancred, Edward Storer, Florence Farr, and later Ezra Pound and others, to talk about poetry in a less dilettante way. The group had in common only a dissatisfaction with current poetry; they suggested as alternatives at various times *vers libre*, the Japanese *tanka* and *haikai*, "poems in a sacred Hebrew form of which 'this is the house that Jack built' is a perfect model," rhymeless poems like Hulme's "Autumn," and of course Pound's favorite Provençal forms. "In all this," Flint wrote later, "Hulme was the ringleader. He insisted too on absolutely accurate presentation and no verbiage; and he and Tancred . . . used to spend hours each day in the search for the right phrase . . . there was also a lot of talk and practice among us, Storer leading it chiefly, of what we

[9] *New Age*, IV (February 11, 1909), 327.

called the Image. We were very much influenced by modern French symbolist poetry." [10]

In a letter of about this time, Hulme boasted that "all the members of my little 'Secession' club are publishing poems next month. Flint with Mathews, Storer, Pound, etc." Hulme, however, published only five short poems in his lifetime (though he published them often — two each in the 1908 and 1909 Poets' Club annuals, and these four with an additional poem in the *New Age* and in Pound's *Ripostes*), and by the time the war came he had stopped writing poetry altogether. Although he regarded himself as the leader of his "Secession Club," his self-appointed role was not that of the *maître* surrounded by imitators, but rather the official theorist whose ideas other people put into practice. "His evenings were diluted with crap like Bergson," as Pound rather inelegantly put it; [11] and it was to the Bergsonian in him that Imagism appealed.

One of the main threads in all Hulme's writing is his enthusiasm for "the general anti-intellectual movement in philosophy throughout Europe." He was attracted to Bergson's belief that the "flux of phenomena" is real but concepts are not, and to his emphasis on intuition as a means of knowledge, the idea that "by intellect one can construct approximate models" but "by intuition one can identify oneself with the flux." Imagism is Hulme's application of these principles to the realm of language: abstractions and conventional locutions are "approximate models," but images identify one with the flux. The former constitute prose, the latter poetry. "There are, roughly speaking," he says, "two methods of communication, a direct, and a conventional language. The direct language is poetry, it is direct because it deals in images. The indirect language is prose, because it uses images that have died and become figures of speech." Prose, being conceptual, is treacherous — it does not correspond to reality. Poetry must therefore carry the whole load of "real" communication: it is the only language that can legitimately be described as meaningful. Thus all writing tends to

[10] *The Egoist*, II (May 1, 1915), 71.
[11] "This Hulme Business," in Hugh Kenner, *The Poetry of Ezra Pound*, p. 308.

be reduced to "objective correlatives," "visual" language purged of "counters."

"Direct language is poetry, because it deals in images." The "Notes on Language and Style" expand this statement: direct language is the *only* poetry, and imagery is the only direct language. The poet starts with an image, which in turn creates other images, and so on: "His sincerity may be measured by the number of his images."

Hulme's remarks on meter are largely a corollary of these views on language; they extend his passion for accuracy to the sound of verse. Imagistic poetry is visual and arresting; its "delicate pattern of images and colour" must not be deadened by "the heavy crude pattern of rhetorical verse." Regular meter is oral and hypnotic, and therefore incompatible with the aims of Imagism.

All this may seem rather like throwing out the baby with the bath by reducing poetry to too bare minimums. But at the time Hulme was writing, such reduction was necessary. English poetry had degenerated at the end of the nineteenth century into "counter-language"; Imagism was a restoration of its natural concreteness and specificity. The best of the poets who were touched by it — notably Pound and T. S. Eliot — went on from there. But the theories of the Imagists were a necessary starting point.

Credit for formulating those theories must go to Hulme. His "Lecture on Modern Poetry" was first delivered in 1908 or 1909, some four years before Pound and Flint laid down their own set of principles in Harriet Monroe's *Poetry*. Hulme was less specific and less doctrinaire than his two friends — he did not try to create a poetic decalogue, and his remarks seem restrained and tentative beside Pound's Mosaic imperatives — but he is more important. Hulme gives the reasons why, the principles behind the practices which Flint and Pound advocated.

Hulme's theories had little immediate effect, largely because they were first delivered to third-rate poets and were not published; Pound could, in fact, refer in his "Prefatory Note" to Hulme's poems to "the forgotten School of 1909." When Hulme gave the lecture again in 1914, the result was equally negative; Hulme's platform presence was that of a frightened schoolboy, and no one could understand him.

But Flint had understood him, and so had Pound, and through Pound particularly, tireless evangelist for the new art that he was, Hulme's theories became current, and changed the face of English poetry. One can scarcely exaggerate Pound's importance to modern poetry, and much honor and credit are due him, but the originator of Imagism was clearly Hulme. By discrediting thought as the source and logic as the method of poetry, he reinstated physical experience as the core of the poem, and imagery as the texture.

In the light of his theories, Hulme's poems are rather disappointing. Poetic revolutions, particularly in their beginnings, are often braver in theory than in practice. One finds in the Fragments collected here much that the Imagists were revolting against — the poetic interjections ("Oh eager page! Oh velvet sand!"), the inversions, the personifications, the clichés, and even an echo of Tennyson. Like many theorists, Hulme was better at formulating theories than he was at applying them. One particularly "poetic" line of Hulme's, which read

> And in the flash of gold heels on the pavement grey

in the Poets' Club volume of 1909, was changed at the insistence of Pound, first to

> And in a flash of gold heels on the pavement hard

and finally to

> And in a flash of gold heels on the hard pavement,

Hulme, with Yeats and Eliot, thus being among the poets who have been improved by Pound's advice.

The fact that Hulme published only five poems has misled some critics into thinking that he wrote only five, and that these are therefore to be regarded as mere *jeux d' esprit*. The fragments included here refute that notion; not only did Hulme write seven times as much as he published, but he carefully worked and reworked images in his "search for the right phrase." On page 217 one can see the steps by which

> Oh God, narrow the sky,
> The old star-eaten blanket,
> Till it fold me round in warmth

becomes "The Embankment," as finally published; and there are other examples. Hulme is not a major Imagist poet, nor did he wish to be; but neither is he simply a poetic joker with a happy facility in making verse. "Poet-philosopher" describes him best, and indeed for Hulme the two terms are not easily distinguishable. In his mind, the distinction which he had set up between poetry and prose had an exact equivalent in philosophy: there are "visual" philosophers and "counter" philosophers, and all his guns are ranged against the latter. Thus his two roles are simply different manifestations of the same convictions about the nature of knowledge and the limited possibilities of human communication.

Hulme's prose style is in many ways more "imagistic" than his poetry. There is in it a more consistent use of direct language, and an absolute avoidance of abstract, involved "counter" language. His arguments are arguments by imagery, and not by the conventional symbolic language of philosophy. His most characteristic phrase is, "I can perhaps put this more clearly in a metaphor," and for him, at least, though perhaps not always for the reader, this is true; for Hulme's mind progressed, like a poet's, by analogies. "A man cannot write," he says, "without seeing at the same time a visual signification before his eyes. It is the image which precedes the writing and makes it firm."

Part of this "imagism" is perhaps due to the influence of Bergson's style, which is also very visual (Hulme discusses Bergson's metaphors at some length in his essay "Bax on Bergson"): but more fundamentally it represents Hulme's deep distrust of words, as counters removed from the "cinders" of reality. He saw knowledge as analogies: "the history of philosophy," he says, "should be written as that of seven or eight metaphors."

Hulme's prose images, often drawn from common, rude sources, and his style, alternately aggressively abrupt and disarmingly conversational, may make Hulme seem less "serious" than he really is.

He was, as he often confessed, a lazy man, and was consequently a deadline writer. Friends recall him rushing off first drafts of essays to the *New Age*, and the mark of that haste is on his work. "His literary remains," Wyndham Lewis has remarked, "are incredibly badly written," [12] and this is often true, though the remark would carry more weight if it came from a writer less barbarous himself. But in even the worst writing there is a vigor and vividness which is the product of Hulme's "physical" philosophy, and which makes his prose lively and lucid, and, at its best, persuasive.

IV

Painters and sculptors were, from the beginning, important members of Hulme's circle. To the Frith Street Friday evenings came Epstein and Gaudier-Brzeska, Wyndham Lewis, Harold Gilman, Spencer Gore, Charles Ginner, Robert Bevan, and C. R. W. Nevinson — the bright young men of the various "modern" groups then forming. One regular recalls that even Walter Sickert came once, "as a consolation prize for George Moore, who didn't." The salon was, if anything, more arty than literary.

This seems to reflect to a degree Hulme's own interests. He talked much about art, but little about literature, at his salon. He was, to the limit of his means, a patron of modern art; he bought two carvings in flenite from Epstein, paying him a pound a week and recording each payment carefully in a little black notebook; and he gave his sister a Gilman painting for a wedding present, admonishing her to give it back if she didn't like it, because he did (she still has it). Even his celebrated knuckle-duster is a kind of abstraction carved in solid brass, which he commissioned Gaudier to make.

Hulme's writings on art, however, cover a very short period, from December 1913 to July 1914. He was just back from Germany, where he had come in contact with the German aestheticians Volkelt and Lipps and the art historian Wilhelm Worringer. The experience had been a catalytic one; it had helped him to organize his random thoughts into an aesthetic which suited his philosophy.

[12] *Blasting and Bombardiering*, p. 107.

From Volkelt and Lipps Hulme borrowed the *Einfühlung-ästhetik* which he defined in a letter to Edward Marsh as " 'feeling oneself into the object.' We 'feel ourselves' in mere lines, for example, ourselves moving along the line, so that if the motion would be agreeable we call the line beautiful . . ." This idea appealed to Hulme because it made the aesthetic experience a motor process, not a rational one; he used it in his lecture "Modern Art and Its Philosophy" (*Speculations*, pp. 73-110) in January 1914. Among Hulme's unpublished notes is another borrowing from Volkelt, a long précis of his argument against the existence of a separate "aesthetic emotion"; the argument appears in this volume in the essay on David Bomberg.

But Hulme's greatest debt was to Worringer, whom he met in Berlin in 1913. Worringer provided the entire framework of Hulme's theory of art — the division of art into vital and nonvital, the relating of that division to the particular society's attitude toward the world, the view that all art since the Renaissance composes a single "vital" period. Hulme cheerfully acknowledged the debt: "What follows," he says in "Modern Art and Its Philosophy," "is practically an abstract of Worringer's views." And so it is.

We may understand the importance of Hulme's contact with German art criticism if we compare his ideas about Renaissance art expressed in the present essays and *Speculations* — "these sloppy dregs," etc. — with those in a note written to his sister from Italy in 1911: "This church in Assisi [he writes] is very interesting for it was practically the beginning of all modern art. It was in the decoration here that people for the first time began to paint things they saw. Instead of the kind of conventional patterns which had done for Christ and the Saints for about 10 centuries . . . Of course it doesn't look much, but when you see the kind of thing that came before it you realize how wonderful it was." This is pretty straight John Addington Symonds; obviously, between 1911 and 1913 Hulme's ideas on "conventional patterns" underwent a radical change. The cause of the change was Worringer.

One important thing which Hulme did *not* derive from Worringer, however, is his *attitude* toward Renaissance and pre-Renaissance art. Worringer is objective, scholarly, and Germanic — there is no emotional loading in his writing. Characteristically, Hulme borrowed the intellectual construction from Worringer, but made it do his own propaganda work, fitted it into the framework of his philosophy. Art was not for Hulme an end in itself — it was evidence, grist for his philosophic mill. He came to art by way of philosophy. "I start," he says, "with the conviction that the Renaissance attitude is breaking up and then illustrate it by the change in art, and not vice versa. First came the reaction against Renaissance philosophy, and the adoption of the attitude which I said went with the geometrical art."

By the end of 1913 Hulme had developed his ideas on modern art well enough to schedule a lecture on the subject for the end of January. He may even have been at work on it, though such foresight would have been out of character. Then the reviews of Epstein's show appeared, and Hulme made a premature debut as an art critic in his "very hurried protest," "Mr. Epstein and the Critics."

The debut was not a success. Readers were too shocked by the violence of Hulme's attack on Ludovici to notice the defense of the flenite sculpture and of sculptural archaism in general. A number of letters appeared in subsequent issues of the *New Age* condemning Hulme's "punch-in-the-nose" methods of argument. Only Wyndham Lewis supported Hulme.

The five essays on art included here are all topical, and inspired by a particular event — an exhibition, a bad review, a published essay. But they are more than that, for Hulme, lacking, as he says, the gift for the prolonged gesture of admiration, could only criticize by "getting up an argument." The sum of these arguments is a sketch of Hulme's aesthetic, as well as a contribution to the history of English art in the years before World War I.

To understand the importance of Hulme's writings on art one must recapture the artistic climate in the England of his time. Only three years before Hulme's first essay appeared, Roger Fry had introduced Gauguin and Van Gogh to a reluctant English public in the first Post-Impressionist show — probably the most controversial, most criticized exhibition in English art history. Two years before that Epstein had unveiled his "Strand statues," and had been roundly condemned as a pornographer by the critics in the public press. English art was firmly in the hands of the Royal Academicians, and the new academicians of the New English Art Club.

The London Group, organized in 1913, was an attempt to break this academic control. It was an amalgamation of several modernist groups — "all the warring elements of Impressionists, Post-Impressionists, Neo-Primitives, Vorticists, Cubists and Futurists," as C. R. W. Nevinson, one of the original members, later described it.[13] The Group originally included Sickert, Epstein, Wyndham Lewis, Nevinson, Bomberg, and a number of others. Roger Fry and Vanessa Bell were admitted later, and some of the original members dropped out.

Hulme's relation to the London Group was very close; its members were in fact precisely those artists who came round to Frith Street on Friday nights. When he came to edit his series of "Contemporary Drawings" for the *New Age*, Hulme selected London Group artists almost exclusively, and announced firmly: ". . . the series includes everyone in England who is doing interesting work of this character. In view of the amount of capable work continually being produced it is difficult to realise that the only part of this which is important, that which is preparing the art of the next generation, may be the work of a relatively quite small group of artists." Like many similar pronouncements by Hulme, this is somewhat hyperbolical; for Hulme, when he was publicizing the ideas he approved of, used the publicist's methods. All his enterprises tended to be The Greatest Show on Earth.

But Hulme was more than a publicist — he was also a serious thinker. He understood what abstract art was about, at a time when not many non-artists did, and he tried in his essays to formulate a theory of art that would contain and explain it. In the perspective of our time, when Cubist art is accepted in public galleries

[13] *Paint and Prejudice*, p. 63.

and Van Gogh hangs in the most bourgeois parlor, some of Hulme's remarks may seem obvious. But in 1914 it was original and even courageous to say flatly, "The pleasure you are intended to take . . . is a pleasure not in representation but in the relations between certain abstract forms." This was a new notion of what happened in art, and like most of Hulme's ideas it was quite contrary to popular taste.

"It was mainly as a theorist in the criticism of the fine arts that Hulme would have distinguished himself, had he lived," says Wyndham Lewis. "And I should undoubtedly have played Turner to his Ruskin." [14] This remark is inaccurate on two counts. Hulme's comments on Lewis' paintings (see below, p. 131) do not indicate any particular admiration, and this is confirmed by Hulme's friends. As for Hulme as a theorist in art criticism, there is little evidence that art was an important interest in the last years of his life. He did apparently work at a book on Epstein, but whatever he had completed of it disappeared after his death, and no one, so far as I can discover, ever saw a page of it. An outline for a book on theories of art exists (see *Speculations*, Appendix B), but only in a sketchy and undeveloped form. In 1914 Hulme's attention was distracted from art, and he turned to another facet of that single comprehensive image of the world which would have emerged in the end as his philosophy. Art had been simply one way of getting at the Truth; war, when it came, offered him another.

v

"I have heard from Hulme when he was at Havre on the way to the trenches," Gaudier-Brzeska wrote to Pound in 1915; "it will change him a bit from the comfort he had at Frith Street." [15] And so it did. Hulme had entered the army immediately and enthusiastically when war was declared; he had persuaded his friends to volunteer (Richard Aldington approached the Honourable Artillery Company at Hulme's suggestion, but was rejected); and he had gone to France like an eager tourist, pleased and excited by the new scenes and experiences.

[14] *Blasting and Bombardiering*, p. 106.
[15] Quoted in Ezra Pound, *Gaudier-Brzeska* (London, 1916), p. 65.

But it was not long before the comfortable London philosopher who considered processions the highest form of art and the sight of soldiers "a symbolic philosophic drama" had become the mud-caked and knowledgeable infantryman, with no illusions about glory. The process of conversion was a rapid one — Hulme was in France less than four months on his first tour of duty. In April 1915 he was wounded by a bullet which passed through his arm and killed the man behind him. Soon after he was returned to England for convalescent treatment.

Hulme's diary of those months in France, written in the form of letters to his aunt, provides a vivid record of the process by which a poet-philosopher becomes a soldier. In some ways the diary is the enlisted counterpart of Wilfrid Owen's letters and of Sassoon's *Memoirs of an Infantry Officer*. Like Owen and Sassoon, Hulme saw war with a poet's eyes, but, because he was of the "other ranks" it was a different war; any ex-enlisted man will recognize in the diary the familiar pattern of rush and wait, the command confusion, the discomfort, the boredom, and the horror. If there is less horror here than in Owen or Sassoon, it is because Hulme was a different sort of man — lazier, calmer, more laconic, more humorous, and therefore better fitted to the common soldier's life. Richard Aldington recalls that Hulme "was pleased that the H.A.C. rejected me on the 5th August 1914 because he said 'war was not for sensitive men.' He thought himself tough. He was, I think." The insensitiveness is obviously a military pose, but the toughness was genuine, and with it went the good soldier's qualities of fatalistic resignation, detachment, and ironic amusement, which run through the diary and give it a saving sanity.

It is always obvious, though, that this is no ordinary soldier writing. One notices first of all the wealth of sharp visual perceptions — the *feeling* of war caught in brief, living images: horsemen against the sky, the fireworks of shell fire. Hulme's poetic theories were clearly developed from, or at least supported by, his natural way of seeing. It was the imagery of existence that appealed to him.

The images stand out more vividly because of the general flatness of the narration — the poet juts through the persona of the common soldier. Hulme's prose style was never jeweled or elegant; here, in his private correspondence, it is often loose, colloquial, and hasty. But it is always honest; the same honesty that drove Hulme to advocate a poetry of exact, precise imagery moved him to qualify constantly his own colorful descriptions: "In reality there is nothing picturesque about it. It's the most miserable existence you can conceive of."

At the same time, one phrase occurs again and again: "It is curious . . ." Hulme the Imagist was sensitive to the incongruity of war, to the way war distorts ordinary peacetime reality. "It's curious how the mere fact that in a certain direction there really are the German lines seems to alter the feeling of a landscape." The private soldier soon ceased to see war as picturesque, but the poet went on seeing it as odd.

Hulme's friends remember that he returned from the front changed — more tolerant, less violent, less aggressive. The war had mellowed him, they thought (though this is not apparent in his writing — his attack on Bell, one of the most violent pieces he wrote, appeared in January 1916). He spent some time in a convalescent hospital, and then the War Office seemed to lose him. He stayed in London, pulling strings to get a commission or a billet in the Naval Air Service, and hanging around the Café Royal, talking to his friends. Ezra Pound made some of that conversation into a poem: [16]

POEM
Abbreviated from the Conversation of Mr. T. E. H.

Over the flat slope of St Eloi
A wide wall of sandbags.
Night,
In the silence desultory men
Pottering over small fires, cleaning their mess-tins:
To and fro, from the lines,
Men walk as on Piccadilly,
Making paths in the dark,
Through scattered dead horses,
Over a dead Belgian's belly.

[16] Ezra Pound, *Umbra* (London, 1920), p. 125.

> The Germans have rockets. The English have no rockets.
> Behind the lines, cannon, hidden, lying back miles.
> Before the line, chaos :
>
> My mind is a corridor. The minds about me are corridors.
> Nothing suggests itself. There is nothing to do but keep on.

(This sounds like authentic Hulme; the dead Belgian appears on p. 170 of the diary, and Hulme complained of the rocket situation in one of his War Notes in the *New Age*.)

Hulme saw that there was "nothing to do but keep on," and in time he returned to the war. But he went back as an officer in the artillery: "I have had my share of the trenches," he wrote to Marsh, and he warned his younger brother against the infantry. In the artillery one sat nine miles back and made war by mathematics; this suited Hulme, who was both lazy and mathematical (he was said to have been writing a book on gunnery at the time of his death). He went back because he was, he said, "in favor of this war," but he also wrote, "I don't have an ounce of bellicosity left." His reasons for returning were intellectual, not emotional.

While Hulme was "lost" in London, he wrote two remarkable series of articles for the *New Age* — the "Notebook of T. E. H.," which appears in *Speculations* as "Humanism and the Religious Attitude," and the "War Notes," which he wrote under the *nom de guerre* of "North Staffs." The latter began in November 1915 and continued almost weekly until Hulme returned to duty in March 1916. Shortly after the first essay appeared, C. K. Ogden, then editor of the *Cambridge Magazine*, invited Hulme to contribute to him "anything he would like to see said." Hulme submitted a series of essays derived from, but not identical with, the *New Age* series on war. The essays included here are those from the *Cambridge Magazine*, which are briefer, more concise, more theoretical and less topical than those in the *New Age*.

At the time that Hulme was writing his first War Notes, Bertrand Russell, then England's most publicized pacifist, was addressing audiences at Caxton Hall, Westminster, on "Principles of Social Reconstruction." Hulme attended some of these lectures, and soon

set Russell up as the specific target for his general remarks on pacifism. The balance of the series was spiced with vigorous attacks on
Russell's "faded Rousseauism" and "progressivism." Russell's more
restrained rejoinders appear in this book as Appendix A.

The Essays on War argue two questions: (1) Is the present war
justifiable? and (2) Can *any* war be "good"? Hulme answers "yes"
to both questions. He argues the first question from topical points
which may seem dated (though they have a certain permanent rele-
vance to the European political situation); but he argues the other
from his total view of man and the world, and in so doing clarifies
and develops the terms of his own philosophy.

To the reader who knows *Speculations,* certain strains in the
Essays on War will be familiar: the attacks on romanticism, the
belief in Original Sin, and the antirational view of the world as
a "cindery chaos." Other beliefs, while consistent with and im-
plicit in the *Speculations* essays, are here enunciated for the first
time. Hulme is, for example, more specific about the necessity of
discipline: ". . . just as man is not naturally good, and has only
achieved anything as the result of a certain discipline, the 'good'
here does not preserve itself, but is also preserved by discipline."
Perhaps because of his military experience, Hulme had become
more explicitly authoritarian.

This authoritarianism is also evident in his discussion of ethics;
he flatly asserts the existence of absolute values which exist outside reason, and are universal. "Values are not relative only to life,
but are objective and absolute, and many of them are above life.
This ethic is not, therefore, bound to condemn all sacrifices of life."
The values "above life," to which Hulme's approval of the war
committed him, are Sorel's "heroic values"; Hulme defends them
against humanistic pacifism.

It is largely on the basis of this authoritarianism that Hulme is
often called a Fascist or "proto-Fascist." The former term is obviously a meaningless anachronism, but we must give more careful
attention to the latter. Hulme made few remarks of a purely political nature in his writing, but the general contours of his political
philosophy are fairly clear: he disliked "liberal, hedonist, pacifist

democracy," he denied the possibility of progress, and he admired authority and military efficiency and "organic" (i.e., stable) societies. Hulme's philosophical sources were, when they were political at all, right-wing; his particular admiration for Georges Sorel is expressed in his introduction to *Reflections on Violence*, and elsewhere he speaks approvingly of "the brilliant set of Neo-Royalist writers grouped around L'Action Française." To these sources we might add Nietzsche, though his influence is less emphatic.

All this, however, adds up to at most a very embryonic Fascism, and we should be wiser, I think, to use Hulme's own term: "I am more than a conservative," he once told a friend, "I am a reactionary." The less attractive characteristics of Fascism — the extreme nationalism, the racial bigotry, the glorification of violence — are absent from Hulme's work. According to Ashley Dukes, Hulme's conversation was more extreme than his writing (he advocated, Dukes recalls, a national costume for all Jews); but Hulme liked to shock his friends, and we should not take such notions any more seriously, I think, than his remark to John Gould Fletcher that "his chief pleasure in life lay in reading Immanuel Kant's *Critique of Pure Reason* while lying prone, at full length, in a well-filled, warm bathtub." [17]

Hulme's disapproval of democracy was partial, never absolute. He disliked some current manifestations of the democratic state, and he found the masses unattractive, but he did not simply reject democracy as a political theory: "No theory," he wrote, "that is not fully moved by the conception of justice asserting the equality of men, and which cannot offer something to all men, deserves or is likely to have any future."

Hulme represented a current of thought in reaction against the prevailing stream of progressive liberalism — a current which included Yeats, Pound, and Eliot in England, and in France Péguy, Maurras, and Sorel. The political issue of the reaction has sometimes been deplorable: of Hulme's own "Frith Street Gang," Pound broadcast for Mussolini, Wyndham Lewis wrote a book in praise of Hitler, and Ramiro de Maeztu died for Franco. But re-

[17] Fletcher, *Life Is My Song*, p. 76.

action is not necessarily Fascism, and the politics of T. S. Eliot seem to me a more logical development of Hulme's ideas than the politics of Pound.

The absolute reversal of the current of English thought in politics, literature and art which Hulme anticipated has not occurred — the Renaissance has not broken up. But there does now exist a legitimate countercurrent, opposed to the liberalism and romanticism which are our legacy from the nineteenth century, and vigorously asserting the values of conservatism and classicism (or, like Mr. Eliot, "classicist, royalist and anglo-catholic"). For this countercurrent in England Hulme is almost entirely responsible. He did not invent it, certainly — the charge that Hulme lacks originality is accurate, though irrelevant — but he was the first to assert it vigorously in England, and he provided the intellectual foundations, and prepared the audience, for the "reactors" who followed him.

TABLE OF CONTENTS

FURTHER SPECULATIONS

APPENDIXES AND INDEX

PHILOSOPHICAL ESSAYS

SEARCHERS AFTER REALITY
1 · Bax

When the clown at the circus puts his head through the paper disc, he appears framed in a ring of torn paper. This is the impression I have of Mr. Bax's position after reading the "Roots of Reality." * He has certainly put his head through a previously unpenetrated system, but he still remains surrounded by the ragged edges of the medium he has destroyed. His own original views appear surrounded with pieces of Kantian tissue-paper. There is no doubt that Bax has brought a really new idea into philosophy — the assertion of the ultimate reality of the alogical. But, alarmed at his own audacity, he seeks to make it perfectly respectable by giving it as a companion a curious mixture of all the German idealists. The frame in which he sets his new conception is antique and thoroughly orthodox, but it ill accords with the central picture.

He has made a brilliant and powerful attack from a new point of view on the Hegelian panlogism. (Why does Mr. Bax pedantically employ the word pallogistic instead of the generally employed panlogistic?) This attack, in its lucidity and directness, is infinitely superior to the fumbling controversial method of Mr. Schiller and the pragmatists, but its significance only comes out when one sees it in its proper perspective in the general movement of European philosophy.

This modern metaphysical movement seems as strange to the layman as the preaching of the simple life would do to a savage. You must have been sophisticated and have sinned before you can experience the relief of repentance. You must first have been a Hegelian before you can get enthusiastic over the general anti-

* Ernest Belfort Bax, *The Roots of Reality* (London, 1907).

3

intellectualist movement in philosophy throughout Europe. Even Nietzsche admitted that perhaps it was better to have had the Wagnerian disease and to have recovered from it than to have merely been continuously healthy and unconscious. (The comedy of it is, however, that the anti-intellectualists are generally so lucid that a class of reader is drawn in which has not previously sinned with Hegel.) The disease in this case is intellectualism. The method of all systems of philosophy, when all the decorations and disguises are stripped off, ultimately resolves itself to this. One takes a little part of known reality and asserts dogmatically that it alone is the true analogy by which the cosmos is to be described. Good philosophy then consists in the choice of a good microcosm, just as surely as genius results from the avoidance of rashness and haste in selecting one's grandparents.

Intellectualism takes a bad analogy, logic and the geometric sciences, which are in essence identical, and asserts that the flux of phenomena which apparently contradicts this is not real, and can really be resolved into logical concepts. Chance is abolished, everything is reduced to law, so that omnipotent intelligence, able to seize the entire universe at a glance could construct from that its past and future. Bax, on the contrary, asserts that there is an alogical element which cannot be reduced to law.

The great antithesis before modern metaphysics is thus the old one between the flux of phenomena and the concepts by which we analyse it in thought. Which term of the antithesis is real? Here I distinguish four solutions. The Hegelian: that only the concept is real; positive significance only attaches to thought or relational elements as opposed to its alogical terms; the other side of the antithesis is argued away. The Bergsonian: that only the flux is real, the concepts being mere practical dodges. The pragmatist: that the concepts are only purposive instruments, but the purpose and will constitute the only reality. Then the Baxian: that both are real, and that the logical is like a serpent engaged in continually swallowing the endless meal of the flux, a task in which it can never succeed. "Reality is the inseparable correlation of these two ultimate terms." There are thus two roots of reality.

Of these four solutions I am here concerned more particularly with the distinction between that of Bax and that of Bergson. There are two ways in which a man may be led to the denial of the possibility of including the alogical under the logical. If one emphasises the character of the flux as motion one sees that the static concepts can never represent it. So Bergson. If one emphasises the infinity of detail in the immediately given, its grittiness, its muddiness, and hence the impossibility of pulling it in the smooth, tidy, geometrical concepts, one arrives at Bax. This difference affects their view of the function of concepts in the flux. This is a rough analogy for Bergson's view. When I see in the changing shape of flame something which resembles a saw edge I may solely for the purposes of human communication call it that. But I have not by that altered the nature of the flame. So with concepts and universals of all kinds. We envisage the flux in certain static geometric shapes entirely for practical purposes, which have no ultimate reality at all. Proteus is god, and he cannot be seized in any formula. Bax, on the other hand, assumes that these forms which describe the flux have some ultimate reality. They do really contain and control the alogical as the hexagons in the comb contain honey. He refuses, however, to go to the length of the intellectualists, who would say that in the last resort matter is abolished and absorbed in form. Bax's position is that there is always something left over, that when you dip the net of concepts and universals some of the reality always escapes through the meshes. He thus occupies a curious midway position which I think will in the end be found untenable.

Here we get to the actual frontier position of modern speculation. The intellectualists, the lay theologians, having been violently expelled from their temple and the final admission made that logical thought is by its nature incapable of containing the flux of reality, what remains? Are we to resign ourselves to ignorance of the nature of the cosmos, or is there some new method open to us?

Bergson says that there is — that of intuition. From a common origin life has divided in two directions; the "élan vital," in its struggle towards the maximum of indeterminism, has employed two methods, the one instinct, the other intellect; one exemplified in animals, the other in man. (Intellect being understood here in a definite way as the capacity for making models of the flux, of reasoning in logic.) But round the central intellect in man there is a fringe, a penumbra of instinct. This instinct, or, as it is better to call it here, intuition, is the faculty that we must use in attempting to grasp the nature of reality. One must carefully guard here against a sentimental use of the word. Bergson gives it a precise technical sense. By intellect one can construct approximate models, by intuition one can identify oneself with the flux.

Here Bax stops and parts company with Bergson. Philosophy, he says, "may not be inaptly defined as the last word of the logical." It is impossible for it to get beyond universals or abstractions. Both realise the unsatisfactory nature of the dry land of concepts on which philosophy has lived, and would not be content with it. Both set out and discovered the turbulent river of reality. Bergson jumped in and swam. Bax looked at it, then came back and merely recorded that the land was not all, that there was a river on which man could not walk, a reality that the logical reason will never grasp entirely. But he forgot that walking is not the only method of progression, and that the logical method of thought may not be the only way of understanding reality.

By many toilsome ways Bax, like Moses, leads us to the Promised Land; then, having privately surveyed it, informs us that, after all, it isn't really interesting, tells us to go back again, but always to bear in mind that there is such a place. That is, the intellect is still for him the only way of getting at Reality, though we are always to remember that by its very nature it can never reach it. What did he see in the promised land of the alogical which prevented him from wandering there? We can only surmise maliciously that somewhere in its pleasant valleys he saw a woman. Is not intuition too dangerous a process for an anti-feminist to suggest as the ultimate philosophic process?

SEARCHERS AFTER REALITY
II · Haldane

The Oriental despot is addressed by his followers as Most High, King of Kings, Son of Heaven, epithets having no accurate or precise meaning, but signifying a general state of admiration. If a western metaphysician had by some unhappy chance been enslaved among the circle of courtiers I feel sure that he would have given praise in the words, "Oh, Ultimately Real." Philosophers desire that their particular obsession shall be dignified with the name Reality as jealously as the hero of Maupassant's "Decoré" desired the badge of the Legion d'honneur, and the desired end is often attained in just as surprising a way. Reality is merely the complimentary word that metaphysicians apply to what they particularly admire. At the present moment they go roughly into two classes, the admirers of Rest and of Motion, and strenuously and ingeniously they labour to identify their preference with Reality.

It is clear from his book * that Mr. Haldane admires order and organization, and from this his metaphysic can be deduced. The flux of sensation by itself would be uninhabitable and uncomfortable. Reaction from its confusion may take two forms: the practical, which requires a mechanism to enable it to move easily in fixed paths through the flux and change, and the aesthetic which shrinks from any contact with chaos. The practical attitude, by the universals of thought, arranges the flux in some kind of order, as the police might arrange a crowd for the passage of a procession. The next step for the man who admires order is to pass from the practical to the aesthetic, to assert that what puts

* Richard Burdon Haldane, *The Pathway to Reality* (London, Vol. I, 1903; Vol II, 1904).

order into the confused flux of sensation alone is real, the flux itself being mere appearance. The mind that loves fixity can thus find rest. It can satisfy its aesthetic shrinking from the great unwashed flux by denying that it is real. This has proved an easy step for Mr. Haldane to take. The constant burden of his book is that Reality is a system; further, that it is an intellectual system, and the flux only has reality in so far as it fits into this system. One might caricature his position by saying that he believes in the ultimate reality of the police, or that a guide-book is superior to an actual visit, for in the former one has sensation systematized.

This is Mr. Haldane's particular trend in prejudice, but in philosophy the correct etiquette is to give excuses for the end we fix beforehand, and one must examine the exact method by which he justifies his assertion that Reality can be identified with Reason. His method and intent, like that of every other philosopher, are anthropomorphic, and narrowly so, for he wishes to prove not only that the cosmos is of the same nature as man, but of a particular faculty of man — the logical Reason. The task does not at first look promising; you are faced with a hard and fast objective world. How are you to explain this as being of the nature of mind, let alone of reason? The method adopted is an old familiar one. Like all idealists since Berkeley, he uses the formula "esse is percipi" as an acid wherewith to break up the apparent solidity of the objective world to a fluid form more suitable for digestion in a spiritual system. Once having reduced it to a flabby condition of this kind, he is in a better position to prove his second step, that it is moulded entirely by the laws of the intellect. There still remains the unfortunate particular, the alogical — the untameable tiger that arouses Mr. Bax's affection. How is it to be murdered that we may at last get a civilised and logical system into the cosmos? If, as Mr. Haldane does, you start off with a sacred conviction that only what is fixed is real, the procedure is quite simple. The immediate sensations of the moment are transient and have no abiding reality; they are different in different people. Reality must consist in the common system, the objective world, that which other people become aware of, when, and on the same ground as

I do, in Mill's permanent possibilities of sensation. The next step consists in proving that this common system, this objective world, is entirely a construction of the intellect. The reason of the actuality of the world round me, the reason why I cannot alter it by my will, lies in the fact that my mind, like the mind of other people, is compelled to think the world according to a system of conceptions. Reality consists in an objective system, and that objective system consists of what we are obliged to think. The nature of the world is thus rational, "Esse is intelligi." The universals of thought are the true foundations of the world. Thought creates things rather than things thought. The phenomenon of experience gets its fixity and definiteness from the universals of reflection. "It is only in the intelligible notions which are embedded in sensation and which give them substance that these sensations have reality." I admit this in so far as it means that the flux is reduced to a practical order for personal life by the intellect, and made habitable, but I refuse to take the further step of saying that it is the only reality. When unhappy proximity forces me to survey Edwardian architecture I am quite aware that what gives fixity to the extraordinary chaos of varied marble is the hidden steel girder, but I cannot console myself, as Mr. Haldane does, by saying that the steel alone is real and that the marble is a passing dream. I am prepared to admit that my mind is compelled to "think" the world according to a system of concepts, but Mr. Haldane and the Hegelians here attribute some transcendental value to the word "think." It does not follow that because the logical faculty is compelled to think in that way that for other purposes other method might be more valid. Thinking might be, and probably is, a method of distorting Reality.

Mr. Haldane, however, is most interesting regarded as a typical example of a certain philosophical manner. He is distinctly a "counter" as distinguished from a "visual" philosopher. I can best get at the meaning I intend by these epithets, by a digression on a certain difference of intention, between verse and prose. In prose as in algebra concrete things are embodied in signs or counters, which are moved about according to rules, without being visualised at all in the process. There are in prose certain type situations and arrangements of words, which move as automatically into certain other arrangements as do functions in algebra. One only changes the x's and y's back into physical things at the end of the process. Poetry, in one aspect at any rate, may be considered as an effort to avoid this characteristic of prose. It is not a counter language, but a visual concrete one. It is a compromise for a language of intuition which would hand over sensations bodily. It always endeavours to arrest you, and to make you continuously see a physical thing, to prevent you gliding through an abstract process. It chooses fresh epithets and fresh metaphors, not so much because they are new and we are tired of the old, but because the old cease to convey a physical thing and become abstract counters. Nowadays, when one says the hill is "clothed" with trees, the word suggests no physical comparison. To get the original visual effect one would have to say "ruffed," or use some new metaphor. A poet says the ship "coursed the seas" to get a physical image, instead of the counter word "sailed." Visual meanings can only be transferred by the new bowl of metaphor: prose is an old pot that lets them leak out. Prose is in fact the museum where the dead images of verse are preserved. Images in verse are not mere decoration, but the very essence of an intuitive language. Verse is pedestrian, taking you over the ground prose — as a train delivers you at a destination.

One result of this difference is that both in prose and philosophy the "derivative" man can manipulate the counters, without ever having been in actual contact with the reality of which he speaks; yet by the use of image the "creative" man can always convey over the feeling that he has "been there." This partial distinction between verse and prose has an exact parallel between the "visual" and the "counter" philosopher. The visual and creative philosopher, like the saint in "Kim," desires the hills, where he can meditate in concrete forms. His method of thinking is visual, and he uses words only secondarily for purposes of communication. He is like a poet delighted with the physical metaphors before him that press directly and actually to be employed as symbols of thought. Once these physical metaphors are embodied in smooth counterwords, the second rank, who have not seen the hills, take them for eternal verities, unaware of the earthy process by which they were born. Philosophy, then, instead of being a kind of institution, becomes a complicated game, the great rule being the "principle of contradiction," in other words, "no two counters must occupy the same square at the same time." Thus, like the priests in the Tower of Manoi, Mr. Haldane sits, moving counters according to a certain ritual, and when all are on the central peg, Buddha will come again — perhaps. Conceive the body of metaphysical notions as a river; in the hills it springs from the earth, and can be seen to do so. But far down stream, on the mudflats where Haldane sits counting his beads with marvelous rapidity, the river seems to be eternal. Metaphysical ideas are treated as sacrosanct, and no one imagines they were born out of humble metaphors, as the river was of earth.

The abstract philosopher has a great contempt for the visual one. Hence the steadfast refusal to recognize that Nietzsche made any contribution to metaphysics. Mr. Haldane constantly informs us that the region of philosophy is not a region of pictorial images, one must beware of similes as the devil. I picture him always standing impressively, holding up a warning finger, saying in an awed whisper, "Hush, I hear a mere metaphor coming"; the supposition being that there is a mysterious high method of thinking by logic superior to the low common one of images. The counter philosopher, taking conceit unto himself, forgets that all his abstract words are merely codified dead metaphors. When we are all descended from monkeys — why put on side? As a matter of fact, the history of philosophy should be written as that of seven or eight great metaphors, and one might even say that the actual physical objects observed by men have altered the course of thought. For example, the mirror in the theory of perception, and the wheel in Eastern thought. One is rather apt in a reaction from Haldane's abhorrence of imagery to swing too much over to the other side. I guard myself against patronising abstraction too extensively, and recognise that the poor thing has after all a function in philosophy, though a secondary one. It is difficult to get the exact relation between the "visual" and "counter" attitudes. One gets it best I suppose by thinking of them as creative and developing functions respectively. The root of metaphor and intuition must rise into the light of abstraction to complete itself, but it should not be allowed to run to seed there. There is no system of philosophy which did not originate in an act of intuition, or as I have previously put it, a perception of a physical analogy. Dialectic is necessary to develop the primary intuition, and to put it into concepts for the purposes of communication. Once having received the impulse from the act of intuition, the philosopher has to continue in the other plane of abstraction. But he must not go too far in this medium or he loses foot and must return to the primary act of intuition. Like Antaeus, he must touch the earth for renewed strength. As in social life, it is dangerous to get too far away from barbarism. This new act of physical vision will destroy a good deal of the work done by the "counter" manipulating of abstractions. For a recent example of this take the word "concept" and the entirely new significance given to it by the pragmatists.

The legitimate function of logic only comes in the elaboration of the original "visual" act. It adds point to it, as a large hat does to the calculated gestures of a woman's head, and as clothing does to flesh. But metaphysics could exist without it, and if I may be allowed to express a personal opinion, I think that what we require now is a race of naked philosophers, free from the inherited embellishments of logic.

Never moving on the physical plane where philosophy arises, but always in the abstract plane where it is finished and polished, Mr. Haldane has his reward in a perfectly extraordinary facility in moving his counter words. Who but he could have given in extempore lectures such a lucid exposition of Hegelianism? The only parallel I can think of here is that of the expert chess player who can mentally follow the game from the written notation. This faculty in moving on the plane of counter words is of course the secret of his versatility. He has the monotonous versatility of the soldier, who in many lands employs the same weapon. It is the very prose of philosophy. He moves his counters, and certainly gets them into new and interesting positions. All the time, however, we cannot believe in their validity, as we are conscious that he is treating as fixed entities things which are not so — which run into one another in inextricable blurs, and are not separate and distinct. He treats the world as if it were ultimately a mosaic, whereas in reality all the colours run into one another. For the purposes of communication we must label the places where one colour predominates, by that colour, but then it is an illegitimate manoeuvre to take these names and juggle with them as if they were distinct and separate realities. I have one particular part of the book in mind, where for fifty pages he performs interesting movements with the four counters, Mind, Subject, Ultimate Reality and Aspect.

The word "Aspect" is indeed a kind of queen and knight, and can move on the board in any direction. Whenever an absurdity of the Hegelian system obstructs the way, "aspect" takes the poor pawn with miraculous ease.

The best way indeed to sum up Mr. Haldane is to say that he believes in the ultimate reality of language. He speaks with contempt of the "thing in itself" as a notion which cannot be expressed in words. It comes to this: "What cannot be expressed in intellectual forms does not exist." What he can't say in a public speech isn't knowledge. It is not difficult to expose the origin of this heresy.

Men for purposes of communication have joined themselves together by an abstract mechanism, a web of language, of universals and concepts. I picture this by thinking of a number of telegraph poles connected by a network of wires, the poles being concrete men, the wires being the abstract, thin concepts of the intellect, the forms in which we think and communicate. It is in the elaboration of this mechanism, and not in the change of the men it joins that all progress in knowledge has taken place. "Science est une langage bien fait." Here comes the great danger for philosophy. The success of the mechanism leads us on to think that it alone is real. The poles come to imagine themselves as built up of some subtle complication of wires. Accustomed to live and think externally in this mechanism of ours, and seeing its success in all the sciences, one comes to think it the only reality, and finally to explain the individual in terms of it. One's gaze being necessarily fixed in life on external communication of which logical thinking is a variety, one by an illegitimate analogy transfers it inward, and explains oneself in terms of what was in the beginning merely a tool.

This intellectual disease has attacked Mr. Haldane more strongly than any of the other Hegelians. The poor men who manufactured the concepts for communication are nothing. He even goes so far as to speak of the self as a mere bad metaphor in the same tone that one might speak of a bad egg.

Surely this is the greatest comedy in human history, that men should come to think themselves as made up of one of their own tools.

SEARCHERS AFTER REALITY
III · De Gaultier

Jules de Gaultier's philosophy is a sign of the times. Taken together with that of Boutroux, Bergson, Le Roy and many others, it is a sign that the centre of interest in philosophy has shifted from Germany to France. The particular characteristic of this movement that first strikes one is the great success of lucidity it has brought. Wilde once asserted that he was the first philosopher to dress like a gentleman. But, unfortunately for this very desirable claim, he was no philosopher. These Frenchmen, on the contrary, while they write like gentlemen and not like pedants, at the same time write metaphysics of a very subtle and distinguished kind. Take de Gaultier for example. In some parts of his work, particularly in his account of what exactly is implied in an act of knowledge, he is treating the most intricate and giddiness-producing part of philosophy. He treats it in an extremely personal way, expressing often views of violent originality. Yet such matters, which a German would not be able even to approach without the creation of an entirely special jargon, he writes of in a charmingly lucid manner, with great literary distinction. This increased lucidity is, I think, more than a mere change of literary manner. It is rather the secondary characteristic of a more general change, that of their whole attitude towards philosophy. They always seem to me to treat it, either explicitly or implicitly, not as science but as an art. This in itself is a relief. Philosophy has released itself from the philosophical sciences.

At this point I want to make a long digression, to express some personal views, which at first sight may appear to have little to do with de Gaultier. I think that this digression, which will occupy the rest of the article, is justified for this reason — that there is a certain attitude of mind, a certain prejudice, which must be attacked before one can appreciate de Gaultier. I want to get this out of the way before giving any detailed account of his philosophy.

There are two aims that metaphysics conceivably might have. It might wish to be considered an art, a means of expressing certain attitudes to the cosmos, or it might be taken as a science, humbly groping after the truth.

If you take the second point of view then probably certain objections would rise up in your mind to de Gaultier's philosophy. The principal conception with which it works may seem so slight, that the extraordinary way in which he makes it account for the whole movement of the cosmos may seem too ingenious to be true. I want to attack the conception of philosophy which gives rise to this hesitation.

One finds it difficult to realise what a baleful fascination the word science has for some people. I never quite realised it until I came across a faded old copy of the once flourishing "Westminster Review," whose gods were Mill and Spencer. In it I read a first review of Buckle's "History of Civilization," which gave me the same kind of sensation one gets from turning up a stone and seeing the creeping things revealed. I don't mean to say that I feel superior, but simply that I was in the presence of an unexpected and quite alien world of things. The reviewer lamented that in the ordered uniform cosmos which science had revealed there had been up to now an impenetrable jungle, the field of human passions and activity. "He rejoiced that at last with the appearance of Buckle's book this had been cleared up, and the whole world made trim and tidy. Law was universal." You saw here what was repugnant to him, the idea of freedom and chance. The ideal was a certitude which should constrain us. This dominant ideal invaded philosophy.

It began to regard itself as a science, to consider itself a systematic structure, solidly built up, which should give us certain unquestionable results. As in the sciences the ultimate nature of the world would reveal itself to continuous and patient work, and not to bold speculation. Philosophy, tempted by science, fell and became respectable. It sold its freedom for a quite imaginary power of giving sure results. It was a solemn structure, in face of which light-heartedness was out of place, and individual idiosyncrasy a sin. One felt uncomfortable in it. Nothing could be done by sudden insight and images; such things were mere folly, here was accumulated wisdom, here were no royal roads. The days of adventure were gone when we could set out to find new lands. Here was no place for the artist to impertinently express an attitude before the cosmos, but rather for the humble professor to work honestly in a corner.

To a certain extent this movement was correct. Logic, psychology, etc., look like, and as a matter of fact are sciences. The artist is here certainly out of place. But the danger was when they began to absorb philosophy itself, when it began to consider itself as merely a scientia scientium.

But with this modern movement, philosophy has at last shaken itself free from the philosophic sciences and established its right to an independent existence. In Bergson's "Idée d'une Métaphysique" one even finds it defined as the exact inverse method to that of science. The old conception of science prisoned us, restrained our vagaries, and made speculation seem childish. My gratitude to de Gaultier and these other critics of science is that they have rescued me from this nightmare and kept philosophy as an art. She has once more escaped the spirit that would make her a dull citizeness. Once more, without the expedient of turning herself into myrtle, Daphne has escaped the god's embraces, which promising love would but result in ungraceful fertility.

This is not a mere piece of reactionary or religious sentiment. We don't assert that a philosopher need not know the sciences, and that the simple man is in the best position to write metaphysics. It is not so; he must know them well.

But we assert that throughout the ages philosophy, like fighting and painting, has remained a purely personal activity. The only effect the advance of science has on the three activities is to elaborate and refine the weapons that they use. The man who uses a rifle uses it for the same purpose as a man who uses a bludg-eon. The results of the sciences merely increase the number of colours with which philosophy paints. The possibilities of the rapier have been worked out till they have become a science, but the process of learning it does not convert the man himself into an automaton. There are not, and can never possibly be, any certain results in metaphysics as there are in science. It is an activity of a different kind, simply an elaborate means for the expression of quite personal and human emotions.

The ultimate point I want to get at here is that philosophy is an art and not a science. The attitude proper to science is this. By work and effort one may discover the truth by which in dealing with this matter one must guide oneself. Science constrains us; we have no freedom, we enter into it humbly to be told the truth. Now philosophy is nothing of this kind. We are free in philosophy. I grant it has all the appearance of a science. Its vocabulary and methods are those of the science, but the driving-power behind it is quite different; it merely uses the scientific terms for a purpose quite different: that of the artist. In it by work one can never dis-cover the secret of the cosmos, one merely finds elaborate and complete ways of expressing one's personal attitude towards it.

From the outside it has all the appearance of a science. But this we might take as a piece of protective mimicry to ward off the multitude, to preserve it in its seclusion as the rarest of the arts.

We have to a certain extent been taken in by the jargon, and taken it for an end in itself, a science; but at last we have won through, and found it to be but part of an art. It is a case some-thing like the old Oriental mysteries; in the lower orders of priest-hood all the ritual was taken literally. But when you had pene-trated to the inner circle, through all the different kinds of magical formula and mysteries, the final secret turned out to be some per-fectly plain human statement. So in philosophy, when one attains the central position, one finds no exact science, but simply an art, a means of ordinary human expression. With this little dif-ference, however: that while the elaboration of ritual and the various mysteries of the Orientals were but means by which the priests controlled the ignorant multitude, in the case of philosophy the scientific terminology is the means by which we control ourselves, i.e., by which we completely express ourselves.

But I should be the first to attack the Philistine who thought he could dismiss this ritual terminology by saying that it corresponded to no reality. It is the finest and most delicately wrought language and means of expression of all the arts. Its elaborate technique enables it to get a leisurely effect of final statement where the other arts can only hint. It is the art of completion. The series of graduated words and definitions, the elaborate balancing and checking of meanings make it possible to isolate an emotion or idea from all accidental relations, so to study it completely. The jargon is a walled garden which enables conceptions to grow to their full expression, or to use a less sentimental metaphor, it is a kind of experimental tank, a laboratory where one can practise "control" experiments on ideas. I give next week an apt illustration of this isolating process in de Gaultier's own concept of Bovarysme, which starting first as a fact of ordinary psychology, he finally fits in a metaphysical setting, in order to state it completely.

One must distinguish the means from the end. The means, the elaborate technique, is certainly a science. But the end, what the Compleat Philosopher practises, is certainly an art. He wishes to express some freely-chosen attitude towards the world. Conceive Plato considering a particular example of love, or a particular scene of beauty. These things in human life are transient. But to him, Stability is more noble than Change. His "Theory of Ideas" is then the expression of this preference. He creates a system in which the ideas of love and beauty are eternal. The particular preference which de Gaultier's philosophy expresses I shall analyse later; roughly it is the exact antithesis of this, change is the only reality.

I anticipated the simple-minded question, "Is it true?" and intended to make the question absurd. There can be no direct answer to that question as there would be to "Is the Eiffel Tower 1,000 feet high?" One is extrapolating the curve of truth outside its proper limits, applying it to fields where it has no meaning. All philosophy is bound to be untrue, for it is the art of representing the cosmos in words, which is just as much a necessary distortion as the art of painting, which represents solidity in a plane of two dimensions. "He is a thinker — that is to say, he understands how to make things seem simpler than they are." One must judge de Gaultier's philosophy as one judges a landscape. One must not ask is it correct? but is it a good picture? The pleasure one takes must be that of a connoisseur and not that of a surveyor. The principal criterion is then, is it a consistent whole? In most of the pictures that philosophy gives us there is a gap right down the middle of the canvas, in that they fail to explain the very possibility of our knowledge. This gap does not exist in de Gaultier; he presents a complete picture on a canvas that is whole. For this reason I delight in him.

NOTES ON THE BOLOGNA CONGRESS

Bologna, April 7 [1911]

One may hold two very different views as to the value of congresses in general. One of these views is always associated with a simple-minded Scotch undergraduate I knew at Cambridge, whose constant topic of conversation at dinner in hall was the extraordinary progress that would take place in science if only the leading people in mathematics and physics could be got together in conference. If only Larmor, Poincaré, J. J. Thomson, Kelvin, and the rest of them could be put together in one room for a month, the exchange of views would solve the problem. It was a real trouble to the poor fellow that the attempt had never been made. I believe that at night, turning over on his pillow for the last time before sleep overcame him, he was lost in amazed wonder that the scandal of the ether's dubious position had been allowed to go on, year by year, when such a simple thing would have finished the matter once and for all.

To show that this congressomania is by no means confined to youth, I can give another example of its ravages. At the last annual meeting of the Aristotelian Society, a member raised an objection to the *variety* of the subjects proposed for discussion in the following year. Let the society take some pressing subject like that of Neo-Realism and discuss it time after time, until the truth had actually been discovered. I make no comment on the fact that a "pressing" subject can easily become "oppressing." What concerns me here is the attitude represented by this request. I was petrified when I first heard it, but after a time, as I looked at the stolid countenance of the reformer, I began to see a kind of halo round him, a coloured landscape of the inside of his mind. His attitude then became less amazing for me. The vision, the sympathetic intuition I formed of his mental make-up, his Weltanschauung was this: Somewhere at a great distance, Truth is hidden. She is always

21

waiting to be discovered, and the reason that during the centuries she has not been found, lies in the perpetual anaemia of the human mind. We cannot keep in one direct path long enough to succeed — or perhaps we keep on dying too often — and so change the line of search. You have, then, a vision of the tragic history of metaphysical thought from Plato to the present time. At many crucial moments in that long and complicated search they were within a foot of Truth, trembling and shrinking in her hiding place, but always at this moment, this fatal anaemia, the desire for variety, turned the hunters off in a new and false direction. Now you see the masterpiece of organised strategy which would infallibly succeed where the ages had failed. Let the Aristotelian Society tie itself down beforehand to keep in one direction. I hasten to say that the society did not set off on this heroic adventure. So what would have happened must for ever remain a subject of pathetic speculation; one of those dreadful "It might have beens" which torment the human mind. "If only Shackleton had not eaten the Manchurian pony, and fallen ill, only 80 miles from the Pole."

However, I have not quite lost hope. Some day a wealthy American lady may endow us, for the precise purpose of taking up the great adventure.

That is one attitude towards congresses. The other is, I think, best explained by a conversation I had with Bergson last July. I told him I was going to Bologna. "I don't know," he said, "whether these meetings actually do any good, but sometimes when you have been puzzled by a man's philosophy, when you have been a little uncertain as to his meaning, then the actual physical presence of the man makes it all clear. And sometimes, as William James used to say, one look at a man is enough to convince you that there you need trouble no further." I went to Bologna in this frame of mind. I wondered how my views on certain people would be affected. I was curious to test the James theory. I wondered how it would work out.

*　　*　　*

I had not long to wait for the first conclusive test. On the way to Italy I stopped two days at Dieppe with Jules de Gaultier, about

whom I have already written a little in this Review. It was a test under most favourable circumstances. Generally in discussing metaphysic one is, apropos of the other man's point, immediately "re-
minded" of something of one's own which one wants to drag out,
and so one never passes outside the limits of one's first concept. But
in this case fate made me a perfect listener, for while I understood
him perfectly, I had not spoken French for so long that all my
uprisings of interruption were stifled automatically before utter-
ance. The result was that I was extremely impressed. Previously,
while I enjoyed reading him, yet I always thought "Bovarysme" to
be a paradoxical though interesting position. While I admired the
dialectic by which it was supported, I had not found it at all "inevitable." But since meeting him I have formed a much clearer
and more definite conception of his philosophy.

This different view I now take of de Gaultier I can only explain
when I have first indicated my rather sceptical opinion of philosophy. Metaphysics for me is not a science but an art — the art of
completely expressing certain attitudes which one may take up
towards the cosmos. What attitude you do take up is not decided
for you by metaphysics itself, but by other things. The number of
such attitudes is, of course, necessarily limited — like the four
points of the compass; the variety of metaphysic can only come
in the different ways in which you can manage to indicate your
preference for the North or South, as the case may be. But de Gaultier has convinced me that there is another attitude beyond the
four traditional ones. It is not an attitude which many people can
take up, but for those who take it de Gaultier has written the
complete metaphysic. I cannot express how intensely I admire
the logical consistency with which it is all worked out.

In so far as philosophers are still peripatetic and like to walk
the road gesticulating, Bologna seems to be the ideal place for
them to meet in.

Walking about its streets for the first time, this evening, I would
go further and say that it is one of the few real towns still left on
this earth. There is a great misconception as to what really constitutes a town. The usual idea is that city and country are a pair

of opposites, and that the progress of events tends to spread the one and destroy the other. Nothing of the kind. The country is not the raw material out of which the town has been evolved. In the beginning was something I can vaguely call desert. Out of this matrix at one period of history civilisation had evolved two perfect correlatives of artificial and deliberate construction: the compact walled town, and the country. That was the ideal State. Now the period of decadence has set in, as you get it, for example, in South Kensington, is fully back to the state of desert again. Well, in so far as a street is to be a street, i.e., a place for strolling and talking in, and not a railway, Bologna seems to me to be the perfect town. It is all compact of little piazzas flanked by arcades, and never a broad straight street or an open vista in the whole place. You feel always, though you may never see it, the bracing feeling of a disciplinary wall keeping it up to the ideal pitch of town I require, and never allowing it to sprawl into desert. It is a quadrangle and cloister raised to the highest power, the only modern substitute for the groves of Academe.

* * *

I have now to chronicle what is perhaps the most important event that has yet happened to a philosopher. I was sitting in the hotel this morning, writing letters, and was vaguely conscious of the noise of bands in the distance, and various tones of shouting. Then after a time, troop after troop of soldiers began to march past the window at which I was sitting. I began to be interested. Surely something important must be happening. I hurriedly left the hotel and rushed to the centre of the town. There were enormous crowds in the Piazza Vittoria Emanuelle. Great red banners hung from the brick Renaissance palaces which surround the square. Lining certain streets were troops with their red pistacchios flicked about by the wind, and behind them a mass of people ten deep, all in their characteristic toga cloaks, with one end thrown over the shoulder. When I say mass of people I ought to correct myself. It was not a crowd in the ordinary meaning of the term, but rather a garden city kind of crowd, for surrounding each man was the large space occupied by his cloak. The more I think of that crowd, the more I admire it. It had a peculiar kind of quality I had never seen before. It had achieved the impossible. It was a crowd without being a crowd. It was simply an aggregation of people who managed the extraordinary feat of coming together without becoming that very low class multicellular organism — the mob. If anyone could invent a kind of democracy which includes, as an essential feature, the possession of large and sweeping brown cloaks, then I will be a democrat. To find out what it was all about I bought a paper. "L'Avveniri d'Italia." With amazement, I saw in enormous letters across the front page, "Filosofia." All this was actually on account of philosophy! Really a world become so self-conscious as to care so much for the "Why" is rapidly leaving the admirable plane of instincts and is nearing its end. This most important event really heralds the rapid approach of the final conflagration.

To descend, however, to detail, this was a welcome for the Duke of the Abruzzi, who had come from Rome to open the Congress on behalf of his cousin the King. I may as well say at once that I have not yet been introduced to him; so that any curiosity the reader of this article may feel about Miss Elkins will have to go unsatisfied.

At this moment circumstance forced on me a frightful dilemma. It was ten o'clock, the time of the official opening of the Congress. I ought at once to go to the "Arch-Gymnasium" and hear the opening ceremony and Professor Enriques' paper on "Reality." But if I did this, I should miss the street scene. I shouldn't hear the bands. I should not solve the question whether the garden city crowd could also cheer with dignity. I had to choose between the two, I could not do both. It was either the street, or the Congress; truly a terrible dilemma for me, for I regard processions as the highest form of art. I cannot resist even the lowest form of them. [I must march even with the Salvation Army bands I meet accidentally in Oxford Street on Sunday night, and here was a procession among processions — and the problem of the behaviour of the crowd. The dilemma was a perplexing one.]

Inside, I knew from the programme that Professor Enriques would speak of Reality. But, alas! Reality for me is so old a lady, that no information about her, however new, however surprising, could attain the plane of interest legitimately described by the word gossip. Outside, officers in wonderful sweeping blue capes were galloping past as the time came for the procession to arrive. The inside seemed to suffer by comparison. My conduct was entirely my own concern, but if Pallas Athene, or the indignant secretary of the Congress had taken it as a piece of lèse majesté and called on me to justify it before a jury of my peers, I could have done so. I would first have appealed to the school which considers that an immediate sensation has reality, and that conceptual notions diminish it. I could have taken the attitude of the aesthetes in the exaltation of the sensation, and said, "Mieux vaut un peu du pain bien cuit, que tout Shakespeare." I could have gone further than that and justified my preference for the particular aspect of sensation represented by soldiers. In the first place, they would be certain to talk inside of progress, while the only progress I can stand is the progress of princes and troops, for they, though they move, make no pretence of moving "upward." They progress in the only way which does not violate the classical ideal of the fixed and constant nature of man.

Then again, there would be much talk inside of the "all" and the "whole," and of the harmony of the concert of the cosmos, and I do not believe in the existence of these things. I am a pluralist, and to see soldiers for a pluralist should be a symbolic philosophic drama. There is no Unity, no Truth, but forces which have different aims, and whose whole reality consists in those differences. To the rationalist this is an absolutely horrible position.

There is one Truth, one Good. It is for this reason that the conception of nationality and everything connected with it appears so extraordinarily irrational to the intellectual. He simply cannot conceive that these are not one truth, but different truths which win or lose. But however symbolic my remaining outside in the street might have been as an assertion of my belief, yet the stage was hardly large enough, the limelight was lamentably absent.

Time passed and here was I presenting this spectacle of indecision on the pavement. Finally inward ridicule decided the thing. To cross Europe with the sole purpose of attending a congress, and then to watch a procession instead, would be too much of a comic spectacle. To my lasting regret I went in. I missed a spectacle I shall never see again. I heard words I shall often hear again — I left the real world and entered that of Reality.

At least, I thought I had, but I was mistaken in thinking of myself as a reversed Faust. There was plenty of the world inside. I passed along long corridors, under many arches, and supporting each arch were several police, and soldiers of the heavy cavalry type, and firemen. I shall return to the subject of the enormous number of firemen which guarded us later. I finally reached the Salla di seduti generale. My general impression is of a broad red line at the end, forming the drapery of the platform, and a regular garden of extraordinary hats; great numbers of pretty women — surely this cannot be the world of "Reality"— I do hope they are not philosophers; and then, vaguely, some drums heard outside.

NOTES ON BERGSON

I

It seems to me that the best way to write about Bergson is to start some distance off. I am the more inclined to this view as it happens to fit in with my secret inclinations. The duty of a small person writing about a big one is, I know, to give as plain an account of his subject as he can, and keep himself out of it. But my anaemic mind shrinks from the kind of concentrated perseverance involved in a straightforward "compte rendu." The prospect of stolidly going through what has been already gone through before fills me with depression. I realise quite clearly that this is no superiority on my part, but is due simply to a certain lack of vitality. I have, however, the excuse that at the present time, when all Bergson's books have been translated, and when all the preliminary panegyric necessary to make his name known has been more than successfully accomplished, any straightforward account would be an entirely unnecessary performance. Those who want any such account cannot do better than read the philosopher himself. No one can improve on the lucidity of his own exposition, and any attempt to cut it short inevitably leaves out all the point. Nor can I emulate the feats of those ingenious people during the last few months, who, in most surprising places, ranging from sporting papers upwards, have managed by the skilful choice and repetition of a few magical phrases, such as "Life overflows the intellect," to create the illusion both in their own and their readers' minds that they have really said something quite definite. I repeat, then, that I do not in these articles intend to give any straightforward account of Bergson's system. I concern myself with a much easier and to me much more amusing undertaking. I intend giving simply a personal confession. At the time when I first read "Les Donnés Immédiates" it represented to me a great influence and a great excitement. All I am trying to do here is fix down exactly what that influence was, and why it was so exciting. My only justification for this kind of treatment is that it amuses me, and further that it does enable me to get the subject into some kind of perspective.

With this I can get back to the beginning of the article and explain what I meant by the first sentence in it. I said that the best way to explain Bergson was to start some distance off. What I meant was that you can only convey over a sense of his importance by first describing the state of things which existed before he arrived, and from which he relieved one. If the reading of "Les Donnés Immédiates" was an influence and an excitement it could only have been so because it bore some relation to something which already existed in my own mind. If he made a tremendous difference to me I cannot explain what that difference was until I have explained the state of things before he arrived. If in my enthusiasm I pictured him as a kind of relieving force I cannot explain what the excitement was about until I have first explained the previously existing state of siege. But while my enthusiasm was due to the fact that reading Bergson put an end to an intolerable state, there was more in it than the feeling of mere relief. If that had been all there would not have been much justification for my describing my previous state of mind merely in order to say, "This is what I was relieved from." It was not simply a case of an intolerable state being changed into a pleasanter one; it was not merely that one state changed into its opposite. On the contrary, there was a certain resemblance between the initial and the final stages. There was a certain continuity between them. The first state might even be considered as a very rough microcosm of part, at any rate, of the second. Certain elements present in one were present in the other. But these elements, which in the first state were tortured, vague, and confused, became in the second clear and definite. It is in this partial correspondence that I find my justification for describing the first state, and which at the same time was the cause of the extent of my enthusiasm. I felt the exhilaration that comes with the sudden change from a cramped and contracted to a free and expanded state of the same thing. It was an almost physical sense of exhilaration, a sudden expansion, a kind of mental explosion. It gave one the sense of giddiness that comes with a sudden lifting up to a great height. One saw clearly outlined in perspective the shape of things which before had only been felt in a muzzy kind of way. My enthusiasm was then a double one, and due to two separate causes. In the first place, there was a simple sentiment of relief. A solution was given to a problem which worried me. I had been released from a nightmare which had long troubled my mind. If I compare my nightmare to imprisonment in a small cell, then the door of that cell was for the first time thrown open. In the second place, the key with which this prison door was opened corresponded to the type of key which I had always imagined would open it. I had constructed for myself imperfect examples of keys of this type. I was shown the perfect and successful one which yet was on the lines I had vaguely imagined might be successful. There had been present in my mind in a very crude form something which did correspond to the solution actually given me by reading Bergson.

The sources of my enthusiasm were, then, the relief from the nightmare, and, in addition to this, the delight of seeing something done perfectly that I had wrestled with clumsily and unsuccessfully. I had the delight of escape, and I had the quite different delight of seeing an expert wield with the ease of Cinquevalli an implement whose shape even I had only just been able to guess at.

I had the purely physical delight of freedom and at the same time the technical delight of seeing the facile and fertile use of an instrument I admired.

If now I am to keep to my announced intention of giving a merely personal account of my relations to Bergson's work and an explanation of exactly what it meant to me, I have, in order to give an adequate account of this enthusiasm, to give first the two elements in my previous state of mind which were responsible for and concerned in this enthusiasm. The enthusiasm I have explained was due to the sudden change in the state of clearness of two elements in my mind. Two things corresponded to what I found in Bergson. In the first place, I was concerned with the same nightmare, and, in the second place, I had a suspicion of his way out of it. Both these were changes from a state of dimness to one of clear light. A dark problem and a vaguely seen way of escape changed to a solved problem with the way out of it clearly defined. In order, then, to give an adequate account of my enthusiasm I must give an adequate account of this double change, and in order to give an adequate account of the change I must commence with a detailed description of these two elements before change of my preliminary state of mind. The first article will be about the nightmare I suffered from, and the second, which I call "the chessboard," will be a description of the roughly-modelled key I had imagined might release me from the nightmare.

This I should have to do in order to explain to what exactly my enthusiasm was due. However, I have a better excuse than this for spending the space of two articles in giving an account of something that Bergson did not say before passing on to what he did. I realise that some better excuse is needed for devoting two articles to something which has no more connection with Bergson than the fact that it gives the reason why I personally found him exciting. It would be rather a thin excuse by itself. Fortunately I can find a better one.

It seems to me to be worth while describing the nightmare, the locked door, in detail, because it enables me to give the state of things that Bergson was heaven-sent to relieve, and so enables me to convey over his immense importance and significance at the present moment. It enables me to show to what circumstances his importance is due. It gives me the age-old problem that he concerns himself with. In the second place, it seems to me to be worth while devoting a whole article to the crude form of escape which had dimly suggested itself to my own mind, as by that means I am enabled to get an easy line of approach to the most difficult part of Bergson and his method — this in the article on "chessboards." When I have got this out I have some kind of basis, some kind of leverage, with which I can get at the explanation of what he means by an intensive manifold.

II

Not exactly, however. I cannot leave it in that precise form, because it embodies a certain inaccuracy. That perhaps would not matter very much were it not that the form of the inaccuracy lays me open to a kind of accusation I particularly detest. I must, therefore, permit myself another digression before I can go straight forward. I have been incautious in the way I have stated things. I have made rather too frequent use of the word enthusiasm, and, worse even than that, I have hinted at the "solution" of a world-old problem. This is where my danger comes in. These things are all signs.

I might be suspected of that particular form of youthful enthusiasm that imagines it has come across the secret of the world for the first time, the kind of enthusiasm that imagines Bergson supersedes all other philosophy.

This would be a most awful accusation. To me personally it would be the most offensive that could be uttered. For this reason, that it would identify me with a type of mentality which I regard with peculiar horror, and which has been particularly prominent in connection with appreciations and criticism of Bergson. It is a type which, while I dislike, I think at the same time that I thoroughly understand. It springs from a kind of mental debility which has left its mark in many other subjects besides philosophy. It is, in fact, one of the normal and common attributes of the human race.

Its external signs are quite easy to recognise. In philosophy you believe that you have got hold of something absolutely "new." You have found the secret of the universe. By the side of this all previous philosophy seems tedious groping. Parallel with this, in social matters, you have the belief that we are on the verge of an entirely "new" state of society which will be quite "different" from anything in the past. Something is going to happen. It may be Home Rule; it may be a social revolution; but, at any rate, when it has happened things will be quite "different."

What is the psychology of this kind of belief? The first step towards a correct explanation of the phenomena is to recognise that your enthusiasm over your particular "new" thing is not caused by the nature of the new thing itself, or only in a very minor degree. The new thing only provides accidentally, as it were, a nucleus round which an over-saturated solution of a certain kind of enthusiasm can crystallise.

One is led to this belief by observing the universality of the phenomena and the widely different subjects in which it is successfully exhibited. If a man believes in the possibility of a new state of society, and at the same time thinks that Bergson has invented an entirely new philosophy, the objects of his enthusiasm have so little connection with each other that you are compelled to believe that the cause of it must lie in some disposition of his mind and not in the things themselves.

It is not so much then anything definite that Bergson says that moves them to enthusiasm as the fact that certain sentences perhaps give a pretext for this enthusiasm to empty itself in a flood. It is not because they have clearly seen in Bergson a completely new system that they are moved to talk in this ridiculous way as that they are in a constant state of wanting to talk like that, and he provides a convenient excuse. They are driven on to beliefs of this kind in all subjects by a certain appetite, a certain craving, which must be satisfied. What happens to satisfy it is quite a secondary matter. They seek, and will have, a certain kind of mental excitement; the desire is the governing factor, not the accidental thing it happens to fix itself on to. It is like falling in love at an early and inexperienced age. You may be under the delusion that it is the object that has so produced the state, but the more aged outside observer of the phenomena could tell you that it is more probably the state which produces the object.

What is behind all this? These are the external signs. What is the internal cause of it all? I should say that it was this.

The type is characterised by a certain malaise, a certain irritation of the mind, which seeks to relieve itself. A certain want of balance, which strives to put itself right, which manifests itself in an insatiable craving for a certain specific kind of excitement and exhilaration.

This malaise can be roughly described as a repugnance to and an irritation at the ordinary and the humdrum. We all suffer from this, but in this type the irritation is raised to a hysterical pitch which can almost be called a disease. It is so strong that it affects the balance of the mind. It can only keep its sanity by hugging to itself a balancing illusion. It must believe, in order that it may continue to exist, that there exists somewhere, or that there is about to come into existence, something emphatically *not* ordinary, something quite "different" from humdrum experience.

This craving for something which can be thought of as "different" might almost be described as the instinctive effort of the organism to right itself. The truth would kill it; this over-belief is necessary in order that it may continue to go on living in comfort. It is like the instinctive action of a man stumbling who throws out his hands to restore his equilibrium. It is an unconscious process. It most generally takes the form of a belief that the future holds possibilities of the perfect which have been denied to the present and the past. This type of debility of mind finds sanity in the belief that it is on the verge of great happenings. It so finds restored equilibrium, but at what a cost! Compared with this fetish worship is an intellectual occupation. Belief of this kind is the most loathesome form of credulity. People in a state of unstable equilibrium support themselves at first sight in very odd ways. A tight-rope-walker carries a long pole; Mr. Balfour, we know, supports himself by holding on to the lapel of his frock coat. But as ludicrous spectacles both these altogether pale when compared with the romancist who prevents himself from falling by leaning on the "future."

* * *

It is at the back of all forms of romanticism. Translated into social beliefs, it is the begetter of all the Utopias. It is the source of all of the idealist support of Revolution. By the use of this word you can indeed generally identify the type. You could get the most condensed expression of it by saying that it believes, and must believe, that something remarkable and revolutionary can happen. All demagogues have built on this fallibility of man. Persuade a people that they are about to make history, and they will proceed to follow you. To take a trivial instance of its workings; the appeal of the phrase about the "rare and refreshing fruit" was not to material interests altogether. There was the much greater consolation involved in the idea that there could be such a thing as a rare and refreshing fruit. Well, just in the same way you persist in thinking that some day a rare and refreshing fruit will be discovered in philosophy. As you believe that a new social order vastly different from everything that had preceded it is about to arrive, so you want as a natural corollary to believe that there is also an absolutely new philosophy to fit in with this brand-new good time coming. It would pain you intensely to think that you had to have any old furniture in the new house. You read Bergson then not so much for any definite views he puts forward; indeed, you very rarely are enabled to give any coherent account of what he says, but simply because there you do get this craving satisfied.

This is the type which I regard with such peculiar horror, and from which I want to dissociate myself. And as the object of writing and of the making of theories is nothing more at bottom than the kind of thing aimed at by the Thirty-nine Articles, that is, the drawing of a peculiarly complicated but quite definite line which will mark you off finally and distinctly from the people you can't stand, I have thought it worth while to examine these people at length.

I want carefully to state that I do not belong to this type. When, therefore, I speak of a new solution to an old problem I do not at all attach the meaning to the phrase that this type would. I believe, on the contrary, that there is nothing absolutely new in either the problem or the solution of it which I am about to describe in Bergson. In substance the problem and its solution are the same in every generation. Every philosopher must deal with an old problem, and must escape from it by an equally world-old solution. It is impossible at this time of day to take up an absolutely new attitude towards the cosmos and its persistent problems. The conflicts of the constant attitudes recur in each generation, and the things we dispute about now are the same in substance as those which occupied the leisure of the theologians of the third and fourth centuries.

It is as impossible to discover anything new about the ways of man in regard to the cosmos as it is to observe anything new about the ways of a kitten. The general conceptions we can form are as limited in number as the possible gestures of the dance, and as fixed in type as is the physiology of man himself. The philosopher who has not been anticipated in this sense of the word does not exist, or, if he does, he breathes forth his wisdom in the ineffectual silence of solitary confinement.

But if that is so, what is the use of bothering about the matter at all? Why should you investigate even the relatively new? Just as one generation after another is content to watch the eternally fixed and constant antics of kittens, so, one might urge, should one generation after another be content to watch the antics of the philosophers without sighing after anything new. There is this obvious objection: that while the antics of the kitten, like the art of the actor, die with it, the same is not true of philosophers.

It is necessary for the kittens of this generation to repeat the gestures of the past in order that we may see them at all, for the dead kittens who did the same things are gone beyond recall; but in philosophy the gestures of the dead are recorded in print. What justification is there for philosophy if it does nought but repeat the same old attitudes? This is a plausible but fallacious objection, and based on an illusion. The phrases of dead philosophers recorded in print are to most people as dead as dead kittens. In order that they may appear alive they must be said over again in the phraseology of the moment. This, then, is the only originality left to a philosopher — the invention of a new dialect in which to restate an old attitude.

This, then, is the sense that I might safely say that Bergson had presented a new solution to an old problem. I should restate the thing, to avoid any suspicion of romanticism, in this way: Bergson has provided in the dialect of the time the only possible way out of the nightmare.

When I said that in my article on the chessboard I should give the suspicion of this way out that was present in my own head, I mean rather that I must give the kind of embryo idea that was present in the minds of this generation ready to be developed. For a philosopher must be anticipated even in this more special way.

The thing that he has to say must already be present in a crude form to the minds of a considerable number of the men of his own generation for him to get a hearing. The ground must be prepared for him. What he says can have very little meaning or significance to the reader unless it hitches on to or resembles some similar idea already present in that reader's head. The egg must be there; all that the philosopher can do is to act as a broody hen. Or perhaps a more correct metaphor would be to say that out of the muddy stream of our own thoughts the philosopher dives in and dries on the bank into a definite and fixed shape the idea that in our own mind was but muddy, transient, and confused. This is in the sense in which every reader who derives anything from the philosopher must have anticipated him. Without you had already something which a little corresponded to what he has to say you would not be able to make very much of him. You anticipate him in this sense, that with several hundred other people in the same state of mind you form the confusion that the particular philosopher is heaven-sent to clear up.

There is nothing in all this derogatory to the originality of a philosopher. It is a grievous mistake to find the originality of a philosopher in his bare ideas. You cannot find the originality and peculiar qualities of an innovator merely in the ideas he brings forward. You wouldn't read him at all did you not find in him much the same ideas that were already present in your own head. There is nothing in having ideas. Anybody can have those much overrated articles of commerce. You or I out for a morning's walk may, if it be the first day of spring, or if we can hear a band in the distance, give birth to a crowd of ideas, each of which might serve as the starting point of a new system of philosophy. Each of them seems to hold the old-world process in its embrace. Probably this is not a matter of seeming only, probably each of them does, or has done so in reality, for the cosmos is by no means a prude in these matters. Surely the history of philosophy is there to prove that the cosmos, like the wife of Marcus Aurelius, has wandered very

37

much. All the disputes come from the fact that the metaphysicians, pitifully lacking not only in physique, but also in the horse sense of the soldiers, are apt in their rapture to think that they are the only ones.

* * *

To return at length to the point, I am giving in the next article, the nightmare, the problem that I conceive Bergson to have finished off. This gives the pedestal he stands on the dark background which throws him into startling relief.

III

We have been treated during the last two weeks to a number of not very profound witticisms on the subject of Bergson.* It has been triumphantly demonstrated that all his conclusions are of extreme antiquity, and great play has been made, both in prose and verse, with "the people who discovered for the first time that they had souls, being told that it was the latest thing from Paris." In any case, this is a fairly mechanical form of wit, because it is the kind of attack which could have been predicted beforehand. The only effective kind of sneer is the one which only your enemy could have thought of, while these things, as a matter of fact, were anticipated in detail by me in the last of my Notes. I knew they would be sure to come and I defended myself in advance.

But my attitude towards the state of mind behind these attacks has become so complicated by the mixture of partial agreement and partial disagreement that I shall try to disentangle the thing out clearly.

I agree entirely with the point of view from which these jokes spring, but, at the same time, I do not see that they have any "point." Some jokes one can never appreciate because they spring from a general mental make-up which one dislikes. I don't appreciate jokes about stupid Conservative candidates, for example. But in this case I am on the same side as the people who make the jokes. Why, then, do they seem to be rather pointless?

* EDITOR'S NOTE. In the correspondence columns of the two preceding issues of the *New Age*, Vol. X, Nos. 2 and 3 (November 9 and 16, 1911).

Take first the sneer about the antiquity of Bergson's conclusions. I agree with the statement it makes. It is so true that it is merely a platitude. But if it is to have any point as an attack, behind it must lie the supposition that philosophers may, and, indeed, ought to, establish some absolutely new conclusion — if they are to be considered of any importance. This is the most vulgar of all superstitions. No new conclusions can ever be expected, for this reason, that when a philosopher arrives at his conclusions he steps right out of the field of philosophy and into that of common knowledge, where nothing new is, of course, possible. I don't mean by this that he has made a step which he ought not to have made; it is, on the contrary, a necessary and inevitable step, which is involved in the very nature of "conclusions." Every philosopher in his conclusions must pass out of his own special craft and discipline into the kind of knowledge which every man may and should have. He passes from the study to the market-place. I use market-place here something in the sense which is intended in the epitaph which I quote below. It is one which is fairly common, but I happened to see it myself first in a churchyard in Sussex. I put in the second verse just for the fun of the thing: —

> Life is a crowded town,
>   With many crooked streets.
> Death is a market place,
>   Where all men meets.
>
> If life were a thing
>   Which money could buy,
> The rich would live
>   And the poor would die.

By the "conclusions" of a philosopher one means his views on the soul, on the relation of matter and mind and the rest of it. If, then, in the above epitaph I take the market-place not to be death itself, but "thoughts and opinions about death," I get the position accurately enough. When the philosopher makes the inevitable step into this market-place, he steps into a region of absolute constancy. Here novelty of belief would be as ridiculous as novelty in the shape of one's body. In these matters, in this market-place, "all men meets." There can be no difference between the philosopher and the ordinary man, and no difference between the men of one generation and the men of another. There is a certain set of varied types of belief which recur constantly.

In this region there could not then be any new conclusion, and expectation of any such novelty could only spring from a confusion of mind.

But though I hold this opinion, yet at the same time I cannot see anything ridiculous in the people who have suddenly discovered that they have souls. I can explain the cause of my apparent inconsistency. To make the task more difficult in appearance I assert that not only do I accept the statement that there is no novelty as a truth, but I welcome it with considerable enthusiasm as the kind of truth I like. My defence of the people who have "discovered their souls" will be the more sincere from the fact that I personally sympathise with the attitude from which they have been laughed at. I find no attraction in the idea that things must be discovered, or even re-stated, in each generation. I would prefer that they were much more continuous with the same ideas in the past even than they are. There is tremendous consolation in the idea of fixity and sameness. If the various possible ideas about the soul at the present moment are represented by certain struggling factions in the market-place, then my own opinion in this flux and varying contests seems, if I confine myself to the present, to be a very thin and fragile thing. But if I find that a certain proportion of the men of every generation of recorded history have believed in it in substantially the same form that I myself hold it, then it gains a sudden thickness and solidity. I feel myself no longer afloat on a sea in which all the support I can get depends on my own activity in swimming, but joined on by a chain of hands to the shore. The difference it produces in the atmosphere of one's beliefs is like the difference which was produced in my outlook on London in the year when I discovered by actually walking that Oxford Street does actually go to Oxford and that Piccadilly is really the Bath road.

I need not be suspected, then, of the kind of excitement about

Bergson which would be caused by the delusion that in him one was for the first time in the world's history, in the presence of the truth. That would have caused my instant flight in some other direction.

Though I do not, then, admit that there can be any real novelty in his "conclusions," yet I can sympathise with the people who find their souls a novelty. I am prepared to defend these people as having instinctively seized an aspect of the truth which the traditionalists had neglected.

The traditionalist view, I take it, is this: To state the thing, I take one definite problem and state, in the terms of the market-place, a certain view of the soul which has always existed, and has always been represented by one of the factions. More than that, the objections to that view have also always existed and always been represented. What excuse is there, then, for the people who became suddenly excited at the discovery of their soul? It is not a new view of the soul that is put forward, and it has not overcome any special obstacles peculiar to this period. Why make this tremendous fuss then?

The answer to that I should put in this way: The opposing sides in this dispute, I supposed, represented by opposing factions in the market-place — always remembering, of course, that the market-place exists in you. These factions represent not only the various views it is possible to hold, but also the force with which these views press themselves on your mind. Beliefs are not only representations, they are also forces, and it is possible for one view to compel you to accept it in spite of your preference for another. Now, while it is impossible to create a new faction, it is possible to alter the weapons with which they are armed and so to decide which shall be predominant.

This is just what has happened in the matter of the beliefs about the soul. The growth of the mechanistic theory during the last two centuries has put a weapon of such a new and powerful nature into the hands of the materialist, that in spite of oneself one is compelled to submit. It is as if one side in the faction fight had suddenly armed themselves in steel breast-plates while the other went unprotected.

It is idle to deny this. It seems to me to be the most important fact which faces the philosopher. If one examines the psychology of belief one finds that brutal forces of this kind decide the matter just as they do more external matters. A candid examination of one's own mind shows one that the mechanistic theory has an irresistible hold over one (that is, if one has been educated in a certain way).

It isn't simply a question of what you would like to win. It is a matter simply of the recognition of forces. If you are candid with yourself you find, on examining your own state of mind, that you are forcibly, as it were, carried on to the materialist side.

It is from this frank recognition of forces that comes my excitement about Bergson. I find, for the first time, this force which carries me on willy-nilly to the materialist side, balanced by a force which is, as a matter of actual fact, apart from the question of what I want, able to meet on equal terms the first force. As the materialist side became for a time triumphant, because it became, to a certain extent, artificial by putting on heavy armour (this is how the effect of the mechanistic theory appears to me), so in Bergson, in the conception of time, I find that the other side, the scattered opposition to materialism, has taken on, for its part, a, to a certain extent, artificial form which is able to meet the other side on equal terms.

It could not be said, then, of me that I had "discovered my soul." But simply that for the first time the side that I favoured was able to meet fairly without any fudging the real force which was opposed to it. It would have been sheer silliness on my part to pretend that this force did not exist, for I knew very well that it did and affected me powerfully.

The attitude behind the sneer seems then to me to be childish, because it takes no account of real conditions. To ignore what one gets in Bergson seems to me to be as silly as to take no interest in Dreadnoughts because one is convinced that one Englishman is a match for fifty Germans. I could not be said to have suddenly discovered that I was an Englishman if I exhibited some delight in a naval victory, but merely that I had some sense of the real forces which move the things. There is, then, nothing comic in the attitude of the people who suddenly discovered their souls, but merely an admirable sense of reality, a sure instinct for the forces that really exist. They had the capacity to understand "the Realpolitik" of "belief."

Summing it all up, then, there exists this constant struggle between the two attitudes we can assume about the soul. But during the last 150 years the balance between the two has been greatly disturbed. The materialist side has clothed itself in a certain armour which makes it irresistible, at least to people of a certain honesty of mind and a certain kind of education. In more concrete terms, what is all this?

* * *

The problem as it has always existed in the market-place, quite independently of its modern manifestations, can be stated quite simply: Is consciousness a mere local phenomenon appearing in certain places where there is a certain highly complex arrangement of matter and entirely at the mercy of the surrounding material circumstances? Or is it a permanent part of reality which only manifests itself under these circumstances, but which exists apart from them?

I put the difference between these two constant views in market-place terminology as a contrast between two different states of mind. I give these states merely as states that occur, without any suppositions as to whether the things we feel in them are true or delusive. They are illustrations by which the problem can be most easily stated. I give them entirely from the point of view of the novelist, then.

This, roughly, is the first state. Among the multifarious contents of a man's mind somewhere in the rubbish heap there is one mood which now and again comes to the top. In certain periods of mental excitement it seems quite clear to one that the active mind whose workings have just excited one, in the working out of a problem, say, or the seizure for the first time of a new idea, must exist independently of matter. When the mind is in full action in this way it seems inconceivable that it is not an independent and persisting entity. It seems ridiculous to think that it is less real than matter. One may get the same kind of sensation in a different way. Sometimes walking down an empty street at night one suddenly becomes conscious of oneself as a kind of eternal subject facing an eternal object. One gets a vague sentiment of being, as it were, balanced against the outside world and co-eternal with it.

Take, on the other hand, an absolutely different state of mind. To make the thing concrete, I will suppose that I am lying in bed ill, in some pain, and unable to get to sleep. This balance I have just talked about seems then upset. The two things that were balanced are no longer so, for all the weights have gone into the one pan. It is now only the material world that seems to be real and enduring. My own consciousness does not seem to me to be an enduring and solid thing at all. It seems as unsubstantial as the flame of a candle and as easily put out.

Now if either of these states occur alone there would be no need for philosophy. You would simply believe the evidence of the state you were in and which you happen to be in. But, unfortunately, for one's peace of mind these states do not occur alone. We pass continually, and sometimes rapidly, from one to the other. At one time one has a firm conviction of the reality and persistence of mind, and at another time one is equally convinced that it is as flimsy as a shadow. The memory of one mood persisting on into the other and forming thus a background of doubt to the firm assurance of the other, we are obliged to search out some system which will enable us to decide which is real and which is a delusion, to decide which is to be taken as a rock-like solidity and which is a temporary aberration of the mind due to the situation of the moment.

I do not, of course, put these two states forward as anything more than two sentiments which do exist and can be described. The question as to whether they correspond to anything real has to be decided in other ways. One can state the question at dispute a little more objectively, in order to bring to a focus the real point of difference which has to be decided. There exist, distributed in space, at this minute, so many centres of consciousness, just as there are so many electric lights in the streets outside. Is there any real resemblance between these two phenomena? Each light exists as the result of certain material conditions, and can be easily extinguished. It is possible for the whole of the lights to be put out. No one pretends that there is a kind of light-world independent of the real world and that light is immortal and endures. Is the same true of consciousness? To all appearances it seems as easy to extinguish a centre of consciousness as to extinguish a centre of light. Is, then, consciousness like light, a phenomenon occurring here and there as a result of certain local physical conditions, having no separate enduring existence? Or is each centre of consciousness, to continue my use of domestic metaphor, better compared to a water-tap, where if you turn off the tap you do not thereby annihilate water?

Is consciousness, then, a temporary phenomenon coming out in spots, or is it a permanent, continuous and enduring entity? The difference between these views is connected somehow with the idea of "separation," and anything which increases your consciousness of your separation from other things increases your conviction that the electric-light view is the right one. Extreme cold, for example, increases your feeling of "separation" from the world, and at the same time tends to convince you that consciousness is nothing but a mere local phenomenon. Personally, I can never walk down the narrow spiral stone staircases that you get in old castles and church towers without feeling what a frail thing consciousness is and how it is caught in the net of matter and is absolutely at its mercy.

On the other hand, we are told that if a man could go to the centre of his own mind and penetrate beneath the surface manifestations of consciousness he would feel himself joined on to a world of consciousness which is independent of matter; he would feel himself joined on to something which went beyond himself, and in no sense an isolated point at the mercy of local changes in matter. The retort to this, of course, would be that he was merely deluding himself.

This is the whole question in as rude a metaphor as I can get. There exist along Oxford Street various entirely separate red buildings known as Tube Stations. As far as outside appearances go, each has no physical connection with the other. Let the phenomenon of conscious life be represented by the ticket clerks at these stations. Suppose that for some mysterious reason they become extremely unpopular and a hostile crowd boards up one of the stations. The crowd represents the world of matter. Would the clerks as a result of this boarding up cease to exist? Obviously not, for they, descending the lift, would find themselves in communication with an underground world which extended beyond themselves. Such is the position of consciousness from one point of view. The position from the opposite point of view would be represented by a number of men living at isolated points, who at the threat of danger dug down under the delusion that they would in that way reach down to an underground passage which did not, as a matter of fact, exist. There are the two views. Either the one or the other must be true. Either consciousness is joined on to something which passes beyond its local appearance in certain physical conditions, or it is not. That is the position as it has always existed. Though appearances, in the shape of death, seem to be in favour of the materialist view, yet the matter was always "open." One could take the opposite side without any flagrant absurdity.

The question in this stage is, then, an open one. The balance of evidence is on the materialist side, but not sufficiently so to turn it into a nightmare. The arrival of the mechanistic view changes all this. It turns the open question into a closed one. It settles the thing definitely in favour of materialism. It is not merely that you may believe that this is the true view, but that you have to. The honest use of your reason leads you inevitably to that position.

IV

Before passing on to a description of this change, it is necessary to state briefly what the mechanistic conception of the world is. It can be given quickly by quotations. I begin with Spinoza: "There is in Nature nothing contingent, but all things are determined by the necessities of the divine nature to exist and to operate in a definite way"; this from a recent book by Munsterberg: "Science is to me not a mass of disconnected information, but the certainty that there is no change in the universe, no motion of an atom, and no sensation of a consciousness which does not come and go absolutely in accordance with natural laws; the certainty that nothing can exist outside the gigantic mechanism of causes and effects; necessity moves the emotions in my mind"; or by Laplace's famous boast: "An intellect which at a given instant knew all the forces with which Nature is animated and the respective situations of the beings that compose Nature — supposing that the said intellect were vast enough to subject these data to analysis — would embrace in the same formulae the motions of the greatest bodies in the universe and those of the slightest atom; nothing would be uncertain for it, and the future, like the past, would be present to its eyes"; and Huxley's, "If the fundamental proposition of evolution is true — that the entire world, living and not living, is the result of the mutual interaction according to definite laws of the forces possessed by the molecules of which the primitive nebulosity of the universe was composed — it is no less certain that the existing world lay potentially in the cosmic vapour, and that a sufficient intellect could, from a knowledge of the properties of molecules of that vapour, have predicted, say, the state of the fauna of Great Britain in 1869 with as much certainty as one can say what will happen to the vapour of the breath on a cold winter's day."

There was a time when this was only a theory which you could adopt if you liked it. In that time it could hardly have been called a nightmare. If you did not like it you could refuse to believe it. But the situation in the last two hundred years has entirely changed. The result of the progress of the sciences has been to exhibit it not as hypothesis to which one might adhere if one wanted to, but as a solid fact which must be taken account of whether one likes it or not. It seems to me personally, at any rate, to be the one thing which overshadows everything else in any attempt to get a satisfactory view of the cosmos.

The arrival of this state of things could be pictured by thinking of a parallel phenomenon which the observer can watch in any public park. You start, say, with a square green plot of grass. Then it occurs to the authorities that there are people who want to cross diagonally from one corner to the opposite one. So two paths are cut along the two diagonals. Then a further difficulty presents itself to the ingenious official. People might want to cross hurriedly from the middle of one side to the middle of the opposite side. Paths are cut for them, and so on until the whole plot is converted from grass into concrete. This is a schematic representation of a process that can be observed each year in Hyde Park. This is what has happened to the cosmos. The pieces of green — that is, the areas of freedom — are constantly disappearing, by a similar process. The whole world will, in the end, be all law — that is, all concrete. As Huxley put it: "The progress of science . . . means the extension of the province of what we call matter and causation and the gradual banishment of what . . . we call spirit and spontaneity. The consciousness of this great truth weighs like a nightmare upon many of the best minds, the advancing tide of matter threatens to drown their souls, the tightening grasp of law impedes their freedom."

The effect of this view of the world on the simple market-place beliefs about the soul is easily traced. It enormously strengthens the materialist side, for by making matter self-sufficing it makes consciousness a by-product and takes away from it all real action on things.

In the picture of the world as it existed before the arrival of the mechanistic theory you had a good deal of freedom in matter itself, and consciousness had this certificate, at least, to it — its independence and reality — that it was able to act directly on and to produce changes in this, the physical world. You might suspect its existence to be a precarious one; but, at any rate, it did exist temporarily, and could prove this existence by real action. But if you accept the mechanistic view of the world, not only does all freedom disappear from the material world, but also from the organic. The world is pictured as a mass of atoms and molecules, which are supposed to carry out unceasingly movements of every kind. The matter of which our bodies are composed is subject to the same laws as the matter outside. The motion of every atom of your brain is, then, subject to the same laws of motion as those which govern all matter. It is, then, completely mechanical and calculable. If, then, at any moment you knew the position of all the atoms of a human body, you could calculate with unfailing certainly the past, present, and future actions of the person to whom that body belonged. Consciousness, then, does nothing; it makes no difference; everything would go on just the same without it.

Before mechanism, consciousness occupied the position of a rather feeble king who still, by the favour of his troops, retained some power. The change produced by mechanism can be compared to the sudden discovery by the troops that they are self-sufficient and can manage things themselves. The monarchy then becomes a very flimsy thing. The effect of the change it produces may be got at also in this way. Suppose a number of figures arranged irregularly with a loose rope passing from one to the other. Let the figures represent consciousness and the rope inorganic matter. If you saw this from a distance you might think that the figures were real people and that the rope was to a certain extent subordinate to their purposes. But if as you watched you saw the rope suddenly tightened, and that as this happened the figures just hung loose on it, then you would recognise that they were merely dummies. Well, that is what happens to us as we gradually arrive at the mechanistic view. We suddenly see the matter under us, and which we to a certain extent felt that we rode, stiffen out to the rigidity of outside matter and move us independently of our own control. It is as if a living horse under us suddenly became a mechanical iron one which was self-acting. But, after all, I think the conception of the rope suddenly tightening gives the sensation best.

Before you can legitimately believe, then, in the existence of the soul, you have got to deal with this nightmare. This is the porch through which you must pass before you can arrive at any spiritual interpretation of the world. You can slip into such beliefs by getting in at side doors, but if you do you have not done the thing properly. There is nothing unusual in this phenomenon. In every age there has been such a porch. I have always been dissatisfied with the traditional division of the future life into heaven, hell, and purgatory. Or rather, I have always been dissatisfied with the conception of these states which makes them correspond as rewards to three divisions of merely ethical conduct. This has always seemd to me to be a singularly crude conception. If the reward is in any way to correspond to the tension and trouble which were necessary to attain it, then it is clear that the highest reward should not be given to a mere ethical perfection. Heaven should be reserved for a more troublesome thing than that — not for those who pursued the good, but for those who had successfully wrestled with the grave doubts they had as to whether the good existed or as to whether the word had any real meaning. A struggle with fundamental unbelief of this kind is much more of a valley of darkness than any mere ethical struggle. It is a much more painful state and deserves a different reward. This kind of unbelief is not an unfortunate accident that comes to a few fidgety people. It is a necessary stage through which all the saints must and should pass, and is a sign of their superiority (1) to the placidly good who go to purgatory, where they are subjected to compulsory doubts before they can pass on, and (2) to the simply bad people who go to hell and stay there.

The saint, then, in every generation has to struggle with an obstacle which stands in the way of any idealist or religious interpretation of the universe. There is some tremendous tendency of things which you have to vanquish before you can legitimately retain your beliefs in any spiritual values. There are some things which you have to conquer before you have any right at all to any spiritual view of the world. If you leave them behind without meeting them fairly you are living on false pretences, or it would perhaps be more accurate to say you are living on credit. You are giving away things that do not in the least belong to you. You have no right to be in a certain position until you have passed to it through a certain struggle. If you have not successfully met this obstacle you are in the position of the philanthropist who has no money. You may have most high falutin' sentiments, but you have no "effective demand," as the economists used to say. It seems that in beliefs about the cosmos there is the same brutal limiting condition. I may spend hours in talking about the soul in the most charming way, but if I have not first removed this obstacle I am then merely giving away something that does not belong to me: I am being merely futile. At the present time there is not the slightest doubt that this belief in mechanism constitutes the obstacle which the saint must surmount.

It is, fortunately, not necessary to labour the point very much that there is an essential incompatibility between the belief in mechanism and any religious attitude whatever towards the world. The incompatibility is so obvious and has been written about at such enormous length that it is certainly not worth while explaining in detail. It may, however, be worth while to indicate briefly two specimen ways of putting the matter. The beginning of any thought about these matters lies in the fact that we have certain preferences; we prefer good to evil, beauty to ugliness, etc. These preferences have of late years been indicated technically in philosophy by the word "values." Now it is the essence of any religious attitude towards the cosmos to believe (1) that these qualities are not merely valuable relatively to us, but are so absolutely, and lie in the nature of fundamental reality itself; (2) that the cosmos is so arranged that these things will be preserved and not perish. Hoffding has, indeed, defined religion as a "belief" in the conservation of values, and the definition is as accurate as definitions of such indefinable things can be. It is more convenient for me to consider first the latter of these necessary beliefs. Can there be any "conservation of values" if the world is to be considered as a mechanism? Obviously not, for the essence of mechanism is that it is self-acting and pays no attention at all to the things that we happen to attach value to. The conception of purpose is quite alien to it, for everything happens as the result of antecedent circumstance. It produced us and our values quite accidentally, and quite as accidentally it will snuff them all out again. Put more concretely in Mr. Balfour's often-quoted though still pleasing rhetoric: — "Man's . . . very existence is an accident, his story a brief and transitory episode in the life of one of the planets — of one of the meanest of the planets. We sound the future and learn that, after a period long enough compared with the individual life, but short indeed compared with the divisions of time open to our investigation, the energies of our system will decay, the glory of the sun will be dimmed, and the earth, tideless and inert, will no longer tolerate the race which has for a moment disturbed its solitude. Man will go down into the pit and all his thoughts perish. The uneasy consciousness which in this obscure corner has for a brief space broken the contented silence of the universe will be at rest. Matter will know itself no longer. 'Imperishable monuments' and 'immortal deeds,' death itself and love stronger than death will be as though they had never been. Nor will anything that is be better or worse for all that the labour, genius, devotion, and suffering of man have striven through countless generations to effect."

A world of this kind cannot concern itself with the "conservation of values." On the contrary, it seems doomed inevitably to destroy them all. In as far as we hold the mechanistic conception and are honest with ourselves we are bound to admit that the world will end either by cooling, or perhaps earlier by collision; but in either case "accidentally," in the sense that this end will take no account of the things we value.

It will end "accidentally," and not when it has fulfilled its purpose or any nonsense of that kind. This automatically knocks on the head any "religion of progress" which attempts to reconcile one to materialism. I would judge any such so-called philosophy by its eschatology. Does it deal with this basic fact or does it attempt to fudge the thing? That it is a difficulty the ingenious authors of such half-baked concoctions evidently feel, for they will explain that by the time this end approaches man will have so "evolved" that he will be able to escape the wrecked planet. Such pieces of childish nonsense are evidences of the truth that it is impossible, if mechanism be a true account of the world, for us to believe in any preservation of values. The world as presented by mechanistic theory is utterly alien and has from our point of view neither rhyme nor reason.

As to the second criterion. It is asserted that we cannot attach any real meaning to our judgments of value if we believe that they are merely personal and relative to man. They must correspond to something in the nature of fundamental reality itself. Is it, then, possible to believe in any values of this kind and at the same time that one holds the mechanistic view of the world? To examine this question I recall exactly what the mechanistic view is by a quotation: — "Every occurrence in the universe is, then, ultimately only a change of position of indivisible particles of which each is completely determined in movement by the preceding movements of the whole system; even the life processes are only physical and chemical occurrences, and every chemical and physical change resolves itself ultimately and finally into mechanical movements of atoms."

Now in such a world the word "value" has clearly no meaning. There cannot be any good or bad in such a turmoil of atoms. There are arrangements which are simple and arrangements which are complex, but nothing gives the slightest warrant for the claim that the complex is better than the simple or the more lasting than the fugitive. If this view of the world is the true one, all the bottom drops out of our set of values. The very touch of such a conception freezes all the values and kills them. It remains as a perpetual menace. As long as it exists no idealist can live a quiet life, for he might at any moment be tripped up by the awful fact. It is a perpetual reminder that you are living in a fool's paradise. I am quite aware that this is a trouble only to a limited number of people — to those who have had a certain kind of education; but to them it is quite as annoying as was Banquo's ghost.

It is, perhaps, necessary to point out that at a certain stage this prospect does not appear to be a nightmare to us. At a certain stage of one's mental evolution the delight in finding that one can completely explain the world as one might solve a puzzle is so exciting that it quite puts in the shade the disadvantages of the conception from other points of view. It is not a nightmare to us — far from it. We delight in it. It is something like the feeling produced by a new toy or a steam-engine that "works" to a boy. It exhilarates us to feel that we have got a neat key to the universe in our pockets, and this delight of acquisition obliterates the nightmarish effect it would naturally produce in a man. One delights in it so much that one resents any attempt to interfere with it or to show that it is not a fact but merely a hypothesis. I recall quite vividly the emotion I felt when I looked, in my school library, at Stallo's quite harmless little book which makes fun of the conservation of energy. I positively detested the sight of the book on the shelves. I would have liked to have it removed from the library. My resentment was of exactly the same nature and due to the same causes as that with which an old lady, all of whose scanty income comes from land, might hear of a proposal for land nationalisation. My toy would have been taken away from me.

But this is only a temporary phenomenon. For the natural man this counteracting emotion would soon be removed and the mechanistic conception would once more become a nightmare. In the few cases in which it does not appear to be a nightmare it is because this kind of delight in the simplicity of a theory and the exhilaration and sense of power it produces have remained beyond the years of puberty to which it is appropriate, and still continue to veil to a man the real horror of his belief.

Those who have read the "Arabian Nights," or failing that, have seen "Sumûrun," will remember the story of the barber who, having swallowed a fish-bone, was taken for dead. How everybody, wishing to be free of the possible unpleasant consequences of having this corpse discovered in their house, passed it on to someone else. The corpse always turned up at some inopportune moment. A man returning cheerful from a banquet found it on his staircase; a bridegroom found it in his bed, and so on. Well, it seems to me that you have an exact parallel here for the nightmare — of the conception of the world which considers that it is a vast mechanism. First Democritus put the fish-bone into the body of the cosmos, then

Lucretius rammed it in; and ever since, after the banquet of an idealist philosophy or the delights of a romantist Weltanschauung we are confronted, when the lights are turned out and our powers of self-delusion with them, with this frightful and hope-killing apparition of the corpse of a "dead world," of a cosmos which is nothing but a vast mechanism.

It is not to be escaped or passed on to your neighbour as long as it exists. No man can honestly hold any optimistic or cheerful view of the world. Of course, there are various ways of hiding it; you can cover it up with various cloths made out of words; you can agree to look at it "sub specie eternitatis." But to the plain man none of these ways is successful. Whatever colour the corpse is painted it remains a corpse. You will remember that at the end of the story the barber was shaken and the fish-bone fell out, whereupon the corpse came back to life to the no small astonishment of the beholders. It seems to me that, as far as I am concerned, at any rate, the fish-bone has been taken out of the corpse of the cosmos; and it is to celebrate the accomplishment of this feat that I am about to execute a war-dance in these pages.

V

A correspondent in a number of this review some weeks ago * pointed out that my parable of the barber and the fish-bone was only correct when properly interpreted. It was necessary to notice that what happened was not that the barber's soul reawoke on a new plane of existence, but that his *body* came to life again. This was precisely what I intended to convey; but as I may not have made my meaning sufficiently clear, I had better emphasise the point in more detail here. I can at the same time use this as a pretext for an examination of the general characteristics which any refutation of mechanism must possess if we are to find it completely satisfactory. I use the word "satisfactory" with a definite intention. I carefully refrain from saying "true." I do not pretend to be discussing abstract philosophy here; I am only estimating things from a personal point of view. I want to find out what must

* EDITOR'S NOTE. *New Age*, X (December 14, 1911), 167.

be the characteristics of that refutation of mechanism which would, as a matter of actual fact, succeed in shifting the hold of mechanism over the emotions of a certain type of intelligence. If I am asked what kind of intelligence, I simply reply: the type of intelligence that *does* find mechanism a nightmare.

That answers, I think, the second point in the same correspondent's letter. He is surprised that anyone, even admitting the truth of mechanism, should find it a nightmare. I understand his point of view; I know that it is possible to look at the matter in that way. It is a possible position even for the man who at one time has felt mechanism to be a great difficulty. For some people, by a kind of slow and gradual change, and not by any definite and conscious process, the difficulty vanishes. Mechanism is never definitely dealt with and routed; it simply seems to lose its importance. In ten years' time you may find you have changed from a belief in materialism to the belief that ultimate reality is a republic of eternal souls, without knowing exactly how it has happened. There has been no definite rational act. It is like the dissolving pictures that one used to see in the pre-cinema age, where one scene melts away into the next and is not shifted to make room for its successor. In your view of the cosmos the things which at one time seemed the solid things melt away, and the flimsy, cloud-like entities gradually harden down till they become the solid bases on which the rest of our beliefs are supported. Whereas at one time you felt sure that matter was the only permanent thing; you now find that you are equally convinced, without any necessity of proof, of the permanent existence of individuals. In any argument you always rest on some base which is taken for granted, and you now find yourself in the position of taking the reality of individuality as such a base. It does not seem necessary to rest it on anything else. In this change mechanism has never actually been refuted; it has just gradually faded away into insignificance, and other things have come into the high lights. But it has not faded away altogether; it remains on the fringe of the mind. It is, however, no longer a difficulty, because all the emphasis and the accent are elsewhere. The best way to put it is to say that all the "values" of the world landscape are altered. Mechanism is still in the picture, but it is no longer the high light, it no longer dominates everything else.

But here a curious situation arises. Pressed on the point, a man in this state would still have to admit that mechanism was a true account of things, yet it no longer seems to him to "matter"; he is no longer disconcerted by the discrepancies between that and the rest of his beliefs. He has never refuted mechanism; time has simply packed the skeleton away. You bring it out of the cupboard and you find that it no longer has the power to startle. It is still the same skeleton, yet it no longer disconcerts. Why?

The process by which the mind manages not to be disconcerted forms a complicated and interesting piece of psychology. The mind executes a set of manoeuvres which, on a different plane, is quite as complicated as the elaborate balancing of personal motives which took place on the lawn at Patterne Hall. I am myself incapable of giving anything more than a very crude outline of these manoeuvres. To commence by a restatement of the preliminary position: the mechanistic theory, while never having been refuted, has gradually come to occupy a very subordinate place in the outlook of a certain type of intelligence. Occasionally, it may be under pressure from outside, or of its own inner buoyancy, it floats up to the surface of their minds; it no longer seems to be a nightmare? Why? The first step towards the solution of the problem is to recognise that the expression "floats up to the surface of the mind" is not an accurate description of what does happen to these people. The idea "the world may be a mere mechanism" does not, as a rule float to the top, but only to a depth at which it is not a clearly-outlined idea, but rather a confused sentiment. In the kind of unconscious reasoning appropriate to this depth the man probably accommodates himself to the momentary chill produced fairly easily in the manner I am about to describe. It does not take the shape of a formulated argument; if it was, he would probably perceive its absurdity himself. It is rather an unformulated reaction to an unformulated doubt. The whole thing takes place on the plane of quality and feeling, rather than that of clear representation. I used the word "chill" a minute ago. That is a more accurate description of the beginning of the process than the words "perception of the consequences of mechanism" would be. Just below the surface of the stream of conscious life you have a vague apprehension of a quality, a sensation which has a disagreeable feeling tone and which contains within it the potency and the capacity for developing into an awkward and unpleasant idea — that of the truth of mechanism. At the depth in the stream of consciousness at which you first become aware of it, it is merely a closed-up parcel; but if you allowed it to come to the top it would pass from the state of feeling to that of representation, and would unpack itself into a clearly-perceived contradiction and fissure in your Weltanschauung. But you do not generally allow it to do that. When its presence becomes felt merely as a chilling shadow thrown on the level of your clearly-focussed conscious life, you deal with it at once on the level at which you perceive it; you meet one sentiment by another. For that reason the arguments which I give here as those by which a man in this state deals with a revival of the mechanistic view in his own mind may seem too like caricature. It must be remembered that they do not represent the actual thoughts which pass through the mind. In fact, the thought-level is not involved at all. But the manoeuvres I give here do represent what the closed parcel of sentiment would develop into were you so foolish as to actually unpack it into definite arguments on the level of clear ideas.

The attitude of mind by which the revival of the mechanism nightmare is generally met consists mainly of the vague kind of idea that the matter has been dealt with and finished long ago. How or by whom is not clearly known. To persist in wanting it done in detail before our eyes is asking too much. There are some questions to which every person of intelligence is expected to know the answer because they are still live questions; but there are others to which no one need know the answer because they are finished with. It might reasonably be expected, for example, of every person interested in the matter, in the time of Copernicus, that they should know in detail the arguments by which the Ptolemaic astronomy was refuted. It is no longer necessary at the present moment to know the arguments in detail, for there is unanimous agreement that the refutation has been made. The people whose mental attitude I am describing are probably of the opinion that this is the case also with mechanism. Forty years ago, in the curiously remote barbaric Huxleyan period, it would have been necessary. Mechanism has been refuted years ago, and it is very démodé and provincial to be ignorant of the fact, to want to see it done again. A persistence in the demand for details would be out of place in the atmosphere in which you find yourself; you feel like a boor in a drawing-room, and you finally stop wanting even to ask questions. I am speaking here of myself as the outside questioner, though, of course, what I really am trying to get at is the state of doubt inside the other man himself. What does fortify these people in dealing with the doubt is really in the end nothing but just a kind of "atmosphere" of this kind — an atmosphere which automatically overpowers certain objections and makes them seem silly. It seems to say: "We don't do these things; we are past that stage." In a certain famous play the nouveau riche tells everybody that he cleans his teeth every day now, the "real gentleman" being supposed to clean his teeth three times a day without mentioning it. Something of the same kind is conveyed to you by the mental atmosphere of this type of people. It is not necessary to refute mechanism "in public" or to talk about it. I must state here that I am not speaking of this state of mind with contempt; I have been perilously near it myself a good many times.

There is also a second type who, like the correspondent I am answering, find it difficult to believe that mechanism can be a nightmare, and who are impatient with the excesssive importance attached to the problem. I heard Mr. Yeats lecturing on "Psychical Research" in a drawing-room the other day. He started by stating that, in his opinion, the whole subject had been distorted by the extraordinary anxiety of most of the people who wrote about it to meet the scepticism of the kind of man they met at dinner. He seemed to imply that, if you put this pusillanimous belief in materialism on one side, you would advance much quicker. Your theories then, freed from the necessity of meeting certain objections, would be much simpler and much more likely to be true. This seems to me to be an exactly similar state of mind to that of the people who dream of the glorious new kind of poetry that would arise if inspiration could only be emancipated from the hampering restrictions of rhyme, metre, and form generally. Everybody can see the absurdity of sentiments of this kind applied to the arts. It is a platitude to say that form here is a liberating and not a restricting thing. But precisely the same statement can be made of theories about the soul. It is not by ignoring mechanism that you will arrive at anything worth having, but by struggling with it. I know this sentence has an uncomfortably ethical flavour, but I hasten to add that it is not intended; it is merely a plain statement of a universal law. The bird attained whatever grace its shape possesses not as a result of the mere desire for flight, but because it had to fly *in air against gravitation*. There are some happy people who can believe any theory they find interesting; others, as soon as they want to believe any theory, feel the full force of certain objections. They are in the position of a man who by jumping may leave the ground, but is at once dragged down again by his own weight. To all kinds of idealistic interpretations of the world there are certain objections of this kind. And just as the whole group of phenomena connected with falling bodies are summed up in the law of gravitation, so all the objections that have in the course of history been urged against the various idealisms seem to me to be summed up and focussed in the mechanistic theory. In it all the ragged doubts and objections seem suddenly to dovetail together and to close up, like certain kinds of box-lids, with a click. It is for that reason that I regard the problem of mechanism with a certain amount of actual enthusiasm. It is not merely an annoying obstacle, but it is the characteristic convention and form which the masters of the philosophic art have to conquer. It is only by dealing with it that any spiritual interpretation of the world can acquire validity, and what is quite as important, a decent shape. Anyone who ignores it will not only have attained his position illegitimately, but, what is definitely worse, he may be accused of being the "Walt Whitman of the soul."

So much for the people who, like the correspondent I have referred to, do not find mechanism a nightmare. I am concerned now with the tougher people who have realised the problem and have attempted to deal with it. For Bergson, of course, is not the only philosopher who has refuted mechanism. It is one of the favourite occupations of the tribe. You could if you liked write the whole history of philosophy, for the last two hundred years, at any rate, from that point of view. The question has been an obsession. One cannot read Coleridge, for example, without seeing what a very real worry it was to him. It seems necessary to mention some of these refutations, if only to be able to define the state of mind which finds them unsatisfactory. The account I give of them must be necessarily so short that it will resemble caricature.

The first and the simplest way of dealing with mechanism is to frankly accept it as a true account of the nature of the universe, but at the same time to hold that this fact makes no difference to ethical values. This is the view generally associated with Huxley's famous Romanes lecture. It has been stated quite recently by Mr. Bertrand Russell in an article which is called "The Religion of a Plain Man," or something of that kind. [It is some time since I read this, and I am rather vague about it. It has since been republished, but the book is always out of the London Library, and I have always felt sure that no new exposition of this ancient view could be worth six shillings. As far as I remember, however, it was very like Lange's phrase: "A noble man is not the least disturbed in his zeal for his ideals, though he be told, and tells himself, that his ideal world, with all its settings of a God, immortal hopes and eternal truths, is a mere imagination and no reality. These are all real for life just because they are psychic ideals."]

Consciousness generally, and ethical principles in particular, are supposed to be mere by-products of a world-process which produces them accidentally and which will in time inevitably destroy them. Yet we are to act as though these ethical principles had an absolute value. The world has no purpose; our ethical values do not, as a matter of fact, correspond to anything in the nature of ultimate reality, and yet we are to act as though they did. The fact that it all leads to nothing is supposed to give an added dignity to man's ethical endeavours. People who take this view can be called stoics in the literal meaning of the word. In my last "note" I called mechanism the "porch" through which you had to pass to arrive at any legitimate spiritual interpretation of the world. These stoics really are "porch" philosophers, for they sit contentedly on the steps and, pointing over their shoulders at the door, say: "This is permanently closed; no one can ever get to the garden inside; but, bless you, we don't mind that — we *like* being outside — we keep on paying the entrance-money as a hobby." I suppose I ought to qualify this a little and point out that I am expressing surprise, not at the fact that ethical conduct can be compatible with materialism, but at the absolute importance that such a view manages to give to such ethical values.

It is an attitude which has a long history, and which at every period has always satisfied a minority. There has always been a certain glamour attached to this form of "resignation." Owing, I suppose, to a certain coarseness in my nature, I have never been able to appreciate it. There has always seemed to me to be something ridiculous in the position, just for this reason: that it is a little "too much"; it is a little pretentious; one instinctively feels that there is something wrong —something a little shoddy about it. One can understand that a man may feel himself compelled by facts to believe that mechanism is a true account of the universe — there is nothing objectionable in that. But it is mere perverse and inhuman romanticism to pretend that this gives added sanction and dignity to our ethical ideals. It violates common experience; it is a little inhuman, and has a certain element of posturing in it.

To assume this position — to believe that the purposelessness of the world gives an added and melancholy dignity to the position of man — may be an "interesting" position to take up at a tea-party — you may then maintain it with vehemence and sincerity as a thesis; but it goes against all honest human instincts. I cannot admire it myself any more than I can ever admire the pale and unearthly high-mindedness of the agnostic who objects to people being good because they want to go to heaven. Shutting himself up in a corner he is condemning universal and legitimate instincts.

The universal instinct has got hold of the truth. I cannot for the life of me see any particular reason for taking life seriously unless it is serious. I cannot see why mankind should be too big for its boots.

This way of dealing with mechanism can be legitimately called sentimentalism, for it clouds over the real outlines of its own position. It shrinks from consistency and refuses to go "to the end" of its belief. Its faith is anaemic. Real belief in the existence of a physical object means that one *acts* in accordance with its perceived shape. If I am convinced that the table is square, I do not try to cut off corners when I am walking past it as I should do if it were circular. So with materialism. To be a materialist should mean to act as a materialist. Consistent materialism is to a certain extent an attractive position. But this other thing — this combination of belief in mechanism and a belief in absolute values — is just irritating sloppiness. The sloppiness is betrayed by the rhetoric in which the position is stated. In the people who take this view you find that heightening of phraseology which always accompanies unconscious untruthfulness. Rhetoric is, I suppose, always unattractive, but it is never more loathsome than when it accomplishes this glazing over of materialism. I say "loathsome" because I think the epithet accurate. I find myself extremely surprised at the adjectives that jump into my mind when I read this kind of stuff. It must be that Nature takes her revenge on those perverted people amongst us, to whom the phraseology of the robustious theatre seems unreal, by turning philosophy itself into a melodrama. At any rate, as I read these modern stoics I gain by an effort of sympathetic intuition an understanding of all those Adelphi phrases which before seen merely from the outside seemed so artificial. I understand now that occasions may arise when the natural expression of one's emotions can only be accomplished by the incoherent use of the words "filth," "sewerage," and the rest of it. My annoyance demands physical expression. I want to do something dramatic with the printed page. I find myself muttering: "You think that, do you? You ———!"

The second method of dealing with mechanism is a little more human.

LITERARY CRITICISM

A LECTURE
ON MODERN POETRY

I want to begin by a statement of the attitude I take towards verse. I do that in order to anticipate criticism. I shall speak of verse from a certain rather low but quite definite level, and I think that criticism ought to be confined to that level. The point of view is that verse is simply and solely the means of expression. I will give you an example of the position exactly opposite to the one I take up. A reviewer writing in *The Saturday Review* last week spoke of poetry as the means by which the soul soared into higher regions, and as a means of expression by which it became merged into a higher kind of reality. Well, that is the kind of statement that I utterly detest. I want to speak of verse in a plain way as I would of pigs: that is the only honest way. The President told us last week that poetry was akin to religion. It is nothing of the sort. It is a means of expression just as prose is, and if you can't justify it from that point of view it's not worth preserving.

I always suspect the word soul when it is brought into discussion. It reminds me of the way that the medieval scientists spoke of God. When entirely ignorant of the cause of anything, they said God did it. If I use the word soul, or speak of higher realities, in the course of my speech, you will know that at that precise point I didn't know of any real reason and was trying to bluff you. There is a tremendous amount of hocus-pocus about most discussions of poetry. Critics attempting to explain technique make mysterious passes and mumble of the infinite and the human heart, for all the world as though they were selling a patent medicine in the market-place.

There are two ways in which one can consider this. The first as a difficulty to be conquered, the second as a tool for use. In the first case, we look upon poets as we look upon pianists, and speak of them as masters of verse. The other way is to consider it merely as a tool which we want to use ourselves for definite purposes. One daily paper compared us to the Mermaid Club, but we are not. We are a number of modern people, and verse must be justified as a means of expression for us. I have not a catholic taste but a violently personal and prejudiced one. I have no reverence for tradition. I came to the subject of verse from the inside rather than from the outside. There were certain impressions which I wanted to fix. I read verse to find models, but I could not find any that seemed exactly suitable to express that kind of impression, except perhaps a few jerky rhythms of Henley, until I came to read the French *vers-libre* which seemed to exactly fit the case.

So that I don't want any literary criticism, that would be talking on another level. I don't want to be killed with a bludgeon, and references to Dante, Milton and the rest of them.

The principle on which I rely in this paper is that there is an intimate connection between the verse form and the state of poetry at any period. All kinds of reasons are given by the academic critics for the efflorescence of verse at any period. But the true one is very seldom given. It is the invention or introduction of a new verse form. To the artist the introduction of a new art form is, as Moore says, like a new dress to a girl; he wants to see himself in it. It is a new toy. You will find the burst of poetic activity at the time of Elizabeth put down to the discovery of America. The discovery of America had about as much effect on the Courtier poets at that time as the discovery of a new asteroid would have had on the poetic activity of Swinburne. The real reason was, I take it, that the first opportunity was given for the exercise of verse composition by the introduction of all kinds of new matter and new forms from Italy and France.

It must be admitted that verse forms, like manners, and like individuals, develop and die. They evolve from their initial freedom to decay and finally to virtuosity. They disappear before the new man, burdened with the thought more complex and more difficult to express by the old name. After being too much used, their primitive effect is lost. All possible tunes have been played on the instrument. What possibility is there in that for the new men, or what attraction? It would be different if poetry, like acting and dancing, were one of the arts of which no record can be kept, and which must be repeated for each generation. The actor has not to feel the competition of the dead as the poet has. Personally I am of course in favour of the complete destruction of all verse more than twenty years old. But that happy event will not, I am afraid, take place until Plato's desire has been realized and a minor poet has become dictator. Meanwhile it is necessary to realize that as poetry is immortal, it is differentiated from those arts which must be repeated. I want to call attention to this point — it is only those arts whose expression is repeated every generation that have an immutable technique. Those arts like poetry, whose matter is immortal, must find a new technique each generation. Each age must have its own special form of expression, and any period that deliberately goes out of it is an age of insincerity.

The latter stages in the decay of an art form are very interesting and worth study because they are peculiarly applicable to the state of poetry at the present day. They resemble the latter stages in the decay of religion when the spirit has gone and there is a meaningless reverence for formalities and ritual. The carcass is dead, and all the flies are upon it. Imitative poetry springs up like weeds, and women whimper and whine of you and I alas, and roses, roses all the way. It becomes the expression of sentimentality rather than of virile thought.

The writers who would be able to use the old instrument with the old masters refuse to do so, for they find it inadequate. They know the entirely empirical nature of the old rules and refuse to be cramped by them.

It is at these periods that a new art form is created; after the decay of Elizabethan poetic drama came the heroic couplet, after the decay of the couplet came the new lyrical poetry that has lasted till now. It is interesting to notice that these changes do not come by a kind of natural progress of which the artist himself is unconscious. The new forms are deliberately introduced by people who detest the old ones. Modern lyrical verse was introduced by Wordsworth with no pretence of it being a natural progress; he announced it in good set terms as a new method.

The particular example which has most connection with what I have to say is that of the Parnassian school about 1885: itself beginning as a reaction from romanticism, it has come rapidly to decay; its main principle of an absolute perfection of rhyme and form was in harmony with the natural school of the time. It was a logical form of verse, as distinct from a symbolical one. There were prominent names in it, Monde, Prudhomme, etc., but they were not very fertile; they did not produce anything of great importance; they confined themselves to repeating the same sonnet time after time, their pupils were lost in a state of sterile feebleness.

I wish you to notice that this was not the kind of unfortunate accident which has happened by chance to a number of poets. This check to the Parnassian school marked the death of a particular form of French poetry which coincided with the birth and marvellous fertility of a new form. With the definite arrival of this new form of verse in 1880 came the appearance of a band of poets perhaps unequalled at any one time in the history of French poetry.

The new technique was first definitely stated by Kahn. It consisted in a denial of a regular number of syllables as the basis of versification. The length of the line is long and short, oscillating with the images used by the poet; it follows the contours of his thoughts and is free rather than regular; to use a rough analogy, it is clothes made to order, rather than ready-made clothes. This is a very bald statement of it, and I am not concerned here so much with French poetry as with English. The kind of verse I advocate is not the same as *vers-libre*, I merely use the French as an example of the extraordinary effect that an emancipation of verse can have on poetic activity.

The ancients were perfectly aware of the fluidity of the world and of its impermanence; there was the Greek theory that the whole world was a flux. But while they recognized it, they feared it and endeavoured to evade it, to construct things of permanence which would stand fast in this universal flux which frightened them. They had the disease, the passion, for immortality. They wished to construct things which should be proud boasts that they, men, were immortal. We see it in a thousand different forms. Materially in the pyramids, spiritually in the dogmas of religion and in the hypostatized ideas of Plato. Living in a dynamic world they wished to create a static fixity where their souls might rest.

This I conceive to be the explanation of many of the old ideas on poetry. They wish to embody in a few lines a perfection of thought. Of the thousand and one ways in which a thought might roughly be conveyed to a hearer there was one way which was the perfect way, which was destined to embody that thought to all eternity, hence the fixity of the form of poem and the elaborate rules of regular metre. It was to be an immortal thing and the infinite pains taken to fit a thought into a fixed and artificial form are necessary and understandable. Even the Greek name ποίημα seems to indicate the thing created once and for all, they believed in absolute duty as they believed in absolute truth. Hence they put many things into verse which we now do not desire to, such as history and philosophy. As the French philosopher Guyau put it, the great poems of ancient times resembled pyramids built for eternity where people loved to inscribe their history in symbolic characters. They believed they could realize an adjustment of idea and words that nothing could destroy.

Now the whole trend of the modern spirit is away from that; philosophers no longer believe in absolute truth. We no longer believe in perfection, either in verse or in thought, we frankly acknowledge the relative. We shall no longer strive to attain the absolutely perfect form in poetry. Instead of these minute perfections of phrase and words, the tendency will be rather towards the production of a general effect; this of course takes away the predominance of metre and a regular number of syllables as the element of perfection in words. We are no longer concerned that stanzas shall be shaped and polished like gems, but rather that some vague mood shall be communicated. In all the arts, we seek for the maximum of individual and personal expression, rather than for the attainment of any absolute beauty.

The criticism is sure to be made, what is this new spirit, which finds itself unable to express itself in the old metre? Are the things that a poet wishes to say now in any way different to the things that former poets say? I believe that they are. The old poetry dealt essentially with big things, the expression of epic subjects leads naturally to the anatomical matter and regular verse. Action can best be expressed in regular verse, e.g., the Ballad.

But the modern is the exact opposite of this, it no longer deals with heroic action, it has become definitely and finally introspective and deals with expression and communication of momentary phases in the poet's mind. It was well put by Mr. G. K. Chesterton in this way — that where the old dealt with the Siege of Troy, the new attempts to express the emotions of a boy fishing. The opinion you often hear expressed, that perhaps a new poet will arrive who will synthesize the whole modern movement into a great epic, shows an entire misconception of the tendency of modern verse. There is an analogous change in painting, where the old endeavoured to tell a story, the modern attempts to fix an impression. We still perceive the mystery of things, but we perceive it in entirely a different way — no longer directly in the form of action, but as an impression, for example Whistler's pictures. We can't escape from the spirit of our times. What has found expression in painting as Impressionism will soon find expression in poetry as free verse. The vision of a London street at midnight, with its long rows of light, has produced several attempts at reproduction in verse, and yet the war produced nothing worth mentioning, for Mr. Watson is a political orator rather than a poet. Speaking of personal matters, the first time I ever felt the necessity or inevitableness of verse, was in the desire to reproduce the peculiar quality of feeling which is induced by the flat spaces and wide horizons of the virgin prairie of western Canada.

You see that this is essentially different to the lyrical impulse which has attained completion, and I think once and forever, in Tennyson, Shelley and Keats. To put this modern conception of the poetic spirit, this tentative and half-shy manner of looking at things, into regular metre is like putting a child into armour.

Say the poet is moved by a certain landscape, he selects from that certain images which, put into juxtaposition in separate lines, serve to suggest and to evoke the state he feels. To this piling-up and juxtaposition of distinct images in different lines, one can find a fanciful analogy in music. A great revolution in music when, for the melody that is one-dimensional music, was substituted harmony which moves in two. Two visual images form what one may call a visual chord. They unite to suggest an image which is different to both.

Starting then from this standpoint of extreme modernism, what are the principal features of verse at the present time? It is this: that it is read and not chanted. We may set aside all theories that we read verse internally as mere verbal quibbles. We have thus two distinct arts. The one intended to be chanted, and the other intended to be read in the study. I wish this to be remembered in the criticisms that are made on me. I am not speaking of the whole of poetry, but of this distinct new art which is gradually separating itself from the older one and becoming independent.

I quite admit that poetry intended to be recited must be written in regular metre, but I contend that this method of recording impressions by visual images in distinct lines does not require the old metric system.

The older art was originally a religious incantation: it was made to express oracles and maxims in an impressive manner, and rhyme and metre were used as aids to the memory. But why, for this new poetry, should we keep a mechanism which is only suited to the old?

The effect of rhythm, like that of music, is to produce a kind of hypnotic state, during which suggestions of grief or ecstasy are easily and powerfully effective, just as when we are drunk all jokes seem funny. This is for the art of chanting, but the procedure of the new visual art is just the contrary. It depends for its effect not on a kind of half sleep produced, but on arresting the attention, so much so that the succession of visual images should exhaust one.

Regular metre to this impressionist poetry is cramping, jangling, meaningless, and out of place. Into the delicate pattern of images and colour it introduces the heavy, crude pattern of rhetorical verse. It destroys the effect just as a barrel organ does, when it intrudes into the subtle interwoven harmonies of the modern symphony. It is a delicate and difficult art, that of evoking an image, of fitting the rhythm to the idea, and one is tempted to fall back to the comforting and easy arms of the old, regular metre, which takes away all the trouble for us.

The criticism is sure to be made that when you have abolished the regular syllabled line as the unit of poetry, you have turned it into prose. Of course this is perfectly true of a great quantity of modern verse. In fact, one of the great blessings of the abolition of regular metre would be that it would at once expose all this sham poetry.

Poetry as an abstract thing is a very different matter, and has its own life, quite apart from metre as a convention.

To test the question of whether it is possible to have poetry written without a regular metre, I propose to pick out one great difference between the two. I don't profess to give an infallible test that would enable anyone to at once say: "this is, or is not, true poetry," but it will be sufficient for the purposes of this paper. It is this: that there are, roughly speaking, two methods of communication, a direct, and a conventional language. The direct language is poetry, it is direct because it deals in images. The indirect language is prose, because it uses images that have died and become figures of speech.

The difference between the two is, roughly, this: that while one arrests your mind all the time with a picture, the other allows the mind to run along with the least possible effort to a conclusion.

Prose is due to a faculty of the mind something resembling reflex action in the body. If I had to go through a complicated mental process each time I laced my boots, it would waste mental energy; instead of that, the mechanism of the body is so arranged that one can do it almost without thinking. It is an economy of effort. The same process takes place with the images used in prose. For example, when I say that the hill was clad with trees, it merely conveys the fact to me that it was covered. But the first time that expression was used by a poet, and to him it was an image recalling to him the distinct visual analogy of a man clad in clothes; but the image has died. One might say that images are born in poetry. They are used in prose, and finally die a long, lingering death in journalists' English. Now this process is very rapid, so that the poet must continually be creating new images, and his sincerity may be measured by the number of his images.

Sometimes in reading a poem, one is conscious of gaps where the inspiration failed him, and he only used metre of rhetoric. What happened was this: the image failed him, and he fell back on a dead image, that is prose, but kept an effect by using metre. That is my objection to metre, that it enables people to write verse with no poetic inspiration, and whose mind is not stored with new images.

As an example of this, I will take the poem which now has the largest circulation. Though consisting of only four verses it is six feet long. It is posted outside the Pavilion Music-hall. We instinctively shudder at these clichés or tags of speech. The inner explanation is this: it is not that they are old, but that being old they have become dead, and so evoked no image. The man who wrote them not being a poet, did not see anything definitely himself, but imitated other poets' images.

This new verse resembles sculpture rather than music; it appeals to the eye rather than to the ear. It has to mould images, a kind of spiritual clay, into definite shapes. This material, the ὕλη of Aristotle, is image and not sound. It builds up a plastic image which it hands over to the reader, whereas the old art endeavoured to influence him physically by the hypnotic effect of rhythm.

One might sum it all up in this way: a shell is a very suitable covering for the egg at a certain period of its career, but very unsuitable at a later stage. This seems to me to represent fairly well the state of verse at the present time. While the shell remains the same, the inside character is entirely changed. It is not addled, as a pessimist might say, but has become alive, it has changed from the ancient art of chanting to the modern impressionist, but the mechanism of verse has remained the same. It can't go on doing so. I will conclude, ladies and gentlemen, by saying, the shell must be broken.

NOTES ON
LANGUAGE AND STYLE

I believe that while the world cosmically cannot be reduced to unity as science proclaims (in the postulate of uniformity), yet on the contrary poetry can. At least its methods follow certain easily defined routes. (Any one can be taught how to use poetry.)

Real work, history and scientific researches, the accidental, the excrescences, like digging, and necessary just as digging is. Poetry the permanent humanity, the expression of man freed from his digging, digging for poetry when it is over.

CLUMSINESS OF PROSE — RELATION OF LANGUAGE AND THE IDEA EXPRESSED

Analysis of the attitude of a man reading an argument

(i) Compare in algebra, the real things are replaced by symbols. These symbols are manipulated according to certain laws which are independent of their meaning. N.B. At a certain point in the proof we cease to think of x as having a meaning and look upon it as a mere counter to be manipulated.

(ii) An analogous phenomenon happens in reasoning in language. We replace meaning (i.e. *vision*) by words. These words fall into well-known patterns, i.e. into certain well-known phrases which we accept without thinking of their meaning, just as we do the x in algebra. *But* there is a constant movement above and below the line of meaning (representation).* And this is used in dialec-

---

* NOTE BY MICHAEL ROBERTS. Hulme illustrates this by a little sketch of a curve rising above a fixed horizontal line (the level of *meaning*) and falling again.

tical argument. At any stage we can ask the opponent to show his hand, that is to turn all his *words* into visions, in realities we can see.

Seeing "solid" things

One facet of the idea may be expressed in this way. Refer back to note on the use of *x* in arithmetic and its analogy in expression. Habitually we may say that the reader takes words as *x without* the meaning attached. Aphra * sees each word with an image sticking on to it, never a flat word passed over a board like a counter.

Perhaps the nearest analogy is the hairy caterpillar. Taking each segment of his body as a word, the hair on that segment is the vision the poet sees behind it.

It is difficult to do this, so that the poet is forced to use new analogies, and especially to construct a plaster model of a thing to express his emotion at the sight of the vision he sees, his wonder and ecstasy. If he employed the ordinary word, the reader would only see it as a segment, with no hair, used for getting along. And without this clay, spatial image, he does not feel that he has expressed at all what he sees.

The ordinary caterpillar for crawling along from one position to another. The hairy one for beauty, to build up a solid vision of realities.

All emotion depends on real solid vision or sound. It is physical.

But in *rhetoric* and expositional prose we get words divorced from any real vision. Rhetoric and emotion — here the connection is different.

So perhaps literary expression is from *Real to Real* with all the intermediate forms keeping their *real* value. In expositional reasoning, the intermediate terms have only counter value. Give an example of *counter* prose (boy's letter to paper).

Watching a class: the difference between their attitude to geography and that to mathematics. Probably having only spatial

---

* NOTE BY MICHAEL ROBERTS. Hulme was going to write a book about a character called Aphra.

imagination, the geography is quite clear and comprehensible. If the mathematics could be got into the same flat form upon a map, with only relative distances to be observed, then their difficulties would vanish.

This suggests that the type of all reasoning is that of arranging counters on the flat, where they can be moved about, without the mind having to think in any involved way. (Cf. this with note in the old book, about chessboard.)

The ideal of modern prose is to be all counters, i.e. to pass to conclusions without thinking.

Visual Poetry

Each *word* must be an image *seen*, not a counter.

That dreadful feeling of cheapness when we contemplate the profusion of words of modern prose. The true ideal — the little statue in Paris.

The contrast between (i) a firm simple prose, creating in a definite way a fairy story, a story of simple life in the country (in the old country). Here we have the microcosm of poetry. The pieces picked out from which it comes. Sun and sweat and all of them. Physical life and death fairies. And (ii) on the other hand, genteel poetry like Shelley's, which refers in elaborate analogies to the things mentioned in (i).

Gibbering ghosts and Morris's tales seem *real*, as (i). Transmigration of souls seems a drawing-room thrill, compounded of goodwill and long words.

Style

With perfect style, the solid leather for reading, each sentence should be a lump, a piece of clay, a vision seen; rather, a wall touched with soft fingers. Never should one feel light vaporous bridges between one solid sense and another. No bridges — all solid: then never exasperated.

A man cannot write without seeing at the same time a visual signification before his eyes. It is this image which precedes the writing and makes it firm.

FURTHER SPECULATIONS

The piece from Morris as an example of poetry always being a solid thing. Seen but not words.

Criticism

Rising disgust and impatience with the talking books, e.g. Lilly and the books about Life, Science, and Religion. All the books which seem to be the kind of talk one could do if one wished.

Rather choose those in old leather, which are *solid*. Here the man did not talk, but saw solid, definite things and described them. Solidity a pleasure.

It is seeing the real clay, that men in an agony worked with, that gives pleasure. To read a book which is *real clay* moulded by fingers that had to mould something, or they would clutch the throat of their maddened author. *No* flowing on of words, but tightly clutched tense fingers leaving marks in the clay. These are the only books that matter — and where are they to be found?

Style short, being forced by the coming together of many different thoughts, and generated by their contact. Fire struck between stones.

Mechanism of Creation

Get rid of the idea that out of vacuo can come writing. Generally following certain practical ends, we throw out writing — comes out as the one in the many. Not as a pure intellectual machine. A cindery thing done, not a pure thought made manifest in some counter-like way.

The idea is nothing: it is the holding on to the idea, through the absolutely transforming influence of putting it into definiteness. The holding on through waves.

That extraordinary difficulty in shaping any material, in moving from the idea to the matter. Seen even in simple matters like going to the tailor's. The difference between the idea and the choice. Material is never plastic. The extraordinary difficulty of the living material. Seen in everything, even in railway meetings, in people, in everything. Write essay on it.

The resistance of the ὕλη, ἐνεργής. The process of invention is that of gradually making solid the castles in the air.

Self-delusion

(i) Whence comes the excitement, the delusion of thinker's creation?

(ii) All inventions spring from the *idea*, e.g. Flaubert and the *purple* bases of Madame Bovary.

(iii) I have a *central* idea like that quite *unworked* out into detail.

(iv) I see a book *worked out* from the same central idea and I unconsciously imagine that I have worked it out myself, and that I could easily have been the author.

(v) But in the working out is required the multiplicity of detail that I lack. The central idea is nothing.

At last come to think that all expression is vulgar, that only the unexpressed and silent . . .

Dead Analogies

All styles are only means of subduing the reader.

(i) New phrases made in poetry, tested, and then employed in prose.

(ii) In poetry they are all glitter and new coruscation, in prose useful and not noticed.

(iii) Prose a museum where all the old weapons of poetry kept.

(iv) Poetry always the advance guard of language. The progress of language is the absorption of new analogies. (Scout, so nearest to flux and real basic condition of life.)

Expression (I)

If I say: putting in the "finer touches," it expresses what I mean by the refinement of language.

But the damnable thing is that if I use that phrase to another person, it produces no equal effect on him. It is one of the rounded counters of language and so has the least possible meaning. What to me is an entirely physical thing, a real clay before me, moulded, an image, is when used nothing but an expression like "in so far, etc."

The pity is that in this all the *meaning* goes.

A word to me is a board with an image or statue on it. When I pass the word, all that goes is the board, the statue remains in my imagination.

Transfer physical to language

Dome of Brompton in the mist. Transfer that to art. Dead things not men as the material of art. Everything for art is a thing in itself, cf. the café at Clapham as a thing in itself.

And the words moved until they became a dome, a solid, separate world, a dome seen in a mist, a thing of terror beyond us, and not of us. Definite heaven above worshippers, incense hides foundations. A definite *force majeure* (all the foundations of the scaffolding are in us, but we want an illusion, falsifying us, something independent of foundations). A long pillar.

Aphra took the words, and they grew into a round smooth pillar and the child wondered and the merchant paused. Putting bricks together to imitate the shape of a dome, but the mist effect, the transformation in words, has the art of pushing it through the door.

Example of Plastic Imagination

The two tarts walking along Piccadilly on tiptoe, going home, with hat on back of head. Worry until could find the exact model analogy that will reproduce the extraordinary effect they produce. Could be done at once by an artist in a blur. The air of absolute detachment, of being things in themselves. Objects of beauty with the qualification as the basis of it. Disinterestedness, as though saying: We may have evolved painfully from the clay, and be the last leaf on a tree. But now we have cut ourselves away from that. We are things-in-themselves. We exist out of time.

Language (I)

(i) Delightful sensation of power in looking at it, as a vehicle, a machine whose ages we can see. The relics of the extravagant fancies and analogies of dead and forgotten poets.

Regard each word as a picture, then a succession of pictures. Only the dead skeleton remains. We cut the leaves off. When the tree becomes a mast, the leaves become unnecessary. But now only the thick lines matter, and the accompanying pictures are forgotten.

(ii) An agricultural implement. Philosophy expressed in farmer's language. All the predominant metaphors are naturally agricultural, e.g. field of thought, flood, stream. Keep present in mind when we look at nature, the curious place of language which is founded on it and *subordinate* to it. When I see a stream now (such as Waterloo Bridge) I imagine it carrying down with it the impermeable language and the *begriffe* of philosophy.

If only the making and fixing of words had begun in the city stage in the evolution of society and not in the nomadic.

(But ideas expressed would have been the same. So thought and language not identical.)

Language (II)

The fallacy that language is logical, or that meaning is. Phrases have meaning for no reason, cf. with nature of truth.

(i) The metaphysical theory. Watching a woman in the street. Is the idea expressed anything like? So ———

(ii) The idea is just as real as a landscape and there is the same difficulty in getting it on to paper. Each word is a different twist to it, something added. Each of the fifty possible sentences that will express it changes its character.

(iii) Another question: growing conviction of the Solidity of Ideas, as opposed to language.

Very often the idea, apart from the analogy or metaphor which clothes it, has no existence. That is, by a subtle combination of allusions we have artificially built up in us an idea, which apart from these, cannot be got at. As if a man took us on a rocky path and said look — and we saw the view. i.e. the analogy is the thing, not merely decoration. i.e. there is no such thing as.

Language (III)

Large clumsy instrument. Language does not naturally come

with meaning. Ten different ways of forming the same sentence. Any style will do to get the meaning down (without childish effect). There is *no* inevitable simple style as there ought to be.

Language a cumbrous growth, a compound of old and new analogies. Does this apply to thought? Is there *no* simple thought, but only styles of thought?

Poetry is neither more nor less than a mosaic of words, so great exactness required for each one.

Language (IV)

(i) Thought is prior to language and consists in the simultaneous presentation to the mind of two different images.

(ii) Language is only a more or less feeble way of doing this.

(iii) All the connections in language, this term including not only prepositions, but all phrases (ready made), which only indicate the precise relation or attitude or politeness between the two simultaneously presented images.

(iv) Connect this with the old scorn, denoted by the black edge theory, cf. Rue de la limite. And hence see the solution of the difficulty, and the use of words for literary purposes, always inferior.

Thought

As merely the discovery of new analogies, when useful and sincere, and not mere paradoxes.

The things bring a kind of going straight, write them as analogy and call it literature, cf. marching in step, the great procession (analogy of creative and sexual pleasure).

Creation

Thought is the joining together of new analogies, and so inspiration is a matter of an accidentally seen analogy or unlooked-for resemblance. It is therefore necessary to get as large as possible change in sense impressions, cf. looking in shop windows, and war-game. The more change of shapes and sights there is the more chance of inspiration. Thoughts won by walking.

Fertility of invention means: remembrance of accidental occurrences *noted* and arranged. (Cf. detective stories.)

Expression (II)

Think of sitting at that window in Chelsea and seeing the chimneys and the lights in the dusk. And then imagine that by contemplation this will transfer itself bodily on to paper.

This is the direct opposite of literature, which is never an absorption and meditation. But a deliberate choosing and working-up of analogies. The continued, close, compressed effort.

The demand for clear logical expression is impossible, as it would confine us to the use of flat counter-images only.

If you only admit that form of manipulating images as good, if you deny all the other grasps, hands, for the cards, all solid images, all patterns, then you can be clear, but not otherwise.

Expression (III)

(i) People who think, pen in hand. Like people who write at twenty, for *Eton College Chronicle*. Writers first, and then afterwards perhaps find thought.

(ii) Think in air. And then years afterwards acquire knack of writing.

Expression (IV)

The chessboard of language expression, where the two players put down counters one after the other. And the player who became interested in the pieces themselves and carved them, and gazed at them in a kind of ecstasy.

Humour and Expression

A joke analysed and viewed as the decadent form into which all forms of literary expression can be shown to pass by degeneration of function (a suitable analogy for this).

(i) The surprise at the end. Resembles novel building.

(ii) Analogies in poetry, like the likenesses of babies, to be taken half seriously, with a smile.

CONTEMPT FOR LANGUAGE

Black Border

All literature as accident, a happy escape from platitude. Nothing new under the sun. Literature like pitching, how to throw phrases about, to satisfy a demand. An exercise for the time being, no eternal body to be added to. So learn phrases "ringed with gold," "in a lens," etc.

To excite certain mild feelings of delight in the reader, to produce a pleasant warm feeling in brain as phrases run along.

Enlightenment when first see that literature is not a vision, but a voice, or a line of letters in a black border.

Vision the sight of the quaint shadows in things, of the lone trees on the hill, and the hills in life; not the deed, but the shadow cast by the deed.

The art of literature consists exactly in this *passage from the Eye to the Voice*. From the wealth of nature to that *thin* shadow of words, that gramophone. The readers are the people who *see* things and want them expressed. The author is the Voice, or the conjuror who does tricks with that curious rope of letters, which is quite different from real passion and sight.

The prose writer drags meaning along with the rope. The poet makes it stand on end and hit you.

Prose

A sentence and a worm are the most stupid of animals and the most difficult to teach tricks. Tendency to crawl along; requires genius, music, to make them stand up (snake charmer).

Uncomfortable vision of all words as line. String lying on paper. Impossibility of getting mystery out of this. Words seen as physical things. Pull gently into rows. Want to make them *stand up*. Must invent new plan.

Words seen as physical things like a piece of string, e.g. walking on dark boulevard. Girl hidden in trees passes on other side. How to get this.

Always a border round, to isolate the sentence as a thing in itself, a living worm to be taught tricks.

FACILITY IN MANIPULATION
Phrases

Two people sitting talking at table. Delight in having counters ready to hand. (French.) Must not be taught how to *make* counters but a list of them.

(i) Collection of phrases. Words fit in and out of phrases. A *cadre* for grammar. Impossibility of grammar because can't think of end of sentence first. *Learn list* of sentences then fix grammar for them as do in English. Get grammar by ear.

(ii) No language but collection of phrases, but phrases on *different* subjects. One wanders as over a country. No fixed guide for everything. Start Good morning.

(iii) All one tense for past. *Je suis allé.*

Sentences

Sentences as units. Given a large *vocabulary of sentence units,* not of words, we are fluent and can express what we want.

Model sentences learnt perfectly. Perhaps three or four in each Berlitz lesson. Gradually get a definite *armoury* of sentences which will help you and be sufficient to you in conversation.

Physical need some people have to be able to make a comment, to exchange comments. Hence proverbs are the most popular authors. Cf. with reading in W.C.

Never, never, never a simple statement. It has no effect. Always must have analogies, which make an other-world through-the-glass effect, which is what I want.

Danger that when all these notes are arranged, the order will kill them in commonplace. When isolated at least there is hope they suggest great unities, which I am at any rate at present quite unable to carry out.

All theories of how to teach a language, all in the air, all null and void, if *each day* you do not learn at your finger's-ends some new phrases. One new *word* and ten phrases as to how to employ it.

Each night. What new phrases. What new *cadres* for the word I already know?

Question of preposition etc. at end of sentence. *Il le faut le faire payer.* Do we think of end first?

In learning foreign language and teaching your own, learn how little is your knowledge of your own. Hesitating for a phrase in your own language. Very few of us learn all the *possible phrases* in our own language, and we must have them all at the tips of our fingers to write well.

So adapt same method to *English*. Read and Read, and copy the phrases like the one about "microscopic detail magnified."

THE IMAGINARY WORLD AND A STANDARD OF MEANING

Literature always possible. Compared with peasant, it only deals with imaginary world. Even my attempt to get to reality (no long words) is in the end only another adjustment of the imaginary toy. Fields left unaltered.

Literary people work in imaginary land, which all of us carry about in desert moments.

Not sufficient to find analogies. It is necessary to find those that add something to each, and give a sense of wonder, a sense of being united in another mystic world.

One must have something to overawe the *reader*. The fact outside him, e.g. in boasting. Take case of *"Oh, Richard, oh mon roi."*

All literature and poetry is life seen in a mirror; it must be absolutely removed from reality, and can never be attained.

The exact relation between the expression and the inside image:
(i) Expression obviously partakes of the nature of cinders, cf. Red girl dancing. (ii) But on other hand, vague hell image common to everybody makes an infinite of limited *hard* expression.

> Over a large table, smooth, he leaned in ecstasies,
> In a dream.
> He had been to woods, and talked and walked with trees
> Had left the world
> And brought back round globes and stone images
> Of gems, colours, hard and definite.
> With these he played, in a dream,
> On the smooth table.

(Cf. the red dancer in his head.)

Expression (Metaphysical)

The red dancer on the stage. A built-up complex of cinders, so not due to any primeval essence. Cinders as foundations for (i) philosophy (ii) aesthetics.

88

The old controversy as to which is greater, the mind or the material in art.

Each dancer on the stage with her effects and her suggestions of intensity of meaning which are not possible, is not herself (that is a very cindery thing) but a synthesized state of mind in me. The red moving figure is a way of grouping some ideas together, just as powerful a means as the one called logic which is only an analogy to *counter-pushing*.

This can be considered more seriously. A picture like this, the comic dancer, fading away into the margin (this the basis of all art), not [this] * which gives the limitations, the furniture, etc.

Must be imaginary world. Trick it out with fancies. Analogies must be substituted for what suggests something, a cloud of fancies, e.g. Waterloo Bridge in the early morning.

The only intellectual pleasure in recognizing old friends.

(i) At a race. Look first and see the horses in the paper described. Then excited about result.

(ii) Picture gallery (*a*) recognition of names. (*b*) progress to recognition of characteristics. Galleries full of strange names no interest.

(iii) Climate and landscape. The only pleasure in comparison, e.g. Waterloo Bridge and Canada by the river in the morning.

Ideal

Typical Phenomena: the yellow girl leaning from the window in the morning. The Baptist meeting seen through the drawing-room window in the evening.

For the first, if it reminds me of an expressible vague something, I must first have been educated into the idea that there was such a vague something.

Observe this something is quite different to the emotional crises of ordinary people when they speak of love and hate. There must be something on which we can hang up our hat. Better something

* NOTE BY MICHAEL ROBERTS. Hulme has two little sketches, one a small central squiggle with half a dozen radiating strokes, the other a small rectangle like a frame.

to which, when for a surging moment we have a feeling (really the cinders drunk for a minute) we can *refer* it.

Literature as the building-up of this *state of reference*. Must avoid the word, the Ideal, like a plague, for it suggests easy comprehension where there is no easy comprehension. It is used by Baptist young men to mean quite other things: it has *moral* contamination.

Ideas Staged

In a sense all ideals must be divorced, torn away from the reality where we found them and put on a stage. They must appear separate and far from all dirt and laughter at their low and common relations. They must be posed and moved dramatically, and above all, their gestures must express their emotions. This is the art of literature, the making of this *other* world.

They must wear high-heeled shoes which make them appear free movers, and not sprung from that low thing Earth. The separation of the high heel and the powdered face is essential to all emotions, in order to make a work of art.

Intensity of Meaning

'By thine agony and bloody sweat.' By common effort, all this many times repeated, gives an *intensity of meaning*. This 'intensity of meaning' is what is sought for.

Christian Mystics and Physical Expression

Read them as analogous with own temper. For the expression of states of soul by elaborate physical landscape analogies, cf. my own walking in the evening by the Thames. Also the Neo-Platonic philosophers. It is the physical analogies that hold me, true kindred spirits in that age, in own poetry, not the *vain* decorative and verbal images of the ordinary poets.

Feminine Form

The beauty of the feminine form, which came to be looked upon even by the halest of the four, as a typical vesture or symbol of

Beauty herself, and perhaps also as the "sovran shrine" of Melancholy.

Rossetti saw the spiritual element in face and form, and desired the spirit through his desire of the body, and at last did not know the one desire from the other, and pressed on, true mystic as he was, in ever-narrowing circles, to some third thing that seemed to lie behind both desires. "Soul is form and doth the body make."

Eye blur

Tennyson seems to have waited for his expression to come to him — to have brooded before a scene with its orchestra of sounds, in a kind of intense passiveness — until the thing beheld *became greatly different from what it was at any other moment or to any other man.*

DWELLING ON A POINT

Perhaps the difficulty that is found in expressing an idea, in making it long, in dwelling on it, by means of all kinds of analogy, has its root in the nature of ideas and thought itself.

Dancing as the art of prolonging an idea, lingering on a point.

This clearly seen gives the relation between the author's and the reader's position. Both can see the points (as visions in their heads), e.g. Moore's hypostatization of the ideas as real. But I am quite unable to dwell on this point at the length of ten pages.

The author is the man who dwells on a point for the edification of the reader, and for his pleasure, thus prolonging the pleasure and luxury of thought in the mind of the reader.

Method: (i) quotation; (ii) analogies from all possible subjects. Write down examples:

(i) Prose — of making a tremendous deal out of a point which can be noted down in one sentence. But perhaps the sentence only represents it to the writer. To get the same effect on the reader as it produces on him, he must work it up into a froth, like stirring eggs.

(ii) Dwelling on a point in poetry. The main function of analogy in poetry is to enable one to dwell and linger upon a point of excitement. To achieve the impossible and convert a point into a line. This can only be done by having ready-made lines in our heads, and so getting at the result by analogy.

The inner psychology of a poet at such a creative moment is like that of a drunkard who pushes his hand forward along a table, with an important gesture, and remains there pondering over it. In that relaxing gesture of pushing comes the inner psychology of all these moments.

Gradually one learns the art of dwelling on a point, of decorating it, of transforming it, until it produces in the reader the sense of novelty.

READER AND WRITER

Personal

The popular idea of poet as in communion with the infinite, cf. account of Yeats walking in the woods, but remember Tennyson and his hair. (The deed and poem always greater than the man.)

The rubbish that authors write in their casual moments, when they talk. We haven't heard the kind of interview Shelley and Keats would have given.

Reason why Whitman did not go to the goldfields and become a frontiersman actually. His hatred of the particular, and desire to be the average American citizen. Desire to find romance even in Brooklyn. Often at theatres, and a journalist and carpenter. When had made money would go for long holidays in the woods and by the sea. Always seen on bus-tops.

The bodily activity and position most favourable to thought requires coolness, comfort, and a table, a strenuous effort. Can't think without words or pencil.

Object and Readers of Poetry

Poetry after all for the amusement of bankers and other sedentary arm-chair people in after-dinner moods. No other. (Not for inspiration of progress.) So no infinite nobleness and function about that. (For one person in a thousand hence uselessness of school teaching.)

Entirely modern view of poet as something greater than a states-man, cf. Frederic the Great.

In old days merely to amuse warrior and after banquet.

(i) amuse banker.

(ii) for use of clerks in love to send to sweethearts.

(iii) temporary moods (in theatres) of cultivated artificial people.

(iv) songs of war.

Author and Reader

Just as Aristotle asserts that Matter the unlimited contains Forms embedded in it, and that they are not thrust upon it from some ideal world, so all the effects that can be produced by the literary man (here assuming his apprenticeship and marshalling of isolated moments to produce a mystic separation, aided by old metaphors), are to be found dormant, unused in the reader, and are thus awakened.

The Reader

The new art of the Reader. (i) The relation between banker and poetry. (ii) Sympathy with reader as brother, as *unexpressed* author.

Literature a method of sudden arrangement of commonplaces. The *suddenness* makes us forget the commonplace.

Complete theory, what was thought, in the old book, of rela-tion between the poet and the reader seen suddenly at a glance in listening to boys going home from music-hall whistling a song. Chelsea Palace. Here a new way (a mental dance) found for them of synthesizing certain of their own emotions. (Even so with per-sonal psychological poetry, mere putting down is for the reader a form of expression.)

Always seek the causes of these phenomena in their lowest ele-ments — their lowest terms, i.e. literati in Chelsea.

The Writer

The effort of the literary man to find subtle analogies for the ordinary street feelings he experiences leads to the differentiation and importance of those feelings. What would be unnoticed by others, and is nothing when not labelled, becomes an important emotion. A transitory artificial impression is deliberately cultivated into an emotion and written about. Reason here creates and modifies an emotion, e.g. standing at street corners. Hence the sudden joy these produce in the reader when he remembers a half-forgotten impression. "How true!"

What is the difference between people who can write literature and people who can merely appreciate it. The faculty of disillusionment and cynicism, of giving the show away, possessed by readers. What is the necessary quality for creation?

Literary man always first completely disillusioned and then deliberately and purposely creative of illusions.

A writer always a feeble, balanced, artificial kind of person. The mood is cultivated feeling all the time. The vibrant and tense fingers, drawing up rhythm, which one knows could be broken at any moment by anyone coming into the room.

Do these doubts, as to authors, vitiate in any way the work they produce?

Poetry not for others, but for the poet. Nature infinite, but personality finite, rough, and incomplete. Gradually built up.

Poet's mood vague and passes away, indefinable. The poem he makes selects, builds up, and makes even his own mood more definite to him. Expression builds up personality.

The life of the literary man being always aiming at the production of these artificial deliberate poises in himself, and so at the creation of his own chessboard.

But what of the relation of this to ordinary life and people? They have their own hereditary (sentimental) chessboards, which remain the same until changed by the survival of some of those of the literary man. The earnest striving after awkward and new points of view, such as that from a balloon, the useful seen from the non-useful attitude.

Literature as red counters moving on a chessboard, life as gradual shifting of cinders, and occasional consciousness.

Unfortunately can now see the trick, can see the author working his counters for the peroration. So very few more possible enthusiasms left. Grit and toothache still to be in any heaven or Utopia.

Literature as entirely the deliberate standing still, hovering and thinking oneself into an artificial view, for the moment, and not effecting any real actions at all. Sunsets no consolation in harvestfield.

(Lovers' sentimental fancies in letters.)

A POEM

It was formerly my idea that a poem was made somewhat as follows: The poet, in common with many other people, occasionally experienced emotions which strangely moved him. In the case of the greengrocer this was satisfied by reading Tennyson and sending the lines he seemed to have experienced to his beloved. The poet, on the contrary, tried to find new images to express what he felt. These lines and vague collections of words he gradually built up into poems. But this I now see to be wrong; the very act of trying to find a form to fit the separate phrases into, itself leads to the creation of new images hitherto not felt by the poet. In a sense the poetry writes itself. This creation by happy chance is analogous to the accidental stroke of the brush which creates a new beauty not previously consciously thought of by the artist.

The form of a poem is shaped by the intention. Vague phrases containing ideas which at past moments have strongly moved us: as the purpose of the poem is narrative or emotional the phrases become altered. The choice of a form is as important as the individual pieces and scraps of emotion of which the poem is made up. In the actual making accidental phrases are hit upon. Just as musician in striking notes on piano comes across what he wants, the painter on the canvas, so the poet not only gets the phrases he wants, but even from the words gets a *new* image.

Creative effort means *new* images. (Lobster and me.) The accidental discovery of effect, not conscious intellectual endeavour for it.

FURTHER SPECULATIONS

The theory that puts all phrases in a box and years later starts to arrange *all wrong*. Don't. Start creating *at once*, and in this very process new ideas spring up, accidentally. So *condemn* card system, red tape leads to nothing. The living method of arranging at once in temporary notebooks.

CROWDS

Drama

The effect produced by multitude (i) one by one as they left the hall; (ii) policemen's dance.

Actors can add to a comedy. All gestures unreal, but add to comedy and subtract and annoy in tragedy.

Music

Fortuitous assemblage of noises.

The mechanical model, music seen for an instant once during a hymn as smooth rolling.*

Conductor's baton and foundation in body rhythm.

Music in its power of seeming to hold an audience or crowd together into an organism. When plays low in park the atmosphere seems to fall to pieces and crowd becomes units again. Cf. Band and Bard.

Sound a fluid beaten up by conductor.

Breaking of waves. Listening is like the motion in a ship.

Big Crowds

(i) Not found in streets which are routes, except in those which are meeting-places, as Oxford Street.

(ii) The old market-places, the gymnasia of the Greeks, Plato, and the pretty youths.

(iii) Churches and theatres to catch the prolific mood. Davidson and railway stations.

(iv) Secular churches in street, to sit, rest and look.

* NOTE BY MICHAEL ROBERTS. Hulme has a small sketch of one circle rolling inside another.

BEAUTY, IMITATION, AND ECSTASY

Tradition

Poetry always founded on tradition. So light-haired woman with upturned face in Regent Street. A bright moon in dark sky over Paddington. All books, history, etc., after all only a record of the opinions of a class, the artificial moments and poses of literary men. The other classes and little worlds inarticulate (cf. villages).

When artistic impressions of miners and artisans seen (Millet) they do not in any way have anything to do with the emotions of the miner, do not in any way dignify his life. Are only blurs in light and shade. There is no *depth* in the mirror.

Beauty

Art creates beauty (not art copies the beauty in nature: beauty does not exist by itself in nature, waiting to be copied, only organized pieces of cinders). Origin of this view, course of etchings has made cranes and chimneys at night seem beautiful.

Landscape makes the ordinary man think pieces of wood beautiful. "Just like a picture."

So one purpose of art to make people like the merely healthy. Necessary to correct false bias in favour of guilt. Plain steel. (Should make all art seem beautiful.)

Beauty is usefulness seen from another point (cf. distant railway line, *not* the one you yourself are on). Point of view above, birds' eye, because *new*. The waiting engine in the trees, *one* line, red light, like animal waiting to kill.

Culture seeks romantic in far regions. Seeks passions and tragedies in peasants. Tolstoy. Then sees it in prostitutes. Why not abandon it all and take supernatural for art.

Whitman had a theory that every object under the sun comes within the range of poetry. But he was too early in the day. No use having a theory that motor-cars are beautiful, and backing up this theory by working up emotion not really felt. Object must cause the emotion before poem can be written. Whitman's theory, that everything in America must be glorious, was his snare, because it was only a theory.

Minor poets, with their romantic jewels, make same mistake from other side — a lost poetic content. Lexicon of beautiful is elastic, but walla-walla not yet poetically possible.

Continual effort necessary to think of things as they are, the constraint necessary to avoid great tendencies to use big words and common phrases without meaning. Cf. Nietzsche and his ambition to say everything in a paragraph.

Imitation

Tendency to begin a tale "It began in the E.M. restaurant" and similarly in poems. The imitation makes one imagine that one is producing stuff of the same calibre and the same effect on other people.

Stupid little poems about flowers and spring, imitations. No *new* emotion in them. Or the infinitely fascinating man (fiction), cf. G. Moore's novels, the infinitely beautiful woman.

Poetasters write in metre because poets have done so, poets because singing, not talking, is the obvious mode of expressing ecstasy. Whitman went wrong through deficiency of selective process. Even Turner had to shroud his railway train in vapour.

What is the exact difference which would be produced if chess or cinders were stated by Andrew Lang. How is the childishness made to disappear? Perhaps they don't state a thing baldly but hint at rounder and counter-like figures behind it.

People anxious to be literary men think there is no work, just as haymaking — but just as monotonous grinding it out. Concerned in the field with ecstasy, but the pains of birth and parturition are sheets and sheets of paper.

W. B. Yeats attempts to ennoble his craft by strenuously believing in supernatural world, race-memory, magic, and saying that symbols can recall these where prose couldn't. This an attempt to bring in an infinity again. Truth that occasionally have moments of poetic feelings in W.C. and other places, banging of doors, etc.

The beauty of London only seen in detached and careful moments, never continuously, always a conscious effort. On top of a bus, or the sweep of the avenue in Hyde Park. But to appreciate this must be in some manner detached, e.g. wearing workmen's clothes (when not shabby but different in kind) then opportunity for conscious reflection. It is the stranger that sees the romantic and the beautiful in the commonplace, cf. in New York, or in strange city, detached and therefore able to see beauty and romance.

Moments of enthusiasm due to a selection seen as a possible *continuously* happy future.

All attempts at beauty necessarily consciously made, open to reaction of the man who talks of "nature," etc.

Life as a rule tedious, but certain things give us sudden lifts. Poetry comes with the jumps, cf. love, fighting, dancing. The moments of ecstasy.

Literature, like memory, selects only the vivid patches of life. The art of abstraction. If literature (realistic) did really resemble life, it would be interminable, dreary, commonplace, eating and dressing, buttoning, with here and there a patch of vividness. Zola merely selects an interesting group of sordid pieces.

Life composed of exquisite moments and the rest shadows of them.

The *gaps* — hence chess.

Drink

They followed the road with the knowledge that they were soaring along in a supporting medium, possessed of original and profound thoughts, themselves and surrounding nature forming an organism of which all the parts harmoniously and joyously interpenetrate each other.

Heroes occasionally, drink influence only for a time like effect of church or music.

The literary man deliberately perpetrates a hypocrisy, in that he fits together his own isolated moments of ecstasy (and generally deliberate use of big words without personal meaning attached) and presents them as a picture of higher life, thereby giving old maids a sense of superiority to other people and giving mandarins the opportunity to talk of "ideals." Then makes attempt to justify himself by inventing the soul and saying that occasionally the lower world gets glimpses of this, and that inferentially he is the medium. As a matter of fact being certain moments of ecstasy perhaps brought on by drink. Surely obvious that drink and drugs have nothing to do with a higher world (cf. Q. and his little safe yacht, a kind of mechanical ladder to the soul world).

All theories as toys.

ESSAYS ON ART

ESSAYS ON ART

MR. EPSTEIN AND THE CRITICS

I begin with an apology. All through this article I write about Mr. Epstein's work in a way which I recognise to be wrong, in that it is what an artist would call literary. The appreciation of a work of art must be plastic or nothing. But I defend myself in this way, that I am not so much writing directly about Mr. Epstein's work, as engaged in the more negative and quite justifiable business of attempting to protect the spectator from certain prejudices which are in themselves literary. This is an article then not so much on Epstein as on his critics. When I see the critics attempting to corrupt the mind of the spectator and trying to hinder their appreciation of a great artist, I feel an indignation which must be my excuse for these clumsy, hurriedly-written and unrevised notes.

An attack on critics could not have a better subject matter than the Press notices on Mr. Epstein's show. They exhibit a range and variety of fatuousness seldom equalled. It is not necessary to spend any time over notices which, like that of "C.B." in the "Athenaeum," are merely spiteful, or that in the "Illustrated London News," which compared him unfavourably with the Exhibition of Humourous Artists. I propose rather to deal with those which, in appearance at any rate, profess to deal seriously with his work.

Take first the merely nervous. Their method is continually to refer to Mr. Epstein as a great artist and at the same time to deplore everything he does. It reminds one of the old philosophical disputes about substance. Would anything remain of a "thing" if all its qualities were taken away? What is the metaphysical nature of an artist's excellence that seems to manifest itself in no particular thing he does? The truth is, of course, that they dare not say what they really think. The particular kind of gift which enables a man to be an art critic is not the possession of an instinct which tells them what pictures are good or bad, but of a different kind of instinct which leads them to recognise the people who do know. This is, of course, in itself a comparatively rare instinct. Once they have obtained a "direction" in this way, their own literary capacity enables them to expand it to any desired length. You can, however, always tell this from a certain emptiness in their rhetoric (cf. Arthur Symons' article on Rodin). There is no one to give them a "direction" about Mr. Epstein's drawings, and they are at a loss. They seek refuge in praise of the "Romilly John," which has been universally admitted to be one of the finest bronzes since the Renaissance. It shows how incapable the critics are of judging even Mr. Epstein's earlier work, that one critic has been found to couple this superb head with Mr. John's thin and unconvincing painting of a child, at present exhibited in the New English Art Club.

I come now to the most frequent and the most reasonable criticism: that directed against the "Carvings in Flenite." It is generally stated in a rather confused way, but I think that it can be analysed out into two separate prejudices. The first is that an artist has no business to use formulae taken from another civilisation. The second is that, even if the formula the artist uses is the natural means of expressing certain of his emotions, yet these emotions must be unnatural in him, a modern Western. I shall attempt to show that the first objection really has its root in the second, and that this second prejudice is one which runs through almost every activity at the present time. These "Carvings in Flenite," we are told, are "deliberate imitations of Easter Island carvings." This seems to me to depend on a misconception of the nature of formulae. Man remaining constant, there are certain broad ways in which certain emotions must, and will always naturally be expressed, and these we must call formulae. They constitute a constant and permanent alphabet. The thing to notice is that the use of these broad formulae has nothing to do with the possession of or lack of individuality in the artist. That comes out in the way the formulae are used. If I or the King of the Zulus want to walk, we both put one leg before the other; that is the universal formula, but there the resemblance ends. To take another illustration, which I don't want to put forward as literally true, but which I only use for purposes of illustration. A certain kind of *nostalgie* and attenuated melancholy is expressed in Watteau by a formula of tall trees and minute people, and a certain use of colour (I am also aware that he got this feeling, in the Gilles, for example, by a quite other formula, but I repeat I am only giving a sort of hypothetical illustration). It would be quite possible at the present day for a painter, wishing to express the same kind of emotion, to use the same broad formula quite naturally and without any imitation of Watteau. The point is, that given the same emotion, the same broad formula comes naturally to the hands of any people in any century. I may say that I have not, as a matter of fact, any great admiration for the particular painters who use this particular formula, but I am trying to give an illustration of a formula which the critics who attack Mr. Epstein would not have attacked. To be legitimate, of course, the formula used must be a natural expression of the feeling you are getting at and not a mere imitation of an exotic or a romantic past. The form follows the need in each case. It may quite easily be the same need divided by many civilisations.

I think that in this way we can force these people back on the real root of their objection, the second prejudice I mentioned, the feeling that it is unnatural for a modern to have the kind of emotion which these formulae naturally express. In getting at this, one is getting at something that is really fundamental in modern life. I do think that there is a certain general state of mind which has lasted from the Renaissance till now, with what is, in reality, very little variation. It is impossible to characterise it here, but it is perhaps enough to say that, taking at first the form of the "humanities," it has in its degeneracy taken the form of a belief in "Progress" and the rest of it. It was in its way a fairly consistent system, but is probably at the present moment breaking up. In this state of break-up, I think that it is quite natural for individuals here and there to hold a philosophy and to be moved by emotions which would have been unnatural in the period itself. To illustrate big things by small ones I feel myself, a repugnance towards the *Weltanschauung* (as distinct from the technical part) of all philosophy since the Renaissance. In comparison with what I can vaguely call the religious attitude, it seems to me to be trivial. I am moved by Byzantine mosaic, not because it is quaint or exotic, but because it expresses an attitude I agree with. But the fate of the people who hold these views is to be found incomprehensible by the "progressives" and to be labelled reactionary; that is, while we arrive at such a Weltanschauung quite naturally, we are thought to be imitating the past.

I have wandered into this by-path merely to find therein an illustration which will help us to understand the repugnance of the critic to the "Carvings in Flenite." It is, says the critic, "rude savagery, flouting respectable tradition — vague memories of dark ages as distant from modern feeling as the loves of the Martians." Modern feeling be damned! As if it was not the business of every honest man at the present moment to clean the world of these sloppy dregs of the Renaissance. This carving, by an extreme abstraction, by the selection of certain lines, gives an effect of tragic greatness. The important point about this is that the tragedy is of an order more intense than any conception of tragedy which could fit easily into the modern progressive conception of life. This, I think, is the real root of the objection to these statues, that they express emotions which are, as a matter of fact, entirely alien and unnatural to the critic. But that is a very different thing from their being unnatural to the artist. My justification of these statues would be then (1) that an alien formula is justifiable when it is the necessary expression of a certain attitude; and (2) that in the peculiar conditions in which we find ourselves, which are really the breaking up of an era, it has again become quite possible for people here and there to have the attitude expressed by these formulae.

I have dealt with these in rather a literary way, because I think that in this case it is necessary to get semi-literary prejudices out of the way, before the carvings can be seen as they should be seen, i.e. plastically.

To turn now to the drawings which have been even more misunderstood by the critics than the carvings. I only want to make a few necessary notes about these, as I am dealing with them at greater length in an essay elsewhere.* I need say very little about the magnificent drawing reproduced in this paper, for it stands slightly apart from the others and seems to have been found intelligible even by the critics. I might, perhaps, say something about the representative element in it — a man is working a Rock Drill mounted on a tripod, the lines of which, in the drawing, continue the lines of his legs. The two lines converging on the centre of the design are indications of a rocky landscape. It is the other drawings which seem to have caused the most bewildered criticism; they have been called prosaic representations of anatomical details, "medical drawings," and so on. It is perfectly obvious that they are not that. What prevents them being understood as expressions of ideas is quite a simple matter. People will admire the "Rock Drill," because they have no preconceived notion as to how the thing expressed by it should be expressed. But with the other drawings concerned with birth the case is different. Take for example the drawing called "Creation," a baby seen inside many folds. I might very roughly say that this is a non-sentimental restatement of an idea which, presented sentimentally and in the traditional manner, they would admire — an idea something akin to the "Christmas crib" idea. If a traditional symbol had been used they would have been quite prepared to admire it. They cannot understand that the genius and sincerity of an artist lies in extracting afresh, from outside reality, a new means of expression. It seems curious that the people who in poetry abominate clichés and know that Nature, as it were, presses in on the poet to be used as metaphor, cannot understand the same thing when it occurs plastically. They seem unable to understand that an artist who

* EDITOR'S NOTE. Hulme had apparently promised to write an essay on Epstein's drawings for Wyndham Lewis's *Blast*; there is no evidence that it was ever written.

has something to say will continually "extract" from reality new methods of expression, and that these being personally felt will inevitably lack prettiness and will differ from traditional clichés. It must also be pointed out that the critics have probably themselves not been accustomed to think about generation, and so naturally find the drawings not understandable. I come now to the stupidest criticism of all, that of Mr. Ludovici.* It would probably occur to anyone who read Mr. Ludovici's article that he was a charlatan, but I think it worth while confirming this impression by further evidence. His activities are not confined to art. I remember coming across his name some years ago as the author of a very comical little book on Nietzsche, which was sent me for review.

I shall devote some space to him here then, not because I consider him of the slightest importance, but because I consider it a duty, a very pleasant duty and one very much neglected in this country, to expose charlatans when one sees them. Apart from this general ground, the book on Nietzsche is worth considering, for it displays the same type of mind at work as in the article on art.

What, very briefly then, is the particular type of charlatan revealed in this book on Nietzsche. It gave one the impression of a little Cockney intellect which would have been more suitably employed indexing or in a lawyer's office, drawn by a curious kind of vanity into a region the realities of which must for ever remain incomprehensible to him. Mr. Ludovici, writing on Nietzsche, might be compared to a child of four in a theatre watching a tragedy based on adultery. The child would observe certain external phenomena, but as to the real structure of the tragedy, its real moving forces, it would naturally be rather hazy. You picture then a spruce little mind that has crept into the complicated rafters of philosophy — you imagine him perplexed, confused — you would be quite wrong, the apperceptive system acts like a stencil, it blots out all the complexity which forms the reality of the subject, so that he is simply unaware of its existence. He sees only what is akin to his mind's manner of working, as dogs out

* EDITOR'S NOTE. In the *New Age*, XIV (December 18, 1913), 213–215.

for a walk only scent other dogs, and as a Red Indian in a great town for the first time sees only the horses. While thus in reality remaining entirely outside the subject, he can manage to produce a shoddy imitation which may pass here in England, where there is no organised criticism by experts, but which in other countries, less happily democratic in these matters, would at once have been characterised as a piece of fudge. I have only drawn attention to this in order to indicate the particular type of charlatan we have to deal with, so that you may know what to expect when you come to consider him as an art critic. I want to insist on the fact that you must expect to find a man dealing with a subject which is in reality alien to him, ignorant of the aims of the actors in that subject and yet maintaining an appearance of adequate treatment with the help of a few tags.

That a man should write stupid and childish things about Nietzsche does not perhaps matter very much; after all, we can read him for ourselves. But when a little bantam of this kind has the impertinence to refer to Mr. Epstein as a "minor personality — of no interest to him," then the matter becomes so disgusting that it has to be dealt with. The most appropriate means of dealing with him would be a little personal violence. By that method one removes a nuisance without drawing more attention to it than its insignificance deserves. But the unworthy sentiment of pity for the weak, which in spite of Nietzsche, still moves us, prevents us dealing drastically, with this rather light-weight superman. To deal definitely then with his criticism. He dismissed Mr. Epstein with the general principle "Great art can only appear when the artist is animated by the spirit of some great order or scheme of life." I agree with this. Experience confirms it. We find that the more serious kind of art that one likes sprang out of organic societies like the Indian, Egyptian, and Byzantine. The modern obviously imposes too great a strain on an artist, the double burden of not only expressing something, but of finding something in himself to be expressed. The more organic society effects an economy in this. Moreover, you might go so far as to say that the imposition of definite forms does not confine the artist but rather has the effect of intensifying the individuality of his work (of Egyptian portraits). I agree then with his general principle: we all agree. It is one of those obvious platitudes which all educated people take for granted, in conversation and in print. It seems almost too comic for belief, but I begin to suspect from Mr. Ludovici's continued use of the word "I" in connection with this principle, that he is under the extraordinary hallucination that the principle is a personal discovery of his own. Really, Mr. Ludo, you musn't teach your grandmother to suck eggs in this way. That you should have read these truths in a book and have seen that they were true is so much to the good. It is a fact of great interest to your father and mother, it shows that you are growing up; but I can assure you it is a matter of no public interest.

Admitting then, as I do, that the principle is true, I fail to see how it enables Mr. Ludovici to dismiss Mr. Epstein in the way he does, on a priori grounds. The same general principle would enable us to dismiss every artist since the Renaissance. Take two very definite examples, Michelangelo and Blake, neither of whom expressed any general "scheme of life" imposed on them by society, but "exalted the individual angle of vision of minor personalities."

The whole thing is entirely beside the point. The business of an art critic is not to repeat tags, but to apply them to individual works of art. But of course that is precisely what a charlatan of the kind I have just described cannot do. It is quite possible for him in each gallery he goes to, to find some opportunity of repeating his tags, but when (as he was in his book on Nietzsche) he is entirely outside the subject, when he is really unaware of the nature of the thing which artists are trying to do, when he gets no real fun out of the pictures themselves, then, when he is pinned down before one actual picture and not allowed to wriggle away, he must either be dumb or make an ass of himself. It is quite easy to learn to repeat tags about "balance," but put the man before one picture and make him follow with his finger, the lines which constitute that "balance" and he can only shuffle and bring out more tags.

Now apply this test to Mr. Ludovici. We have seen him dismiss Mr. Epstein with a tag. When he makes individual judgments about individual pictures in The New English Art Club, what kind of judgments are they? We start off with Mr. John. Here he thinks he may be fairly safe; here is a reputation ten years old which has at last reached him. But, alas! we are not dealing with Mr. John as a painter, but with one painting by Mr. John. Mr. Ludovici falls. He picks out for extravagant praise Mr. John's cartoon "The Flute of Pan," a thing universally admitted to be the worst thing John has ever exhibited, a macédoine of Botticelli-Mantegna drapery, Rossetti faces, rocky backgrounds from Leonardo, and a ridiculous girl on the right pretending to be dancing in order that she may show a Botticelli leg and foot, on the left a sort of crapulous Michelangelo and the little Peter Pan boy so much admired by Mr. Ludovici, the whole messy, smudged and in parts badly drawn, the design itself so clumsy that the right third of the picture is left so empty that one feels a girder should be run up from the corner to prop up the rest, which seems in imminent danger of toppling over. The whole thing expresses, with the impotence of old age, the kind of dream appropriate to puberty. It lacks precisely that quality of virility which Mr. Ludovici finds in it, and is admired by precisely those "spinsterly," sloppy and romantic people whom, he imagines, dislike it. It is the result of no personal creative idea, but is entirely a derivative conglomeration of already existing pretty ideas. I emphasise this point because your critic insists so much on a picture being the expression of a definite "scheme of life." I am not dealing with this picture as Mr. Ludovici did with Mr. Epstein, contemptuously, but pointing out that it marks a degeneration, temporary perhaps, of a great talent.

Of the other pictures that he praises, it is only necessary to mention Von Glehn's No. 2, which is merely a bad fake, and Mr. D. G. Well's hackneyed Victorian cliché, and Mr. Steer's "Sunset," which expresses nothing but a romantic nostalgia. Are these the feeble derivative things the "creators of new values" admire?

That a critic of this calibre should attempt to patronise Mr. Epstein is disgusting. I make this very hurried protest in the hope that I may induce those people who have perhaps been prejudiced by ignorant and biased criticism to go and judge for themselves.

MODERN ART
1 · The Grafton Group

I am attempting in this series of articles to define the characteristics of a new constructive geometric art which seems to me to be emerging at the present moment. In a later series, to be called the "Break-Up of the Renaissance," I shall attempt to show the relation between this art and a certain general changed outlook.

I am afraid that my use of the word "new" here will arouse a certain prejudice in the minds of the kind of people that I am anxious to convince. I may say then that I use the word with no enthusiasm. I want to convince those people who regard the feeble romanticism which is always wriggling and vibrating to the stimulus of the word "new," with a certain amount of disgust, that the art which they incline to condemn as decadent is in reality the new order for which they are looking. It seems to me to be the genuine expression of abhorrence of slop and romanticism which has quite mistakenly sought refuge in the conception of a classical revival. By temperament I should adopt the classical attitude myself. My assertion then that a "new" art is being formed is not due to any desire on my part to perceive something "new," but is forced on me almost against my inclination by an honest observation of the facts themselves.

In attempting thus to define the characteristics of a new movement a certain clearance of the ground is necessary. A certain work of dissociation and analysis is required, in connection with what is vaguely thought of as "modern" in art. A writer on art may perform a useful function in pointing out that what is generally thought of as one living movement consists really of many parts, some of which are as a matter of fact quite dead. The words

"modern," "Post-Impressionist" and "Cubist" are used as syno-
nyms, not only in the more simple form of instinctive reaction to
an unpleasing phenomenon, but also in a more positive way,
the psychology of which seems to me to be rather interesting. The
Post-Impressionist or Cubist appearances, at first perceived chaoti-
cally as "queer" and rejected as such, became after a mysterious
act of conversion, a signal for exhilarated acceptance, irrespective
of the quality of the painting itself. They give every picture, good
or bad, which possesses them, a sort of cachet. But although this
complex of qualities passes from the stage in which it is repulsive
to that in which it is attractive, yet for most people it remains
unanalysed. It must be pointed out that what has been grouped
together as one, really contains within itself several diverse and
even contradictory tendencies. One might separate the modern
movement into three parts, to be roughly indicated as Post-Im-
pressionism, analytical Cubism and a new constructive geometrical
art. The first of these, and to a certain extent the second, seem to
me to be necessary but entirely transitional stages leading up to
the third, which is the only one containing possibilities of development.

This show at the Alpine Club provides a convenient illustration of these points. Mr. Fry organised the first Post-Impressionist
exhibition in London and was thought to have established a corner in the movement. He probably regards himself, and is certainly
regarded by many others, as the representative of the new direction in art. The earlier shows of the Grafton group were sufficiently
comprehensive and varied to make this opinion seem plausible.
. . . * There was a mixture of a sort of aesthetic archaism and a
more vigorous cubism which corresponded very well to the loose
use of the words "modern art" which I have just mentioned, and
helped to maintain the illusion that the whole formed in reality
one movement. But the departure of Mr. Wyndham Lewis, Mr.
Etchells, Mr. Nevinson and several others has left concentrated

---

*EDITOR'S NOTE. Hulme's use of three periods is reproduced throughout from
the original essays in the *New Age*. The periods are not ellipsis marks, but a
kind of punctuation peculiar to him.

in a purer form all the worked-out and dead elements in the movement. It has become increasingly obvious that Mr. Fry and his group are nothing but a kind of backwater, and it seems to me to be here worth while pointing out the character of this backwater. As you enter the room you almost know what to expect, from the effect of the general colour. It consists almost uniformly of pallid chalky blues, yellows and strawberry colours, with a strong family resemblance between all the pictures; in every case a kind of anaemic effect showing no personal or constructive use of colour. The subjects also are significant. One may recognise the whole familiar bag of tricks — the usual Cézanne landscapes, the still lifes, the Eves in their gardens, and the botched Byzantine. As the Frenchmen exhibited here have really no connection with the Grafton group, I will omit them and confine myself to the English painters. In Mr. Fry's landscape you can see his inability to follow a method to its proper conclusion. The colour is always rather sentimental and pretty. He thus accomplishes the extraordinary feat of adapting the austere Cézanne into something quite fitted for chocolate boxes. It is too tedious to go on mentioning mediocre stuff, so I should like to point out the two things which are worth seeing, No. 29, a very interesting pattern by Mr. Roberts, and M. Gaudier-Brzeska's sculpture.

However, I find it more interesting to escape from this show for a minute, by discussing a general subject which is to a certain extent suggested by it — the exact place of archaism in the new movement. I want to maintain (i) that a certain archaism was a natural stage in the preparation of a new method of expression, and (ii) that the persistence of a feeble imitation of archaism, such as one gets in this show, is an absolutely unnecessary survival when this stage has been passed through.

In the first place then, how does it come about that a movement towards a new method of expression should contain so many archaic elements? How can a movement whose essence is the exact opposite of romanticism and nostalgie, which is striving towards a hard and definite structure in art, take the form of archaism? How can a sensibility so opposed to that which generally finds satisfaction in the archaic, make such use of it? What happens, I take it, is something of this kind: a certain change of direction takes place which begins negatively with a feeling of dissatisfaction with and reaction against existing art. But the new tendency, admitting that it exists, cannot at once find its own appropriate expression. But although the artist feels that he must have done with contemporary means of expression, yet a new and more fitting method is not easily created. Expression is by no means a natural thing. It is an unnatural, artificial and, as it were, external thing which a man has to install himself in before he can manipulate it. The way from intention to expression does not come naturally as it were from in outwards. It in no way resembles the birth of Minerva. A gap between the intention and its actual expression in material exists, which cannot be bridged directly. A man has first to obtain a foothold in this, so to speak, alien and external world of material expression, at a point near to the one he is making for. He has to utilise some already existing method of expression, and work from that to the one that expresses his own personal conception more accurately and naturally. At the present moment this leads to archaism because the particular change of direction in the new movement is a striving towards a certain intensity which is already expressed in archaic form. This perhaps supplements what I said about the archaism of Mr. Epstein's "carvings in flenite." It perhaps enables me to state more clearly the relation between those works and the more recent work represented by the drawings. You get a breaking away from contemporary methods of expression, a new direction, an intenser perception of things striving towards expression. And as this intensity is fundamentally the same kind of intensity as that expressed in certain archaic arts, it quite naturally and legitimately finds a foothold in these archaic yet permanent formulae. But as this intensity is at the same time no romantic revival, but part of a real change of sensibility occurring now in the modern mind, and is coloured by a particular and original quality due to this fact, it quite as naturally develops from the original formula one which is for it, a purer and more accurate medium of expression. [That the great change in outlook is coming about naturally at the present moment, I shall attempt to demonstrate later by a consideration which has nothing whatever to do with art. I shall then be able to explain what I meant by the "dregs of the Renaissance."]

To return then to the discussion from which I started. A certain archaism it seems is at the beginning a help to an artist. Although it may afterwards be repudiated, it is an assistance in the construction of a new method of expression. Most of the artists who prepared the new movement passed through this stage. Picasso, for example, used many forms taken from archaic art, and other examples will occur to everyone. It might be objected that a direct line of development could be traced through Cézanne, even in much of his later work, that he seeks expression through forms that are to a certain extent archaic. So much then for the function of archaism. Apply this to what you find in the Grafton group. If it were only a matter of serious experimentation in archaic forms, after the necessity for that experimentation had passed by, the thing would be regrettable but not a matter for any violent condemnation. But you do not find anything of that kind, but merely a cultured and anaemic imitation of it. What in the original was a sincere effort towards a certain kind of intensity, becomes in its English dress a mere utilisation of the archaic in the spirit of the aesthetic. It is used as a plaything to a certain quaintness. In Mr. Duncan Grant's "Adam and Eve," for example, elements taken out of the extremely intense and serious Byzantine art are used in an entirely meaningless and pointless way. There is no solidity about any of the things; all of them are quite flimsy. One delightful review of the show described Mr. Fry's landscapes as having "the fascination of reality seen through a cultured mind." The word "cultured" here explains a good deal. I feel about the whole show a typically Cambridge sort of atmosphere. I have a very vivid impression of what I mean here by Cambridge, as I have recently had the opportunity of observing the phenomenon at close quarters. I know the kind of dons who buy these pictures, the character of the dilettante appreciation they feel for them. It is so interesting and clever of the artist to use the archaic in this paradoxical way, so amusing to make Adam stand on his head, and the donkey's ear continue into the hills — gentle little Cambridge jokes.

It is all amusing enough in its way, a sort of aesthetic playing about. It can best be described in fact as a new disguise of aestheticism. It is not a new art, there is nothing new and creative about it. At first appearance the pictures seem to have no resemblance to pre-Raphaelitism. But when the spectator has overcome his first mild shock and is familiarised with them, he will perceive the fundamental likeness. Their "queerness," such as it is, is not the same serious queerness of the Pre-Raphaelites, it is perhaps only quaint and playful; but essentially the same English aesthetic is behind both, and essentially the same cultured reminiscent pleasure is given to the spectator. This being the basic constituent of both arts, just as the one ultimately declined into Liberty's, so there is no reason why the other should not find its grave in some emporium which will provide the wives of young and advanced dons with suitable house decoration.

What is living and important in new art must be looked for elsewhere.

MODERN ART
II · A Preface Note and Neo-Realism

As in these articles I intend to skip about from one part of my argument to another, as occasion demands, I might perhaps give them a greater appearance of shape by laying down as a preliminary three theses that I want to maintain.

1. There are two kinds of art, geometrical or abstract, and vital and realistic art, which differ absolutely in kind from the other. They are not modifications of one and the same art, but pursue different aims and are created to satisfy a different desire of the mind.

2. Each of these arts springs from, and corresponds to, a certain attitude towards the world. You get long periods of time in which only one of these arts and its corresponding mental attitude prevails. The naturalistic art of Greece and the Renaissance corresponded to a certain rational humanistic attitude towards the universe, and the geometrical has always gone with a different attitude of greater intensity than this.

3. The re-emergence of geometrical art at the present day may be the precursor of the re-emergence of the corresponding general attitude towards the world, and so of the final break-up of the Renaissance.

This is the logical order in which I state the position. Needless to say, I did not arrive at it in that way. I shall try to make a sweeping generalisation like the last a little less empty by putting the matter in an autobiographical form. I started with the conviction that the Renaissance attitude is breaking up and then illustrate it by the change in art, and not vice versa. First came the reaction against Renaissance philosophy, and the adoption of the attitude which I said went with the geometrical art.

Just at this time I saw Byzantine mosaic for the first time. I was then impressed by these mosaics, not as something exotic or "charming," but as expressing quite directly an attitude which I to a certain extent agreed with. The important thing about this for me was that I was then, owing to this accidental agreement, able to see a geometrical art, as it were, from the inside. This altered my whole view of such arts. I realised for the first time that their geometrical character is essential. It seemed clear that they differed absolutely from the vital arts because they were pursuing a different intention, and that what we, expecting other qualities from art, look on as dead and lifeless, were the necessary means of expression for this other intention.

Finally I recognised this geometrical re-emerging in modern art. I had here then very crudely all the elements of the position that I stated in my three theses. At that time, in an essay by Paul Ernst on religious art, I came across a reference to the work of Riegl and Worringer. In the latter particularly I found an extraordinarily clear statement founded on an extensive knowledge of the history of art, of a view very like the one I had tried to formulate. I heard him lecture last year and had an opportunity of talking with him at the Berlin Aesthetic Congress. I varied to a certain extent from my original position under the influence of his vocabulary, and that influence will be seen in some, at any rate, of the articles.

*   *   *

To turn now to Mr. Ginner's defence of Neo-Realism.* His article having somewhat the character of a painter's apologia, inevitably raises points over the whole range of the subject. I confine myself therefore to the main argument, which, put shortly, is that (1) All good art is realistic. Academicism is the result of the adoption by weak painters of the creative artist's personal method of interpreting nature, and the consequent creation of formulae,

* Charles Ginner, "Neo-Realism," *New Age*, XIV (January 1, 1914), 271–272.

without contact with nature. (2) The new movement in art is merely an academic movement of the kind, springing from the conversion of Cézanne's mannerisms into formulae. (3) The only remedy is a return to realism. Only a realistic method can keep art creative and vital.

These statements are based on such an extraordinarily confused and complicated mass of assumptions that I cannot give any proper refutation. I shall just try to show exactly what assumptions are made, and to indicate in a series of notes and assertions an opposite view of art to Mr. Ginner's. I can only give body to these assertions and prove them much later in the series.

Take first his condemnation of the new movement as academic, being based on the use of formulae. My reply to this is that the new movement does not use *formulae*, but *abstractions*, quite a different thing. Both are "unlike nature," but while the one is unlike, owing to a lack of vitality in the art, resulting in dead conventions, the other is unlike, of deliberate intent, and is very far from being dead. Mr. Ginner's misconception of the whole movement is due to his failure to make this distinction, a failure ultimately arising from the assumption that art must be realistic. He fails to recognise the existence of the abstract geometric art referred to in my prefatory note.

If you will excuse the pedantry of it, I think I can make the matter clearer by using a diagram:

$$R \ . \ . \ . \ . \ . \ p_{(r)} \ . \ . \ . \ . \ . \ a_{(r)} \ . \ . \ . \ . \ . \ A$$

I take R to represent reality. As one goes from left to right one gets further and further from reality. The first step away being $p_{(r)}$, that is the artist's interpretation of nature. The next step $a_{(r)}$ being an art using abstractions (a), with a certain representative element (r). The element a owes its significance to, and is dependent on the other end A of this kind of spectrum — a certain "tendency to abstraction." I assert that there are two arts, the one focussed round R, which is moved by a delight in natural forms, and the other springing from the other end, making use of abstractions as a method of expression. I am conscious that this is the weak point of my argument, for I cannot give body to this conception of the "expressive use of abstraction" till later on in the series.

Looking at the matter from this point of view, what is the source of Mr. Ginner's fallacy? He admits that $p_{(r)}$ is the personal interpretation of reality, but as he would deny the possibility of an abstract art altogether, any further step away from reality must appear to him as decay, and the only way he can explain the a in $a_{(r)}$ is to look on it as a degeneration of p in $p_{(r)}$. An abstraction to him then can only mean that decay of mannerism in formulae which comes about when the artist has lost contact with nature, and there is no personal first-hand observation. When, therefore, Mr. Ginner says the adoption of formulae leads to the decay of an art, it is obvious that this must be true if by art you mean realistic art. Inside such art, whose raison d'être is its connection with nature, the use of formulae, i.e., a lack of personal, creative and sincere observation, must inevitably lead to decay. But here comes the root of the whole fallacy. Realistic art is not the only kind of art. If everything hangs on the R side of my diagram then the a in $a_{(r)}$ gets its whole meaning and significance from its dependence on the other end of the scale A, i.e., from its use by a creative artist as a method of expression. Looked at from this point of view, the position of *abstraction* is quite a different one. The *abstractions* used in this other art will not bring about a decadence, they are an essential part of its method. Their almost geometrical and non-vital characters are not the result of weakness and lack of vitality in the art. They are not dead conventions, but the product of a creative process just as active as that in any realist art. To give a concrete example of the difference between formula and abstraction. Late Greek art decays into formulae. But the art before the classical made deliberate use of certain abstractions differing in kind from the formulae used in the decadence. They were used with intention, to get a certain kind of intensity. The truth of this view is conveniently illustrated by the history of Greek ornament, where abstract and geometrical forms precede natural forms instead of following them.

To these abstractions, the hard things Mr. Ginner says about formulae have no application.

We shall never get any clear argument on this subject, then, until you agree to distinguish these two different uses of the word formula. (1) Conventional dead mannerism. (2) Abstraction, equally unlike nature, but used in a creative art as a method of expression.

The first effort of the realists then to give an account of abstraction comes to grief. Abstractions are not formulae. In their effort to make the matter seem as reasonable as possible the realists have a second way of conceiving the nature of abstractions which is equally misleading. They admit the existence of *decorative* abstractions. When they have managed to give partial praise to the new movement in this way, they then pass on to condemn it. They assert that the repetition of empty decorative forms must soon come to an end, that pure pattern does not contain within itself the possibility of development of a complete art. But their modified approval and their condemnation are alike erroneous. This second misconception of abstractions as being decorative formulae, is as mistaken as the first conception of them as being conventionalised mannerisms. Like the first, it springs from a refusal to recognise the existence of an art based on the creative use of abstraction, an art focussed on the right hand side *A* of my diagram. As long as that is denied, then abstractions must inevitably be either conventionalised mannerisms or decorative. They are neither.

Now to apply the first distinction between *formulae* and *abstraction* to Mr. Ginner's argument about the new movement in art. This art undoubtedly uses abstraction. Are these abstractions *formulae* in his sense of the word or not? If they are, then his argument is valid and we are in presence of a new academic movement.

I deny, however, that the abstractions to be found in the new art are dead formulae. For the moment, I do not intend to offer any proof of this assertion, as far as Cubist art itself is concerned. I intend to deal rather with the precursor of the movement, that is Cézanne himself. The point at issue here then is narrowed down to this. The Cubists claim that the beginnings of an abstract art can be found in Cézanne. Mr. Ginner, on the contrary, asserts that Cézanne was a pure realist. It is to be noticed that even if he proved his case, he would not have attacked the new art itself, but only its claimed descent from Cézanne.

One must be careful not to treat Cézanne as if he actually were a Cubist; he obviously is not. One must not read the whole of the later movement into him. But there are in his paintings elements which quite naturally develop into Cubism later. You get, contrasted with the Impressionists, a certain simplification of planes, an emphasis on three-dimensional form, giving to some of his landscapes what might be called a Cubist appearance. It is true that this simplification and abstraction, this seeing of things in simple forms, as a rule only extends to details. It might be said that simplifications are, as it were, "accepted" passively, and are not deliberately built up into a definite organisation and structure.

The first thing to be noticed is that even supposing that Cézanne's intentions were entirely realistic, he initiated a break-up of realism and provided the material for an abstract art. Picasso came along and took over these elements isolated by Cézanne, and organised them. If the simplifications in Cézanne had passed beyond details and become more comprehensive, they would probably of themselves have forced him to build up definite structures.

But not only are the elements of an abstract art present in Cézanne, I should say also that there was an embryo of the creative activity which was later to organise these elements.

I put again the opposed view to this. I have already said that the simplification of planes is based on that actually suggested by nature. The realist intention, it might be said, is directed towards weight and three-dimensional form, rather than towards light, yet it still remains realist. This is quite a conceivable view. It is quite possible that a realist of this kind might prepare the material of an abstract art automatically. The abstractions might be produced accidentally, with no attempt to use them creatively as means of expression.

It seems to me, however, that there are many reasons against the supposition that this was the case with Cézanne. In looking for any traces of this abstract organising tendency, one must remember that Cézanne was extraordinarily hampered by the realism of his period; in some ways he might be said to have carried out the complete impressionist programme. Yet showing through this you do get traces of an opposed tendency. I should base this assertion on two grounds:

(1) Though the simplification of planes may appear passive and prosaic, entirely dictated by a desire to reproduce a certain solidity, and from one point of view almost fumbling, yet at the same time one may say that in this treatment of detail, there is an energy at work which, though perhaps unconscious, is none the less an energy which is working towards abstraction and towards a feeling for structure. If one thinks of the details, rather than of the picture as a whole, one need not even say this energy is unconscious. In this respect Cézanne does seem to have been fairly conscious, and to have recognised what he was after better than the contemporary opinion which looked upon him as an impressionist. I should say that expressions like "everything is spherical or cylindrical," and all the forms of nature "peuvent se ramener au cône, au cylindre et à la sphère," yet show the working of a creative invention, which had to that extent turned away from realism and showed a tendency towards abstraction. (It is obvious that these words were not used in the same sense in which a Cubist might use them; they apply to details rather than to wholes. Yet a denial of the wider application does not, as many people seem to suppose, justify the idea that they were meant in the sense in which a Cubist might understand them.) These sentences seem to me to destroy the whole of Mr. Ginner's argument, unless, of course, you go a step further than those who explain Cézanne's painting as the result of astigmatism and incompetence, and assert that the poor man could not even use his mother tongue. The simplification of planes itself, then, does seem to show a tendency to abstraction which is working itself free. (2) But the fact that this simplification is not entirely realistic and does come from a certain feeling

after structure, seems to me to be demonstrated in a more positive way by pictures like the well-known "Bathing Women." Here you get a use of distortion and an emphasis on form which is constructive. The pyramidal shape, moreover, cannot be compared to decoration, or to the composition found in the old masters. The shape is so hard, so geometrical in character, that it almost lifts the picture out of the realistic art which has lasted from the Renaissance to now, and into the sphere of geometric art. It is in reality much nearer to the kind of geometrical organisations employed in the new art.

That is a theoretical statement of the errors Mr. Ginner makes. I think it might be worth while to go behind these errors themselves, to explain the prejudices which are responsible for their survival.

As a key to his psychology, take the sentence which he most frequently repeats. "It is only this intimate relation between the artist and the object which can produce original and great works. Away from nature, we fall into unoriginal and monotonous formulae." In repeating this he probably has at the back of his mind two quite different ideas, (1) the idea that it is the business of the artist to represent and interpret nature, and (2) the assumption that even if it is not his duty to represent nature that he must do so *practically*, for away from nature the artist's invention at once decays. He apparently thinks of an artist using abstractions as of a child playing with a box of tricks. The number of interesting combinations must soon be exhausted.

The first error springs from a kind of Rousseauism which is probably much too deeply imbedded in Mr. Ginner's mind for me to be able to eradicate. I merely meet it by the contrary assertion that I do not think it is the artist's only business to reproduce and interpret Nature, "source of all good," but that it is possible that the artist may be creative. This distinction is obscured in Mr. Ginner's mind by the highly coloured and almost ethical language in which he puts it. We are exhorted to stick to Mother Nature. Artists who attempt to do something other than this are accused of "shrinking from life." This state of mind can be most clearly seen in the use of the word simplification. There is a confusion here between the *validity* and *origin* of simplification. The validity of simplification is held to depend on its origin. If the simplification, such as that for example you get in Cézanne's treatment of trees, is derived from Nature and comes about as the result of an aim which is itself directed back to Nature, then it is held to be valid. I, on the other hand, should assert that the validity of the simplification lay in itself and in the use made of it and had nothing whatever to do with its descent, on its occupying a place in Nature's "Burke."

Take now the second prejudice — the idea that whatever he may do theoretically, at any rate practically, the artist must keep in continual contact with Nature — "The individual relying on his imagination and his formula finds himself very limited, in comparison with the infinite variety of life. Brain ceases to act as it ceases to search out expression of Nature, its only true and healthy source."

You see here again the ethical view of the matter — the idea of retribution. Get further and further away from dear old Mother Nature and see what happens to you: you fall into dead formulae.

My answer to this argument is: that while I admit it to be to a certain extent true, I deny the conclusion Mr. Ginner draws from it.

I admit that the artist cannot work without contact with, and continual research into nature, but one must make a distinction between this and the conclusion drawn from it that the work of art itself must be an interpretation of nature. The artist obviously cannot spin things out of his head, he cannot work from imagination in that sense. The whole thing springs from misconception of the nature of artistic imagination. Two statements are confused: (1) that the source of imagination must be nature, and (2) the consequence illegitimately drawn from this, that the resulting work must be realistic, and based on natural forms. One can give an analogy in ordinary thought. The reasoning activity is quite different in character from any succession of images drawn from the senses, but yet thought itself would be impossible without this sensual stimulus.

FURTHER SPECULATIONS

There must be just as much contact with nature in an abstract art as in a realistic one; without that stimulus the artist could produce nothing. In Picasso, for example, there is much greater research into nature, as far as the relation of planes is concerned, than in any realist painting; he has isolated and emphasised relations previously not emphasised. All art may be said to be realism, then, in that it extracts from nature facts which have not been observed before. But in as far as the artist is creative, he is not bound down by the accidental relations of the elements actually found in nature, but extracts, distorts, and utilises them as a means of expression, and not as a means of interpreting nature.

It is true, then, that an artist can only keep his work alive by research into nature, but that does not prove that realism is the only legitimate form of art.

Both realism and abstraction, then, can only be *engendered* out of nature, but while the first's only idea of living seems to be that of hanging on to its progenitor, the second cuts its umbilical cord.

MODERN ART

III · The London Group

This group has been formed by the amalgamation of the Camden Town Group and the Cubists. It thus claims to represent all the forward movements in English painting at the present moment. Judging from its first exhibition, it is probably destined, since the decline of the New English, to play a very important rôle in the next few years. Of the more realist section of the society I shall not say much here, as I intend to write about it at greater length later. Mr. Spencer Gore's "The Wood," and Mr. Harold Gilman's "Eating House" show in very different ways the same intimate research into problems of colour. Mr. Charles Ginner's "La Balayeuse" is the best picture of his that I have seen as yet. His peculiar method is here extraordinarily successful in conveying the sordid feeling of the subject. Mr. Bevan exhibits a characteristic and interesting painting of horses. Although at the moment I am more in sympathy with the other section of the society, yet I am bound to say that the work of the painters I have just mentioned is better than that one finds at the New English, and infinitely better than the faked stuff produced by Mr. Roger Fry and his friends. It is possible to point out, however, in looking at this kind of painting, the dissatisfaction which inclines one towards Cubism. These pictures are filled by contours which, when one is moved by the dissatisfaction I am speaking of, one can only describe as meaningless. They are full of detail which is entirely accidental in character, and only justified by the fact that these accidents did actually occur in the particular piece of nature which was being painted. One feels a repugnance to such accidents — and desires painting where nothing is accidental, where all the contours are closely knit together into definite structural shapes.

The Cubist section is particularly interesting, as it shows very clearly the unsettled state of the new movement. Though it has finally got clear away from its Post-Impressionistic beginnings, it cannot be said to have reached any final form. Two different tendencies can be distinguished. The main movement is that which, arising out of Cubism, is destined to create a new geometric and monumental art, making use of mechanical forms. It is possible, I think, to give an account of this movement, which will exhibit it as an understandable and coherent whole, closely allied to the general tendency of the period, and thus containing possibilities of development.

But this has now generated a second movement based simply on the idea that abstract form, i.e., form without any representative content, can be an adequate means of expression. In this, instead of hard, structural work like Picasso's you get the much more scattered use of abstractions of artists like Kandinsky. It seems, judging by its development up to now, to be only a more or less amusing by-product of the first. Lacking the controlling sensibility, the feeling for mechanical structure, which makes use of abstractions a necessity, it seems rather dilettante. It so happens, however, that all explanations of the new movement as yet given, have been explanations of this second tendency only. In this way the real importance of the main tendency has been veiled. It has seemed rather in the air, rather causeless. The driving force behind it remained hidden.

What is really behind the main movement, what makes it important is the re-emergence of a sensibility akin to that behind geometrical arts of the past. At first, at its rather fumbling search for an appropriate means of expression, it naturally went back to these past arts. You thus got a period in which the work produced had a certain resemblance to Archaic, Byzantine and African art. But this state has already been left behind. The new sensibility is finding for itself a direct and modern means of expression, having very little resemblance to these past geometric arts.

It is characterised, not by the simple geometric forms found in archaic art, but by the more complicated ones associated in our minds with machinery. Minor effects of this change of sensibility are very obvious in the pictures here. They do not shrink from forms which it is usual to describe as unrhythmical, and great use is made of shapes taken from machinery. The beauty of banal forms like teapot-handles, knuckledusters, saws, etc., seems to have been perceived for the first time. A whole picture is sometimes dominated by a composition based on hard mechanical shapes in a way which previous art would have shrunk from. It is not the emphasis on form which is the distinguishing characteristic of the new movement, then, but the emphasis on this particular kind of form.

But it is easy to see how this main movement, with its necessary use of abstraction of a particular kind for a particular purpose, has engendered on the side of it a minor movement which uses abstractions for their own sake in a much more scattered way. I do not think this minor movement is destined to survive. I look upon it rather as a kind of romantic heresy, which will, however, have a certain educative influence. It will lead to the discovery of conceptions of form, which will be extremely useful in the construction of the new geometrical art. But temporarily, at any rate, most of the painters in this exhibition seem to be very much influenced by an enthusiasm for this idea. One has here, then, a good opportunity for examining this heresy. Theoretically it is quite plausible. It seems quite conceivable that the directions of the forms in a picture, the subordination of the parts to the whole, the arresting of one form by the other, the relation of veiled to exposed shapes, might make up an understandable kind of music without the picture containing any representative element whatever. How does it work out in practice? Take Mr. Wyndham Lewis's large canvases, which at first look like mere arbitrary arrangements of bright colours and abstract forms. Judged from this point of view, what can be said about them? They fail, in that they do not produce as a whole, the kind of coherent effect which, according to the theory, they ought to produce. The forms are not controlled enough. In the "Eisteddfod," for example, long tranquil planes of colour sweeping up from the left encounter a realistically painted piece of ironwork, which, being very large in proportion to the planes, dwarfs any effect they might have produced. The second picture, "Christopher Columbus," is hard and gay, contains many admirable inventions, but is best regarded as a field where certain qualities are displayed, rather than as a complete work of art. In Mr. Lewis's work, there are always certain qualities of dash and decision, but it has the defects of these qualities. His sense of form seems to me to be sequent rather than integral, by which I mean that one form probably springs out of the preceding one as he works, instead of being conceived as part of a whole. His imagination being quick and never fumbling, very interesting relations are generated in this way, but the whole sometimes lacks cohesion and unity. The qualities of Mr. Lewis's works are seen to better advantage in his quite remarkable drawing, "The Enemy of the Stars." Equally abstract is Mr. Wadsworth's work. In the most successful, "Scherzo," a number of lively ascending forms are balanced by broad planes at the top. The painter whose work shows the greatest advance is Mr. C. F. Hamilton. His "Two Figures" shows a great sense of construction, and is one of the best paintings in this section. Mr. F. Etchells' drawings are admirably firm and hard in character; but it would obviously be premature to form any sure judgment about this artist's work at a time when he almost seems to be holding himself back, in a search for a new method of expression. His fine "Drawing of a Head" shows this state of hesitation and experiment very clearly. Mr. Nevinson is much less abstract than the others. His best picture is "The Chauffeur," which is very solid and develops an interesting contrast between round and angular shapes. I admire the ability of Mr. Gaudier-Brzeska's sculpture; the tendencies it displays are sound though the abstractions used do not seem to me to be always thoroughly thought out.

In all the painters I have mentioned so far abstract form has been used as the bearer of general emotions, but the real fanatics of form reject even this abstract use as savouring of literature and sentiment. Representation has already been excluded. They want to exclude even the general emotions conveyed by abstract form, and to confine us to the appreciation of form in itself *tout pur*. Some such intention must be behind the largest picture in the show, Mr. Bomberg's "In the Hold." Stated in more detail, the theory on which it is based seems to be this. In looking at a picture one never sees it as a whole, one's eye travels over it. In doing so, we continually find certain expectations fulfilled — a boot is followed by a leg, and even when there is no representation at all, certain abstract forms are naturally continued by other forms. Apparently this fulfilled expectation is an added non-aesthetic emotion, and must be excluded by those who wish to take an absolutely "pure" pleasure in form itself. Mr. Bomberg therefore cuts his picture up into sixty-four squares, and as each square is independent of its neighbours, the "fulfilled expectation" I spoke of above is excluded, and whatever pleasure we take must be in the arrangement of shapes inside each square. The picture appears to have started off as a drawing of an actual subject, but that apparently was only because a purely mental invention of form would have inevitably produced those "sequences" it was desired to avoid. The representation of the outside scene generates, in its passage through a square, an entirely accidental and "unexpected" shape. The square I might call K.Kt.6, for example, makes an interesting pattern. That the picture as a whole is entirely empty is, I suppose, on the theory I have just put forward, no defect. All the general emotions produced by form have been excluded and we are reduced to a purely intellectual interest in shape. This particular picture, then, is certainly the reductio ad absurdum of this heresy about form. I see no development along such lines, though such work may be an excellent discipline. I look forward, however, to Mr. Bomberg's future work with interest; he is undoubtedly an artist of remarkable ability. For the present, I prefer his drawings. "The Acrobats" breaks away from the sculptural treatment of his recent work and seems to me to be admirable.

Most of the work I have been talking about is experimental and is interesting because it is on the way to something else. Perhaps the only really satisfying and complete work in this section is that of Mr. Epstein. He possesses that peculiar energy which distinguishes the creative from the merely intelligent artist, and is certainly the greatest sculptor of this generation; I have seen no work in Paris or Berlin which I can so unreservedly admire. At the present moment he has arrived at an interesting point in his development. Starting from a very efficient realism, he passed through a more or less archaic period; he seems now to have left that behind and, as far as one can judge from the drawings for sculpture he exhibits, to have arrived at an entirely personal and modern method of expression. The "Carving in Flenite" comes at the end of the second period. Technically it is admirable. The design is in no sense empty, but gives a most impressive and complete expression of a certain blind, tragic aspect of its subject — something akin perhaps to what Plato meant by the vegetable soul. The archaic elements it contains are in no sense imitative. What has been taken from African or Polynesian work is the inevitable and permanent way of getting a certain effect. The only quite new work Mr. Epstein exhibits, the "Bird Pluming Itself" is in comparison with this profound work, quite light in character, but the few simple abstractions out of which it is built are used with great skill and discretion.

MODERN ART
IV · Mr. David Bomberg's Show

Mr. Bomberg stands somewhat apart from the other English Cubists. I noticed that in signing the collective protest, published a few weeks ago, he added in a footnote that he had nothing whatever to do with the Rebel Art Centre — very wisely, in my opinion, for his work is certainly much more individual and less derivative than the work of the members of that group. The tendency to abstraction does seem in his case to have been a logical development of tendencies which were always present even in his earlier drawings, and not merely the result of a feverish hurry to copy the latest thing from Paris. The fact that his work shows these individual qualities justifies much more than is generally the case a one-man show, and separate consideration. But while I have great admiration for some of Mr. Bomberg's work, that does not make it easier for me to write an article about it. An article about one man's pictures is not a thing I should ever do naturally. The only absolutely honest and direct and straightforward word expression of what I think as I go round such an exhibition would be a monotonous repetition of the words "This is good or fairly good. How much does that cost?" for I would certainly rather buy a picture than write about it. It seems a much more appropriate gesture. Any more rotund or fluent expression than these short sentences must, however admirable, be artificial. Only the expert art critic can prolong the gesture of admiration artificially by cliché — that, of course, is his métier. I wish I could do it myself. The fact that naturally one's expression is inadequate, springs entirely from a certain physical difference of *pace*. What you feel before a picture is long, slow, seems important. The rattle of sounds which expresses it is quick, short and unimpressive. The body as a tool of expression is obviously a failure, it is too light weight. Your sentence over, you feel you have finished too soon; you feel uncomfortable and want to prolong the gesture. Hence is born the whole system of cliché; a system enabling you to "last out" the feeling; hence also we might even say to the whole mechanism of literary expression. It all exists to cover the body's inefficiency. If only our arms were so heavy that an appreciative sweep lasted ten minutes we should be saved from literature. Opera, of course, can "last out" by raising the sentence into *aria*. The American has his drawl, and consequently has no literature — not needing any. But I haven't these expedients; nor as an outsider in this business have I the necessary cliché at my command. I can only then write an article on one man's pictures by using the only form of incense natural to me; I can get up an argument about them — which I therefore proceed to do.

Mr. Bomberg starts off by stating in the preface to his catalogue that his object in all his painting is the construction of "pure form," and that he appeals constantly to a sense of form. We might all admit that this is true as a description of pure fact, at any rate. All the paintings are of the character he describes. They do appeal to very little else but a sense of form. Take, for example, one of the best of the drawings (No. 6) "Ju Jitsu." What strikes you first as excellent is the contrast between the bareness of certain parts as contrasted with the complex and intricate liveliness of others. Wherever it was felt to be necessary, representation has been sacrificed. The body line of one figure, which would be in reality hidden behind another figure in the foreground, is clearly shown. The realist would here urge that if that line was necessary in order to get a certain arrangement of form, it should have been continued by a line on the front figure, so that representation should not have been sacrificed. I will deal later with the validity of this kind of objection; I only mention the point here to show that the intention of the artist is clearly what he announces it to be. It is still clearer in the remarkable drawing, "Zin" (No. 26), which contains hardly any representative element at all. In the upper part, which strikes me as best, there are no recognisable forms at all, but only an arrangement of abstract lines outlining no object. It is very difficult to state why one considers a drawing of this kind good when one hasn't it before one. Perhaps the best way of describing it would be to say that it looks like a peculiarly interesting kind of scaffolding. It is obvious, therefore, that the only interest in it must be an interest in form. I should probably find it difficult to say what I found interesting in it if I had the drawing here before me and could show it you. Its interest depends on qualities peculiarly indescribable in words. Indescribable not for any mysterious reason, but because forms are of their nature indescribable, and even difficult, to point out. They depend, for example, very often on a three-dimensional relation between planes which is very difficult to get at. The artist in front of a picture endeavouring to explain it, by inexpressive motions of his hands, has often been laughed at; but laughed at, I think, for a wrong reason. It is supposed that he waves his hands, makes strange gestures with his thumbs, peculiar twists with his wrists, because he lacks the power of expressing himself in words; because he is a painter, in fact, and not a literary man. This I believe to be a mistaken view of the phenomenon. He is not using his hands through poverty of words, through lack of the ability to express himself in the proper manner. He is trying to describe the qualities of the picture in the only way they can be described. But he is a figure for laughter because he is employing a miserably inadequate tool. It is impossible to suppose that those ancient prehensile implements, our hands, could ever be turned to this new use — a description of subtleties and intricacies of form. It cannot be done, and surely the designer of the universe never intended that it should be done. I think of designing a little brass instrument which shall adequately perform the function which the hands now so inefficiently perform. An arrangement of revolving graduated spheres will enable you to indicate at once all the complicated twists and relations of form that you perceive in a picture. This invention would have two advantages. It would do away with the art critic. On each picture would be an indication as to how you must graduate your instrument, in order to grasp the relations of forms the artist was after; this would do away with any necessity for the confused and stuttering metaphors by which the critic endeavours to express the inexpressible; one painful scene the less in this world of trouble. Moreover, it would please the conservatives in these matters, for the manufacture of my instrument would soon fall into the hands of a trust, who, whenever a new generation began to experiment with a new kind of form unprovided for by the instrument, would see that the Press unanimously denounced it.

To return, however, to Mr. Bomberg's exhibition. Those who are curious as to the genesis of abstract form, as to the way in which it is actually constructed in the artist's mind, should find Nos. 23, 11, 1 which probably represent three stages in the development of the same idea, interesting. The first step towards the understanding of this process of genesis is to recognise that the mind cannot *create* form, it can only *edit* it. In this, as in other very different matters, existing here in this world, bound to this body, we have little spontaneity. Asked to fill a space with a *new* abstract design, and told at the same time to empty his mind of all recollection of the external world, an artist would produce nothing but a few arbitrary and uninteresting repetitions. The first suggestion must always come from some existing outside shape. This sets the mind going. Consider now the three things I mentioned above. No. 23 is the first drawing. The artist probably got the lines of his main design from some accidental material arrangement. The suggestions of form this contained were then probably continued and developed by thinking of them as parts of human figures. (This use of doll-like human figures is a characteristic of Mr. Bomberg's work, as those who saw his drawings in the New Age will remember.) In the final stage, these figures are so abstract that they are not recognisable as such. In all this process what suggestions of real objects occur, are only as a means of getting the mind going, as fertiliser of the design. In themselves they are of no importance, the controlling interest all the time being the selection and production of abstract form. The first of these three works, No. 23, I do not think successful, taken by itself. One notes it as interesting, but it produces no definite effect. The two paintings developed from it, however, are much more interesting; No. 1, "The Mud Bath," being one of the best things Mr. Bomberg has done; the colour in it being much more vigorous than in the earlier study, No. 11 of the drawings, which, while being abstract, at the same time contains recognisable representative elements. No. 5, reading from Torak, seems to me to be the best. The abstract shapes here do reinforce a quite human and even dramatic effect, at the same time being interesting in themselves, merely as a construction of shapes. They would probably be even more interesting carried out as three dimensional shapes in wood or something of that kind. Another extremely good drawing of an almost sculptural quality is "Chinnereth," about which, however, I need say nothing, as it has already been reproduced in this paper.*

So far I have only been concerned to show that on the assumption that an interest in pure form is a sufficient basis in itself Mr. Bomberg's work is, as a matter of fact, good work. It may be worth while here to examine that assumption. Is pure form alone a sufficient basis for interest in art? The best answer is, of course, that certain people do find it enough. They find that they are moved by, and interested in, the suggestions of abstract form they see about them, and do feel themselves prompted either to then organise these suggestions, or to look for them in art. When a man simply says: "I do feel interested in abstract form, as another might in atmosphere and landscape," no objection can be made to his statement. But there is an erroneous way of transforming the statement into a theory, which makes it impossible for the layman to understand the motives of abstract art. For this reason I want to contradict it. The theory is that we contemplate *form* for its own sake — that it produces a particular emotion different from the ordinary everyday emotions — a specific *aesthetic* emotion. If this were a true account of the matter, it would be incomprehensible to the layman. "Pictures with some dramatic or human interest I like, . . . but this damned stylistic bunkum. . . . " And

* *New Age*, X (April 2, 1914), 689.

he would be right. If form has no dramatic or human interest, then it is obviously stupid for a human to be interested in it.

But the theory is erroneous. There is no such thing as a specific *aesthetic* emotion, a peculiar kind of emotion produced by *form* alone, only of interest to aesthetes. I think it could be shown that the emotions produced by abstract form, are the ordinary everyday human emotions — they are produced in a different way, that is all.

What happens, then, is not

$$S_{(f)} \quad . \quad . \quad . \quad . \quad . \quad . \quad . \quad . \quad . \quad . \quad . \quad F$$

where S is the spectator, F the outside form, and (f) the specific form emotion, but much more this —

$$S_{(de)} \quad . \quad . \quad . \quad . \quad . \quad . \quad . \quad . \quad . \quad . \quad F_{(if)}$$

where (de) stands for quite ordinary *dramatic human emotions*, which occur in daily life, and not only in the contemplation of works of art. I do not say that in looking at pure form we are *conscious* of this emotion they produce. We are not fully conscious of it, but *project it* outside ourselves into the outside form F, and may only be conscious of it as (if) "interesting form." But the (if) only exists because of the (de).

After all this possibility of living our own emotions *into* outside shapes and colours is the basic fact on which the whole of plastic art rests. People admit it in the case of atmosphere, colour, and landscape, but they will not admit it in the case of abstract form. Very possibly the number of people who can thus be affected by form is much more limited, but the phenomenon is the same. There is nothing mysterious in this process by which *form* becomes the *porter* or *carrier* of internal emotions. It admits of a simple psychological explanation which I need not give here, however; all that concerns us for the moment is the *fact*. Bare abstract form can be dramatic; the mere shape of a tree as tragic has a long explicit history. As a rule, of course, much milder emotions of tension, balance, contrast, etc., are called up. But it remains possible to say all one wants about arrangements of pure form without once using the word beauty and employing always the vocabulary with which one would speak of a man's character, commonplace . . . vigorous . . . empty, etc.

It must be insisted that there is nothing esoteric or mysterious about this interest in abstract forms. Once he has awakened to it, once it has been emphasised and indicated to him by art, then just as in the case of colour perception and impression the layman will derive great pleasure from it, not only as it is presented to him organised in Cubism, but as he perceives it for himself in outside nature. He will feel, for example, probably for the first time, an interest in the extraordinary variety of the abstract forms suggested by bare trees in winter (an interest, I must repeat, which is really an interest in himself as these forms, by an obscure psychological process, become for him the bearers of certain emotions) or in the morning, he may contemplate with interest the shapes into which his shirt thrown over a chair has fallen.

Here comes a common objection. Admitting the existence of this special interest in form, it is asked, why cannot these forms, instead of being abstracted, be given *in* the objects in which they actually occurred, i.e. *in* a realistic setting? If an artist looking out of a high window on the street beneath is interested in the fish-like interweaving of the motor traffic, why cannot that interweaving be given in a representation of the motor? Why attempt to give the interweaving alone? Why attempt to give the soul without the body — an impossible feat? Why could not Mr. Bomberg have given the shape-design of his "Men and Lads" or his "Acrobats," embodied *in* a more realistic representation? For two reasons: first that the only element of the real scene which interests the artist is the abstract element; the others are for that interest irrelevant, and, if reproduced, would only damp down the vigour of the naked form itself. And secondly, the fact that the abstract element did occur as a matter of fact in external nature mixed up with other things is of no importance. The forms are either interesting in themselves, or not. They derive no justification from their natural occurrence. The only importance of nature in this connection is that it does suggest forms, which the artist can develop; the mind here, as elsewhere, having very little natural spontaneity.

The use of form is then constructive. The same may be said of Mr. Bomberg's use of colour. The relations of colours used are not *right* because they are the kind of sets of colour that do, as a matter of fact, actually occur in nature. In some of his earlier work, however, this is the case. (No. 23) "The Song of Songs," a very beautiful work, is an example of this older use of colour. The combination of greys, dead black and gold strikes one as distinguished, but at the same time the pleasure it gives may be partly the pleasures of association; it is the kind of colour that might occur in nature at times of the day which have a certain emotional accompaniment. In the "Mud Bath," on the contrary, the colour is used in an entirely constructive way, and in no sense derivative from nature. Here I might deal with a quite reasonable objection which is frequently brought against this kind of art. I went round Mr. Bomberg's show with a very intelligent painter of an older school. "Although I find these abstract drawings extremely interesting," he said, "yet if I were buying I should get this" — pointing out No. 32, I think. "I feel abstract work would become tiring when one continually saw it in a room." Though this sounds plausible, yet I don't think that it would as a matter of fact turn out to be the case. Personally, I think I should find drawings in which your imagination was continually focussed in one direction by a subject more fatiguing. The proportions of a room or the shape of a good window, though they exercise a definite effect on one, do not become tiresome. And the pleasure to be got from good abstract art is of the same kind, though infinitely more elaborate, as the pleasure you get from these other fixed elements of a room.

To turn now to Mr. Bomberg's earlier work. Here I have a convenient opportunity of dealing with an entirely fallacious argument which I am now thoroughly tired of reading. The baffled art critic, being entirely at sea in dealing with quite abstract work, and feeling himself unable to pass any secure judgment on it, turns to the artist's earlier and more conventional work, and says, "This

earlier work which I *can* understand is commonplace, I can therefore legitimately infer that this abstract work which I cannot understand is also entirely commonplace." Now this argument, although attractively simple, is a *non sequitur.* Suppose that the
qualities of a good naturalistic drawing are ABC . . . . . . F
where F is a sense of form. In any particular case F might be good,
but the man's attention and interest might be so concentrated on
F that ABC were comparatively uninteresting, so that on the whole
the drawing might be pronounced commonplace. I see, however,
that one critic has already applied this faulty criterion to Mr.
Bomberg's earlier work. "This earlier work," he says, "shows energy without patience . . . is very ordinary student's work . . .
he has never had the patience to master form," and so on. These
judgments I consider to be entirely unjust. Bearing in mind what
I said in the last paragraph, I find it decidedly *not* commonplace,
because all of it shows emphasis on, and understanding of, that
quality which, while it may only be one element in the excellence
of a naturalistic drawing, is yet the whole of a more abstract one —
a sense of form. That seems to have been always excellent. He has
all the time, and apparently quite spontaneously, and without
imitation, been more interested in form than anything else. Take
No. 46, a bedroom picture, for example. I mention it because it
shows the transitional period very clearly — the bed and room
quite in the Sickert tradition, quite realistic and with Sickert's
ideas about paint, the figure of the girl in it treated quite differ-
ently, very much simplified, getting on to abstraction, and looking
consequently very unreal in the midst of the other very solid realistic things. All the early drawings show a preoccupation with
form — the heads, though, less than the figure studies. In all of
them, there is an insistency on shapes running through. You can
see this most clearly in the figure study in the first room. Done
realistically the lines of the deltoids in the two arms, and the line
of the chest, would form three broken parts of one line. As he has
done it, the three are joined to make one line running through. I
am quite aware, of course, that this sort of thing has always been
one element in good drawing, but I do think you find it empha-

sised here in a way which makes his later development very understandable. No. 32 is good, and gets a certain monumental effect.

That his work shows the impatience the critic regrets is only to
be expected. People with any guts in them do not have catholic
tastes. If they realise in a personal and vivid way the importance
of *one* element, if they feel that they have anything fresh to say
about that, they are naturally impatient with the other elements.
Why, if you are only interested in form, should you be asked —
once you have got down the elements of that form adequately — to
add to it the alien elements which would make it into a solid
realistic representation? The water-colour "Rehoboam" (No. 21)
admirably expresses the idea it is based on. Why should it be carried any further? Why not stop with the idea which started it —
why artificially prolong it into something not present on that initial idea?

To sum up, then — in my notice of the London Group I said
that I thought Mr. Bomberg was an artist of remarkable ability.
This show certainly confirms that impression. It also adds something. It convinces me that his work has always been personal and
independent — much more independent than that of most Cubists — and never reminiscent. If I am to qualify this, I should add
that as yet his use of form satisfies a too purely sensuous or intellectual interest. It is not often used to intensify a more general
emotion. I do not feel, then, the same absolute certainty about his
work that I do about Epstein's. In Mr. Epstein's work the abstractions have been got at gradually, and always intensify, as abstractions, the general feeling of the whole work. But then Mr.
Epstein is in a class by himself. I think that in this merely intellectual use of abstraction Mr. Bomberg is achieving exactly what he
sets out to achieve. But at the same time it is quite legitimate for
me to point out why I prefer another use of abstraction. In any
case, I think he will develop remarkably, and he is probably by this
kind of work acquiring an intimate knowledge of form, which he
will utilise in a different way later.

DIARY FROM THE TRENCHES
AND ESSAYS ON WAR

DIARY FROM THE TRENCHES

Dec. 30th, 1914

We left Southampton about 4 p.m., after marching down the principal street, all out of step, and all the girls waving from the windows. (On the way down on Sunday, people waved to us from the back windows; all the troops go down that line so they have formed a habit.)

We had a very smooth crossing, 700 of us in a tramp steamer which was fitted out to carry cattle or horses. We slept in the stalls, hurriedly whitewashed to make them clean, with notice painted over our heads "This is for urine only not for dung." It sounds dreadful but it's really all right.

We were accompanied all the way by two English destroyers, as escort, got to the port I said we should come to about 4 a.m., but did not leave till about 9. As we entered the harbour, some French soldiers, drilling on the quayside in white trousers looking from the distance exactly like penguins, called out "Air we down-hearted." We marched then, with all our equipment up a fearful hill about 4 miles to what is called a Rest Camp, a fearful place, deep in mud, where we have to sleep in tents which makes me very depressed. I hope we shan't stay here long. All my clothes are wet through with sweat.

I am writing this in a little café, by the camp. Crammed full of Tommies of all sorts, where we are eating tremendously. We are all dreading the night for we are 12 in one tent & it looks like rain. The town seems absolutely empty but for the soldiers in red trousers, of all ages.

I thoroughly enjoy all the events, like being seen off at the dock, except that there were only about 10 people to cheer us as the ship left the side, but its all very amusing — and the girls at the windows.

We are in one of a series of similar Rest Camps on the top of a hill.

Send the first part of this letter to my Aunt. Ask her to send me a large pair of chauffeurs gloves, line with felt. (Any socks must be long in the leg). Also a piece of soap & a night light each week.

Jan. 5th, Sunday. Rest Camp

We are leaving here to-day. A wire came at midnight that we were to be ready. I shan't be sorry to leave this mud. You must imagine a large space of clayey earth, no grass, like an undeveloped building plot, all pulped up into mud and covered with tents with large trenches round them. We get up at 5:30 & march down to the docks, as a rule without breakfast. Here we do ———* work in an enormous shed. Here is the base for the army & here is all the food. The shed is 5/8 of a mile long & 79 yrds wide. On one side are the ships coming in and on the other a luggage train of ——— covered in vans and the same length as the shed. Each truck is marked with chalk with the amount of stuff that has to go in. So many boxes of corned beef, pepper, salt, bran, hay, oats etc. We work in gangs and have to fill so many trucks from the piles inside the shed. The train goes off in 4 parts each night, to feed the whole army. The shed inside is quite nice, as it's quite new, all light iron work and has of course immense distances in it, men and horses at the end of long avenues, between the mountains of boxes looking quite tiny. There are two cafés inside the limit of the camp (otherwise we have no leave) & we go and talk to the Tommies there. There are all people from all kinds of regiments, some wounded, some lost etc., a kind of sorting camp. We spent one evening with some Belfast Tommies, men about 35, who had re-joined, very simple people with faces like pieces of wood, who told us fearful stories of this sort. Some Ghurkas were left in charge of German prisoners. In the morning all the Germans were found

---

* EDITOR'S NOTE. Spaces in the text of the diary indicate similar gaps in the Hulme family manuscript, which is a transcript of the original letters made by a member of the family. The gaps apparently represent words which could not be deciphered from Hulme's extremely difficult handwriting, though some may also be due to military censorship.

with their heads off. Asked for an explanation, they opened their haversacks, each of which had a German head in it & said, "Souvenir Sahib." All this in the most wonderful accent you ever heard. — Three men have been sent back with pneumonia already & I'm not surprised. In the enormous shed we worked in, were batches of English prisoners, people sent back from the front for various reasons, a sergeant 5 years for cowardice, another 15 years for looting. At one end of the shed was an enormous cage, in which all the rum was kept. This was to keep it from being stolen by the A.S.C. men, who are really London dockers enlisted for the war. It was really impressive to see all the piles of food, all done up into cases a convenient size for men to handle. It makes the word "base" & "lines of communication" seem much more real to have seen it. It was all guarded by English Territorials who slept in a little enclosure made of packing cases in the middle. All the men doing clerks work live in little houses made of packing cases put together. They say that when the Germans were 12 miles off some months ago they had to shift the whole contents in a day.

Monday. I was called off suddenly at this part of the letter, as we were told we must fall in to leave at once for Rouen. We left about 12, marched 7 miles to the station got here about 8 & then they left us in a railway siding till this morning. We did not know where we were going — it's rather amusing travelling in this way. It was a fearful night however. I woke with a pain behind my right back & could hardly walk. However after going about 200 yds it passed off. We marched off in the morning about 7 miles to an enormous camp up here, through acres of mud, but finally to quite a dry new camp, where we are again under canvas, but much more comfortable. I've got a bad headache so can't write much — am writing this in the Y.M.C.A. shed, there are dozens of them about the camps. I expect we shall be off to-morrow, or in a few days, to the trenches. We have had our fur coats issued to us — I have a kind of goat or wolf skin, look like a bear, great long fur stretching out all over from me. I haven't had my clothes off since I left Southampton. I have chucked my extra pair of boots away, as I couldn't stand the weight. With these heavy packs we perspire like anything on the march, though we go very slowly, very different to marching in England. This camp is on a kind of plateau on the hills outside Rouen & is enormous.

Tuesday, Jan 12th

We did not have such a long journey as I expected. We left about 4 p.m. and arrived here at the frontier (& the front) about 10 this morning. We travelled up in wagons between 30 & 40 in closed horse or cattle trucks. They are fitted up inside with rough seats down the centre. We marched down to the station, to a kind of railway siding where the cattle train was waiting for us. They kept us standing about for ¾ hour, so that we should be thoroughly uncomfortable and then we had to scramble in, everyone of course fighting for the corners. As it got dark people dug their clasp knives into the sides of the truck and fastened their candles to them, so the whole place looked dark and mysterious eventually, with little groups playing cards under the candles. Trucks as you know are fastened with a kind of iron sliding door. It was fearfully uncomfortable. The rain made the floor a pool of black mud, & the few of us who could get down to sleep there had to do it in the mud with continually feet fighting all the night.

As we got near here, we saw on the flat kind of horizon lines of cavalry on horseback, exercising their horses I suppose. When we got here we were marched up into a kind of greenhouse for grapes. It's a very large one and there are about 300 or 350 of us sleeping in it. It's a steel thing, looking like a small Olympia. We have strict instructions not to hang anything on the vines. Just now when everyone is writing letters or getting to bed, it looks like the opening of one of the scenes of the "Miracle."

I have just been outside the greenhouse now 7:30 p.m. You can hear all the heavy guns going off. It's like the sound of summer thunder a long way off. We are only about 8 miles from the firing line here and from the part of the trenches, we shall probably march to to-morrow. To continue, every now & then on the horizon, you see a flash, its a kind of illuminating shell used to light up things so that the artillery can fire at anything they see moving. If you listen carefully you can hear from time to time, quick firing by the men's rifles in the trenches. The men are standing watching it by ——— fire outside, as if it were a fireworks exhibition. We have just met some men I used to know in the 1st Battalion. They are very gloomy about the trenches. An officer and two men have just been killed by snipers. We shall either move up to the trenches to-morrow, or else in 6 days time when the rotation comes round again. We have not rejoined the regiment who are in billets 3 miles nearer the fighting line. There's no doubt about us actually being at the front at last.

Wednesday, Jan. 13th

We left the place I last wrote from on Wednesday. It was pouring with rain and we had to march about 6 miles altogether I should think. It sounds very little but when you have all your equipment and very heavy packs it becomes very tiresome. We were told before we set out that we should, in a few miles, be inside the area of shell fire. The roads are simply fearful with mud and you keep meeting supply motors and carts which push you to the side of the road in the mud. All you can think of on the march, is various ways of shifting the weight of your pack from one shoulder to another, every now and then you rest and you bend down something like this * in order to save the weight of your pack on the shoulders. You look reflectively at your feet & the patterns of the mud as you do this, & that will be the predominant impression I shall carry away from this war. The first thing that looked at all characteristic of war (in the old Boer War scene) was when we were overtaken by a transport wagon taking food, guarded by men on horseback with rifles slung across their shoulders. These we met at the corner of a road where we seemed to have lost our way. Our feet of course were all wet through. About midday we passed through a village, where a lot of our H.A.C. men were resting & people recognised each other. They kept us standing here 20 min. without letting us take our packs off, every man swearing.

* Editor's note. Here Hulme has inserted a sketch of a man with a pack on his back, bent at the waist and leaning on his rifle.

Finally about a mile further on, after the man on horseback who was supposed to be guiding us, had cantered up to various farmhouses, one about 100 yards off the main road was pointed out to us as the one where we were to eat. There was a big barn there, where we could shelter from the rain. We waded across a field & through a farmyard with mud above our ankles, only to be turned back by a staff officer who said we had made a mistake. This was the last straw — some of us wandered off by ourselves and found a little cowshed where we took off our packs at last and ate bully beef. When we got a ¼ mile from the village we were making for, we had to stop and wait till dusk, as it is rather exposed to shell fire. We heard fearfully unpleasant noises of guns going off, but they were our own batteries just behind us. After dusk we got in the village where our men were. About half the houses have one side or a roof missing, as this place has often been bombarded and there are great holes at the side of the road made by Jack Johnson shells. All the houses in this place are empty, a few of the whole and shelled houses being used as a billet for our men. We could see some of them asleep & some washing as we came in. There is a very incongruous bandstand in the centre, surrounded by barbed wire entanglement ready to be moved to the trenches.

We were marched up to some large schools where we were billeted. In the evening I went round to see some of the people I used to know in the 1st Battalion. All looked very different, their faces & clothes a sort of pale mud colour, all very tired of it and anxious to get back.

Thursday, Jan. 14th

We had to mend the holes in the road made by the shells, great holes that are very dangerous at night.

Friday, Jan. 15th

We had to dig a deep trench to clear away the water from a lot of dug outs (holes made as a protection from shell fire). All the time we were doing this the Germans were dropping shells onto a hill above us. One fell about 70 yds away, by the bandstand. You hear a noise like a train high up in the air appearing to go very slowly, then you see a thick cloud of black smoke going up where they have burst, then you hear the bang, then after that the whistling noise seems to end.

Nobody is in the least frightened because they are all being aimed at a point a few hundred yards away, where they think an English battery is. Everybody stopped digging when they heard the first whistling noise in order to run to a place where they could see them burst. How we should behave if they started shelling us I don't know. This village has several times been bombarded & probably will be again, only the Germans don't know we are here. In order that they shan't find it out, no fires are allowed at night, all candles must be kept on the floor and window spaces blocked up. A regiment near here neglected this and got a shell in the middle of their place, killing about 10 men.

Friday, Jan. 15th

They have not amalgamated us yet with the 1st Battalion, so we did not go into the trenches with them. I wanted to see what the trenches were like, so I volunteered to go as one of a party which was going up to the trenches at night, to take up large bundles of wood to put at the bottom of them for the men to stand on. These parties go up almost every night. They are fairly safe, though it so happened that the party that went the night before had one man killed. But they go night after night and nothing happens. There were about 100 of us. We wore our overcoats & carried rifles. We were formed up about 5 o'clock when it was dark, told to load our rifles & then we filed past a barn where each man drew a long bundle of faggots about 8 ft long. We then went off in single file, down a long road lined with poplars, nearly all the way. The Germans kept firing off rockets & star shells. These latter hang in the air for a few minutes & light up the whole road. We were told that whenever one of these went off we were to stand still & bend our heads down so that the white of our faces could not be seen. After a time we began to hear bullets whizzing over our heads all fairly high. All that worries anyone is the uncomfortableness of the faggots. Also I had not put the sling of my rifle on properly & was wondering all the while whether it would not slip off my shoulder on to the ground & draw attention to me personally & my clumsiness. After about a mile along the road, we turned off along the fields & made for the trenches. Here the uncomfortable part started. It seemed to be absolutely all mud. Its bad enough walking over uneven ground in the dark at any time when you don't know whether your foot is landing on earth or nothing the next step. Every now & then you fell over & got up to your knees in the mud. As the trenches here are rather this shape ——— you got bullets flying over your head from the German trenches in all directions. Nobody worries about these however, all you can think of is the mud. What makes it infinitely worse is that, every now & then you lose sight of the man in front of you. The line ahead of you runs over a rather more dangerous part & you must keep up at all costs, though it's all in the dark & you are floundering about all the time. You simply must keep up, because if you once lost the man in front, you wouldn't know what on earth to do, you might even walk up to the German lines. We finally had to cross a series of great ditches of mud & deposit the faggots under the shelter of some rising ground about 40 yds behind the trenches. Its fairly quiet up in the trenches, & all we heard was an average of about 20 a minute & as we were a short distance behind the trenches they were flying over our heads all the time. The only thing that makes you feel nervous is when the star shells go off & you stand out revealed quite clearly as in daylight. You have then the most wonderful feeling as if you were suddenly naked in the street and didn't like it. It isn't that really but the impression it makes on you, as if you were walking across a flat heath or common at night & along a long line in front of you the lights were shooting off all the time silhouetting all the trees & bushes. It's really like a kind of nightmare, in which you are in the middle of an enormous saucer of mud with explosions & shots going off all round the edge, a sort of fringe of palm trees made of fireworks all round it. One thing I forgot to mention, when you do lose the man in front of you, if you crouch down low in the mud you can see the profile of the men in front of you, but with these faggots in a sort of frieze — like the procession in Scheherezade, or rather very unlike it. It took me the *whole* of the next morning to scrape the mud off my clothes, it was all over my coat up to my waist.

Saturday, Jan. 16th

At 7 o'clock on Saturday we had to parade in the road outside the school where we lived, to march back in the dark, some 3 or 4 miles to a place further back from the firing line, out of range of shell fire, for 4 days rest. After that we shall go back for 4 days in the firing line again & so on. It was an awful confusion as we marched out in the dark, as the other regiments to take our place, were entering the place & we got mixed up in the road with another regiment also leaving for the night. We seemed to be about 3 different regiments abreast going different ways. We marched in single file all the way, it was pitch dark. When we got to the next town we were told off to different cottages where we were billeted. There are 36 in the room I'm in. Here in the time during the 4 days rest, I'm spending all my time with my old section & am really quite comfortable. They have been here for weeks & know the ropes. They have things sent them out from England, have made friends with a Flemish cobbler & we all 12 of us, sit in their back room all day, cooking our meals ourselves on the stove that all the villages have here. You must feed well these days of rest in order to keep well in the trenches. Here is where we find a little money useful. We can buy ourselves eggs etc. & all kinds of things. The bully beef gives everyone bad dysentery. In the afternoon we go up a hill where we can see for miles our own & beyond the German lines, the flash from an English gun, & then later see, it seems miles away, the white smoke of the shell bursting. Then you see all over the landscape the white puffs from which German shells are bursting over our trenches. We can see a town about ———— miles away that was bombarded. I can't go into details about anything or the letter would be torn up.

FURTHER SPECULATIONS

To-morrow, Wednesday we go back to the trenches for 4 days. It so happens however that the next 4 days, all No. 2's officers are away on leave, so to my annoyance my company will not go to the trenches this time, but will act as reserve, but we shall probably go up to the trenches to carry up things.

Jan. 27th

I have had a very uncomfortable time this week. As I told you last week after 4 days rest we go down to a place near the trenches. We marched off there last Wednesday, late in the day so as to get there after dark, or we might be shelled on our arrival. We never know whether we shall get a good or a bad billet when we arrive there, it's always different. We were led into the chapel attached to a school and our section managed to get a corner by the altar. It looks very curious to see a lot of troops billeted in a place like this, rifles resting on the altar, & hanging over statues of the saints, men sleeping on the altar steps. (You had better leave this part out in sending it to Stanbrook).* It was rather cold as all the windows were smashed & we have no blankets now. We lit a brazier, i.e. an old bucket with holes knocked in it, burning charcoal & coke. We had nothing to do the first night, as it was some other company's turn in the trenches. Next morning one of the men went out & dug up some vegetables from a deserted garden & made a kind of stew without meat. We get no cooked meat in the 4 days. The next night we went up to a kind of circular reserve trench. You go up a long file, as I described in my last letter. We were challenged at the entrance & then entered a narrow passage going down to the level of the trenches. I don't think I've been so exasperated for years as I was in taking up my position in this trench. It wasn't an ordinary one but was roofed over most of the way, leaving passage about 4 ft: absolutely impossible for me to walk through. I had to crawl along on my hands & knees, through the mud in pitch darkness & every now & then seemed to get stuck altogether. You feel shut in and hopeless. I wished I was about 4 ft. This war isn't

* EDITOR'S NOTE. A convent near Worcester where two of Hulme's aunts were nuns.

for tall men. I got in a part too narrow and too low to stand or sit & had to sit sideways on a sack of coke to keep out of the water. We had to stay there from about 7 p.m. till just before dawn next morning, a most miserable experience. You can't sleep & you sit as it were at the bottom of a drain with nothing to look at but the top of the ditch slowly freezing. It's unutterably boring. The next night was better, because I carried up a box to sit on & a sack of coke to burn in a brazier. But one brazier in a narrow trench among 12 men only warms about 3. All through this night, we had to dig a new passage in shifts. That in a way did look picturesque at midnight – a very clear starry night. This mound all full of passages like a mole hill & 3 or 4 figures silhouetted on top of it using pick or shovel. The bullets kept whistling over it all the time, but as it's just over the crest of a hill most of them are high, though every now & then one comes on your level & it is rather uncomfortable when you are taking your turn at sentry. The second night it froze hard, & it was much easier walking back over the mud.

In reality there is nothing picturesque about it. It's the most miserable existence you can conceive of. I feel utterly depressed at the idea of having to do this for 48 hours every 4 days. It's simply hopeless. The boredom & discomfort of it, exasperate you to the breaking point.

It's curious to think of the ground between the trenches, a bank which is practically never seen by anyone in the daylight, as it is only safe to move through it at dark. It's full of dead things, dead animals here & there, dead unburied animals, skeletons of horses destroyed by shell fire. It's curious to think of it later on in the war, when it will again be seen in the daylight. We had to do this for every night for 12 hours. Next week we shall be in the firing line, in two periods of 24 hours each. On our way down we generally meet someone being brought up wounded or killed to cheer us up.

Feb. 10th

The last day of the last 4 days rest here was like summer. We had breakfast outside the cobbler's cottage and in the afternoon went up to the Inn on the hill and they all drank wine outside. A regular who was up there said "Who says there's a war now" & it certainly did seem absolutely remote from it, though we could see here and there the ———— of heavy artillery firing at the Germans. The same evening we marched straight from here up to the trenches. We went to the firing line again. But this time it was not a new properly constructed trench like the last one I told you of but an ———— average trench. We had to spend the night in the open air as there were very few dugouts. There was a German rifle trained on a fixed part of the trench just where we were. It's very irritating to hear a bullet time after time hit the same spot on the parapet. About lunch time this rifle continually hitting the same place, spattered dirt from the parapet over my bread and butter. It gets very irritating after a time & everybody shouts out "Oh stop it." It showed however that it was a dangerous corner and the next day another company of our regiment took our place in this trench, a man in exactly the place where our section was, getting curious at the repetition of a shot in the same spot, got up to look with his field glasses. He stayed up a second too long and got shot through the head dead. Field glasses are rather a temptation, they make you stay up too long. Towards the end of our ———— the same day, the Germans started to shell our trench. It was a dangerous trench for shelling because it was very wide so gave no protection to the back. Our N.C.O. told us to shift to a narrower part of the trench. I got separated from the others in a narrow communication trench behind with one other man. We had seen shells bursting fairly near us before and at first did not take it very seriously. But it soon turned out to be very different. The shells started dropping right on the trench itself. As soon as you had seen someone hurt, you began to look at shelling in a very different way. We shared this trench with the X regiment. About 10 yds away from where I was a man of this regiment had his arm and ¾ of his head blown off a frightful mess, his brains all over the place, some on the back of that man who stands behind me in the photograph. The worst of shelling is, the regulars say, that you don't get used to it, but get more & more alarmed at it every time. At any rate the regulars in our trenches behaved in rather a strange way. One man threw himself down on the bottom of the trench, shaking all over & crying. Another started to weep. It lasted for nearly 1½ hrs and at the end of it parts of the trenches were all blown to pieces. It's not the idea of being killed that's alarming, but the idea of being hit by a jagged piece of steel. You hear the whistle of the shell coming, you crouch down as low as you can and just wait. It doesn't burst merely with a bang, it has a kind of crash with a snap in it, like the crack of a very large whip. They seemed to burst just over your head, you seem to anticipate it killing you in the back, it hits just near you and you get hit on the back with clods of earth & (in my case) spent bits of shell & shrapnel bullets fall all round you. I picked up one bullet almost sizzling in the mud just by my toe. What irritates you is the continuation of the shelling. You seem to feel that 20 min. is normal, is enough — but when it goes on for over an hour, you get more & more exasperated, feel as if it were "unfair." Our men were as it happened very lucky, only three were hurt slightly & none killed. They all said it was the worst experience they have had since they were out here. I'm not in the least anxious myself to repeat it, nor is anyone else I think. It was very curious from where I was; looking out and over the back of the trench, it looked absolutely peaceful. Just over the edge of the trench was a field of turnips or something of that kind with their leaves waving about in a busy kind of way, exactly as they might do in a back garden. About 12 miles away over the plain you could see the towers & church spires of an old town very famous in this war. By a kind of accident or trick, everything was rather gloomy, except this town which appeared absolutely white in the sun and immobile as if it would always be like that, and was out of time and space altogether. You've got to amuse youself in the intervals of shelling and romanticising the situation is as good a way as any other. Looking at the scene the waving vegetables, the white town & all the rest of it, it looks quite timeless in a Buddhistic kind of way and you feel quite resigned if you are going to be killed to leave it just like that. When it ceased and we all got back to our places everybody was full of it. We went back that night to a new billet in a barn, so near the line that we weren't allowed to have light at all, but spread our bread & butter in the dark, or by the intermittent light of electric torches pointed down. The next night we went up to new trenches altogether. This time we weren't in the firing line, but in a line of dug-outs, or supports.

These dug-outs were about 2 ft deep, so you can imagine how comfortable I was. They put me in one by myself. It felt just like being in your grave, lying flat just beneath the surface of the ground & covered up. And there I had to be for 24 hours unable to get out until it was dark next night for we could be seen from the German lines. — We were relieved very late and altogether were out 30 hours instead of 24. We had a couple of men wounded on the road up, so we went back by a safer way across the fields. A man I know quite well had a bullet entered one side of his nose & came out near his ear. They have sent him back to England & say he will remain.

I'm getting more used to this kind of life and as long as I don't get hurt or it doesn't rain too much, don't mind it at all.

Feb. 20th

We went down to the trenches on a Saturday. We form up at dark in the one street of the town here. There is generally a lot to be done on the last day as we have to clean up all our billets ready for the other brigade marching up after their 4 days at the trenches. While we are formed up there in the street waiting, some of the other regiments of our brigade who go to the trenches at the same time as we do are sure to march past. A regiment on the march here is a very curious sight. In spite of the fact that they have to clean themselves and their clothes in their 4 days of rest, they all look a general pale, washed out, dusty muddy colour. The officers march on foot generally at the head of their platoons, looking very little different to their men, except that they generally carry a roughly trimmed piece of wood, about as long as a shepherds crook, as a walking stick. They find these useful in the muddy paths up to the actual trenches. Very few are in any kind of step and they slouch along generally two deep, for only the centre of the road is really passable. The exception to the slouching is an occasional section when the two front men play a mouth organ or bones, when they march well to-gether. Their packs look a good deal lighter than ours, they don't get so many parcels. At intervals come the officers horses, generally unmounted (they ride them however at the end of 4 days when they are coming *back* from the trenches & are more tired). At the end come the mules carrying extra ammunition, the transport & finally the field kitchens, usually boiling something & stuffed up with odd bits of wood ready for fuel & the cooks leaning on them as they walk behind. This time we did not go straight up to the trenches but into "close billet" for the night. This is a large barn. It's comfortable except that it's well within range & if only the Germans one day find out we are here, they will drop a shell on us, and then we should most of us be done for. On the morning of the next day we had all suddenly to get ready & come downstairs, because shells were falling uncomfortably near. We always have a guard outside to report aeroplanes & the nearness of shells for this purpose. None of us are ever allowed out in the daytime. How near it is to the trenches may be judged from the fact that this time one of our sentries was shot dead by a stray bullet. The next night we went up to the trenches. I think I told you in my last letter that we are now holding a different part of the line, a mile or so N of our old trenches, worse trenches and a worse path up to them. Last time we went up to them by a road but we had one man wounded (there are too many stray bullets passing over it) so we went up by a new way over the fields. Suddenly when we were going up a fearfully muddy field by the side of a wood in a long line & single file, a shell whizzed over us & burst a few yards behind the last man. I happened to be looking backward when it burst. Being night it was very bright & looked more like a firework than anything else. We at once got the order to lie flat in the mud on our faces and although it isn't pleasant to be flat on your face in pure mud, yet the presence of the shells makes us do it without any reluctance. I didn't see much after that, for I had my head down flat, but they put about 20 shells over us, rather smallish shells they must have been which seemed to go whizz-bang — very quickly. They fell all along the line of the 50 men, but all a little wide. We got bits of earth flung over us but nothing more. They all thought their last hour had come for to be caught & shelled in the open like that is the most dangerous thing that can happen to you. You have no protection like you have in a trench. It was soon over however & then we got up and continued our walk to the trenches, most of us expecting suddenly to hear the same explosion again. We had to cross several shell & Jack Johnson holes full of water bridged by a single plank & in the dark most of us fell in once before we got there. We got to miserable trenches where we were not allowed to have a brazier and we sat there absolutely wet through up to the pips for 24 hours. That's the worst of getting wet here, it isn't like after a day's shooting when you can get home & change. The next night when we got back, an attack from the Germans was expected. We had to sleep in our boots etc all night & couldn't take anything off. That made 48 hours thoroughly wet through. The extraordinary thing is that it doesn't hurt you. It hasn't hurt us at any rate, though when the regiment last spent 3 days in the trenches before Xmas they lost 250 men & 11 officers through sickness. It makes you very depressed however & weakens you — it gave me diarrhoea. This last 6 days have been unusual for all kinds of things have been happening to the N of us of which we hear rumours. We are told over night that further up the line certain trenches are to be retaken & next day we hear they have been taken. I expect you have read all about it in the papers & of course as it is only a few miles from us, it affects us. We have to be ready for a counter attack. That first night we were up we could tell that something was up. It was a pitch black night, one of those nights that exasperate you because you are afraid of losing the man in front of you. All the heavy guns on both sides were firing, never a minute without a report and you could see the flashes from the muzzles all round the horizon. In the trench that day (it couldn't properly be called a trench, just a ditch with sandbags on the top) we sat all day and watched shells burst in the field behind us. Fortunately never nearer than 20 yards. In the next trench, a different company of our regiment in, they killed one man & wounded 15 that afternoon. The most annoying part of being in the trenches is the waiting for the "relief." You get ready long before it comes. Sometimes it comes hours after you expect it. You listen & think you hear voices & feet. At last it's coming. Then it turns out that you were mistaken. Finally a German star shell reveals them to you half-way across the field. They are all standing immobile in the middle of the field bent down. It is curious how this continuous shelling and the apprehension of it has altered some men. They keep very quiet all day long & hardly say anything. This day in the trenches I should think 50 or 60 dropped in the one field, making holes all over it like a sort of smallpox. It is these holes filled with water which make walking up the roads at night so annoying. The 4 days when we came back we were told we shouldn't be relieved for some days. However we were relieved after 6 days and marched back very late to our rest town, everyone fearfully exhausted. I have written much too long a letter. I want to post it at once so that it won't be delayed like the others were. I can't tell you much, but as a result of the recent fighting there are all kinds of changes. We are now in a different brigade etc.

[NOTE BY CENSOR. Please inform sender next letter of this length will not be passed. H. P. G. M——]

March 2nd

The first time up we went back again into the trenches where we were shelled. This is a bad trench in which you just have to sit out in the open all night. It froze hard and all the rifles were white in the morning. The next time it was our turn to have a rest, but they gave us (the platoon about 40 men) a fatigue up to the trenches, carrying up hurdles and barbed wire. Except for the danger from stray bullets, this is compared to going into the trenches, a pleasure trip. You are very light carrying only a rifle. It was a bright moonlight night, and the way up to the trenches is a straight narrow road. There were far too many men to carry the stuff and 4 of us carried one hurdle ragging each other all the way up, suggesting that the fat man should sit on top of it and we would carry him up. Half way up we met the stretcher bearers, carrying down one of our men who had been killed during the day. They hurry along quite in a different way when they are carrying a dead and not a wounded man. I think they break step and hurry along like lamplighters to avoid getting caught by a stray bullet themselves. It's curious how the mere fact that in a certain direction there really are the German lines, seems to alter the feeling of a landscape. You unconsciously orient things in reference to it. In peacetime, each direction on the road is as it were indifferent, it all goes on ad infinitum. But now you know that certain roads lead as it were, up to an abyss.

When we came back from this fatigue it so happened it was very quiet no bullets about at all, and we strolled back exactly as though we were walking home late from a party on a moonlight night. These fatigues are not always so lucky. Last week the tennis player Kenneth Powell was killed carrying up corrugated iron. (It seems curious the way people realize things. I heard a man say "It does seem a waste. Kenneth Powell carrying up corrugated iron." You see he was interested in games.) This is a curious life — in that there is nothing certain or fixed. You never come back to the same billets. You can never leave anything. You have no place that belongs to you. You really are as nomadic as an animal. You never depend on any routine. You may be there 4 or 6 or 10 days. You may come back to a different place altogether. The only fixed thing seems to be the letters you get from home. It's very difficult to describe anything to you, to at all make you realize what it is *actually* like. Not that it is above the common place, & too difficult to describe, for that reason it isn't. But just actually in its own peculiar way. If I describe a tiring day in the trenches to you & the weary march back at night to the farm, in the dark, you go wrong at once, because when I use the word farmhouse, you must have some fixed idea in your head of a farmhouse, which isn't at all the ——— of the one we ——— in.

We have not gone back to the trenches to-day as we generally do, the 4 days rest being up, but are to stay up here an extra 2 days.

I suppose it will mean that when we do go to the trenches it will be for 6 days, so it's not as pleasing as it might otherwise have been. So that we shouldn't enjoy the extra rest too much, they had us out in the middle of a field to do company drill — we were all drawn up to hear an announcement — we all expected something dramatic, but it was only to say that Gen. Smith Dorrien was very pleased with us, or something equally uninteresting, finishing up by saying that they hoped we should continue to uphold our reputation "till the end of the campaign." This fell very flat as all everyone hopes is that we shall get back as soon as possible. I am afraid we are in for it. We may get a fortnight's rest but there's no chance of us getting back at all. It still continues wonderful weather & the country looks absolutely different. One can see now how it will look in the Spring. I don't suppose any of us ever waited for the Spring with so much interest. One does notice physical things here tremendously. You reckon up when it will be full moon, it means a very uncomfortable clear walk up to the trenches. To-day it's frosty, but a hard wind, everything is very clear and bright. Along the crest of a hill I have just seen a lot of Indians, leading donkeys & mules, leaning forward to meet the wind, & silhouetted on the sky line, looking just like the conventional illustrations of the East. You have no idea what a difference the hard weather makes.

Must stop here.

March 21st, Sunday

I think I told you that for the first nine days we were continually in a kind of reserve trench. The second morning there we saw what so far I think has been the most complete war scene yet. I mean the most conventional, shut off, the most like war in a theatre as it were. Just below us about 300 yards away was a large farm with its buildings (on a position very like that of Gratton * (on a hill, below another hill) looking at it from Dunwood but about half the distance away). To make the thing comprehensible I must explain that after 24 hours in the trenches, troops go back for the

---

* EDITOR'S NOTE. Hulme's birthplace, in Staffordshire.

next 24 hours to what are called "close billets" i.e. places where they are still under shell fire & so where they must remain invisible all the time. It is the business of the artillery on both sides to shell likely "close billets," sometimes getting the information as to which farms & villages are close billets from spies. Most of the farms round about have been destroyed only the walls standing & another man said early in the morning that it was curious that this farm was entirely untouched looking very peaceful (& as I say exactly like Gratton about the same size.) In the middle of the morning we suddenly heard a shell whistling over which burst just over the roof. Then a second, whose smoke was all red showing that it had hit the roof, the red tiles broken up into dust mixing with the smoke. Three or four more shells & then we saw two pigs rushing out of the courtyard. We thought the place was empty & that the Germans were wasting their shells. Then we saw one figure going across a field on the other side of the farm but we couldn't tell whether a soldier or perhaps a Belgian civilian. The shelling went on dropping all over the roof till one caught fire. Then we caught sight of about 30 bent figures creeping along the road along the ridge from the farm. To make you realize the actual scene, there was a hedge on this side of the road & an avenue of trees. There were more shells & finally the whole of one roof burning. More & more groups of men creeping along the road (at this distance we could only see a kind of bent silhouette). This went on till I should think several hundreds more had left (they were probably all asleep resting after the trenches). Then there was a fearful row of ammunition popping off sounding exactly like continuous rifle fire in the trenches. Then another building caught fire (in which I suppose those wounded by the shells had been put). One man came out of an open door & ran across a field & behind a haystack after a minute another followed, then there were about ten there, when the Germans dropped a few shells over it. Then along the road men began to come back & fetch out the wounded from the burning barn. As they came back along the road very slowly helping the men along they were spotted & got

German rifle fire at them. The place went on burning for nearly two days. The whole scene being extremely depressing. Enormous red flames, exactly like a poster of war & destruction & then miserable looking black figures & probably very tired people crawling out. What happened later in the week I can't tell you about for it would probably be crossed out by the censor. I was on sentry one night & saw a whole regiment passing up in single file to take up their position for an attack. One man was shot about 20 yds from me. I saw in the dark, the line stop & people cluster round him, the line pass on & then finally stretcher bearers carry him off. I saw his equipment ———— in the place where he had fallen. I had myself too one night up there the unpleasant job of carrying down one of our men who had been shot dead through the heart. This is a very unpleasant job when you have to go in pitch darkness a way you don't know very well over mud & ditches. I'm glad it wasn't a man I knew but it's very queer as you carry him down shoulder high, his face is very near your own. One day after an attack I saw a man come staggering across a field as if he were drunk, holding his head, finally falling down just outside our barbed wire entanglement. It turned out to be a Tommy who had been blown right out of our trenches by our own artillery. All that day there had been a terrific bombardment, English shells whistling over our heads every second.

Must stop now.

If you don't hear from me again, you will know I have gone to the trenches again for 4 or 6 days.

April 19th 1915

We left the filthy barn we are billeted in about seven o'clock, marched down a side road over a hill about three miles to a smashed up village just behind the new trenches we were going to. We were marched up to a chateau all blown to pieces. When we got there we had to wait about 2 hours outside while they tried to find places for us inside. That's how they do things in the army. They never seem to think 5 minutes before they do a thing. Eventually some of us were stowed in a dug-out just deep enough for us to crawl through, just like a rabbit hole and told we were to stay there for 48 hours a perfect nightmare for people of my size. Eventually they came and after looking round had found us a room in a house in a village that had a roof on it. The room had no windows and was filled with layers of straw which we daren't move for fear of what might be underneath. However it was very comfortable after the dug-out. Here we stayed for 48 hours, the second night being out from 10 till 2 carrying barbed wire up to the trenches. This was a hideous affair. When we got there nobody knew where they were to go and so we stopped there for 30 minutes behind the firing trench while they found out, a very uncomfortable time. One bullet hit the trestles the fat man was carrying and a piece of the wood flew up his arm. It's the kind of fooling unnecessary business which makes one so fed up. After 48 hours we went up to the trenches. A wretched night continually soaking and through a blunder the ———— fully equipped as we were carrying up boxes about 1000 rounds of ammunition over ditches and soaked fields. I dont know how some of the men ever got up. We got into an open trench about 1:30 having started at 10, so you may tell what sort of a job it was, to go along 2 miles. There were no shelters and it poured continually for several hours. Fortunately the next 36 hours it was finer and then we marched back about 10 p.m. to a rest barn. After going about a couple of miles we stopped at some cross roads for nearly an hour and a half absolutely tired out. It's the kind of thing ———— you more than anything. You try to sleep on the side of the road but it's too cold. And now for our rest here. Every night we have had to march back to the trenches about 4 miles and dig. The night before last we were out from 8 p.m. till 4 in the morning. We have only had a proper night's rest in the last three weeks. This isn't a proper diary I have just told you in a hurry what we have been doing. I'll write a proper account in the trenches directly. I've no time here, as ———— to sleep all day. We are back again to the trenches to-night for four days continuously. We shall be glad when we do get our rest, this three weeks is all for some special reason when that is over I hope we shall go back to the old system. This is a curious thing, we move as you know always at night and troops going always in the same direction make definite paths, One of our snipers walking about in the daylight discovered that one of these paths that we walk over led right over the chest of a dead peasant (Belgian).

ON LIBERTY

When the pacifist speaks on the "loss of liberty" involved in conscription, or in the alteration of trade union rules his opponents
do quite sincerely think that he is using empty phrases to disguise
sordid motives. They are really unable to imagine what meaning
he attaches to the words under such conditions. In the same way
the pacifist never really at heart thinks that our "liberty" would
be in any way endangered by the loss of this war.

Perhaps, then, I may get a pacifist favourably inclined to admit
that I do mean something when I say we are fighting for liberty,
when I admit that there is considerable danger to liberty at home
in the process. I do fully recognise how much of our liberties we
do surrender under the various "Defence of the Realm" Acts, and
the really considerable danger that we shall not recover all of
them at the end of the war. The middle classes, as a whole, are
inclined to be impatient of such talk when it is concerned with
Trade Unions privileges. The reality of the danger may be brought
home to them by the trivial example of the freedom we alone,
among European nations, enjoyed from the irksome necessity of
registration, of filling up forms at hotels, etc. Once lost, this trivial
liberty may be difficult to regain, for there are many of the *good*
who would like to see us all registered. What is our reply to this?

We assert that the danger to liberty involved in this Act, and
in the use of compulsion, is infinitesimal in comparison with the
loss of liberty that would follow our defeat. The controversies
which these things create are like disputes as to relative position
inside a structure which may at any time be *overturned* by external
causes. But this is entirely ineffective as an argument, for it depends on an assumption to which the other side do not agree. We
assume that defeat would involve a very great curtailment of our

liberty. It is evident from everything they do and say that the pacifists do not believe there is any such danger. Though they make perfunctory reference to it, they do not at heart believe in it. They take no real interest in the matter, their enthusiasm is directed to other ends. Loss of liberty in this connection is to them an empty phrase, and they treat it with the same impatience that the middle classes treat the same phrase when it is applied to Trade Union troubles under the Munitions Act.

This scepticism about the consequences of defeat springs from two sources.

(1) The fatuous belief that liberty cannot at any rate be permanently endangered, for "Germany herself will *inevitably* develop toward democracy."

(2) The inability to see that Europe will be really altered in structure by this war. The facile and false analogy with wars like the Crimean or the Franco-Prussian, which, while they increased the power of one nation, or diminished that of another, yet still left Europe a society of independent nations. *There is no analogy between this war and other wars.* A German victory means an end of Europe as a new Hellas, a society of nations. It means a Europe under German leadership. The pacifists cannot see this, for, curiously enough, while they *repudiate the balance of power as a doctrine of policy, they do so because they unconsciously assume that the balance of power will take care of itself, being grounded on the nature of things.* Being assumed, like democracy, to be of the nature of the law of gravitation, it would be absurd to fight for it.

I realise the source of your incredulity. "You may make out a case for the danger to liberty — but it lacks reality. Europe has had many wars — many spoke of them as a danger to liberty — but always things were much the same after."

But this time they won't be. Forget easy analogies and examine carefully the obvious facts.

You are slowly realising the nature of that irrational thing, Force. Force does settle things, does create facts, which you have henceforth to deal with. The situation round the Dardanelles has probably now crystallised. Russia will not get through to the Mediterranean, and we shall be unable always to prevent Germany's access to Asia. Another situation created by force is being prepared for us nearer home. Europe is in flux; it will settle after the war into a physical structure which will probably endure for a century.

The most accurate metaphor for the new structure that will follow the victory of Germany is that of the emergence of a mountain in a plane. You are not to think that such an emergence leaves surrounding countries unaffected. It produces the same effect on them as putting a parcel under the tablecloth would do — all of them have to live on an inclined plane.

As evidence of the existence of the intention of Germany really to alter the framework of Europe in this way, I may conveniently quote a few sentences from a recent book on the war by Max Scheler. Scheler is not a sensational journalist, or a military writer like Bernhardi, but one of the most intelligent of the younger German philosophers, and one who, moreover, belongs to the school that is beginning to have the greater influence on this generation of students.

After a long preliminary discussion on the real nature of "international" and "cosmopolitan" the main object of the war is stated to be the destruction of the balance of power: and the creation for the first time of a solidarist Continental Europe under *German military leadership*. . . . "Then we shall see the creation of a new Mediterranean culture grounded on the *military power* of Germany."

To attain this end, Russia must be finally driven out of Europe, and France completely crushed.

What is the position of England then?

He attacks the Germans, who are surprised and shocked at our entry into the war. "It is inevitable that England should come in. Her whole existence as an Empire was threatened by the building of the German fleet." He reproves those who, "with an imitation of English cant," have pretended that the fleet was built for defensive purposes.

"The only possible aim in the building of the German Fleet was directed against England." "Our first object always must be the destruction of the English naval supremacy, for this stands between us and the fair division of the earth. If this object is not attained now further struggles must and will follow."

INEVITABILITY INAPPLICABLE

I think the writer who said the war was the most important European event since the French Revolution and probably since the Reformation, was right in this point, though he has been wrong in almost everything else. You probably reject such a statement as exaggeration, because you are very much aware of the sordid motives and the petty unimaginative people who brought it about. You prefer to look at it as a small event on a very large scale. In doing so you exhibit a certain romanticism about the past, an ignorance of the way in which really great events have been brought about. But even taking the war at your estimation, the statement quoted still remains true. You admit that it is on a very large scale — it is the mere material consequences that will follow the war as a material *fact*, that create its importance. Perhaps it is better to speak of the *conditional* importance of the war. It would be comparable to the Reformation if the Germans won; if they don't it is not an important event in the same sense. Why would it then be so important? Because a German victory means an end of Europe as we know it, as a comity of nations; the whole framework would be changed. If you ask, further, why that is important, the answer is in the enormous reactions inside the beaten nations that would follow this enormous change in their external situation. When a box is turned over on to another base, the arrangement of the loose things inside alters with it. In our own case, our liberties have to a great extent depended on our securities, and our security would now have disappeared. We shall all be obliged to become conspirators.

There are certain habits of thought, which make a realisation of the actual nature of Force, very difficult. This applies not only to the opponents of the war, but to its supporters. Take the case of writers like Mr. Wells. You remember the old story of the man who was taken ill suddenly. The strange doctor who was called in exhibited a certain hesitation. "I'm not exactly a doctor," he said, "in fact, I'm a vet. I don't know what's the matter with you, but I can give you something that will bring on blind staggers, and I can cure that all right." Now Mr. Wells had never taken the possibility of an Anglo-German war seriously — he was pacifist by profession. It was not exactly his subject then, and last August may have found him somewhat baffled as to what to say. So he gave it blind staggers, he turned it into a "war to end war," and there you are. Such writers, in dealing with a matter like war, alien to their ordinary habits of thought, are liable to pass from a fatuous optimism to a fatuous pessimism, equally distant from the real facts of the situation.

Of all these ordinary habits of thought, perhaps, the one that has the most unfortunate influences is the belief in *inevitable* progress. If the world is making for "good," then "good" can never be in serious danger. This leads to a disinclination to see how big fundamental things like liberty can in any way depend on trivial material things like guns. There is no realisation of the fact that the world *may* take a wrong turning. In a pacifist lecture by Mr. Bertrand Russell I read "the only things worth fighting for are things of the spirit, but these things are not subject to force." ("The Philosophy of Pacifism," p. 9) Make the matter more concrete by taking liberty as an instance as a "thing of the spirit." The things not subject to force may be, then, one or two things: (1) The *principle* of liberty or (2) the *fact* of liberty. If the first, the statement is self-evident and entirely unimportant. A *principle* . . . the ethical principle, e.g. that "liberty is good," is true timelessly and eternally. It cannot be affected by force, any more than the truth that two and two make four. But he cannot have meant this trivial statement; he must mean, then, the "good" which follows from the *fact* of liberty. But in that case the statement could only be true, if you suppose some tendency at the heart of things which is all the time "making for an increase of the *facts* of liberty," — in other words, you must believe in *inevitable* progress. But we know from other sources that Mr. Russell believes nothing of the kind. What does he mean, then?

Consider now two specific examples of the way in which the habit of thought distorts the pacifist perception of the facts:

(1) Even admitting that the facts as put forward by you are true; even admitting that our defeat will be followed by a German hegemony, we refuse to see in this any permanent danger to liberty. To do so would be to "assume that Germany lacks the power of development . . . her *natural* line of development towards a tolerant liberalism." There is a richness of fallacy in this quotation, which makes choice somewhat embarrassing. For our purpose here, of course, the important word is *natural*. It is natural to progress; Nature herself tends of her own accord to progress, etc. This is complicated, however, by a further assumption, an example of what the Germans call the characteristic English view of mistaking *Umwelt* for *Welt*, in other words, of mistaking the conditions of our own particular environment for universally valid laws. Even if the Germans must *naturally* develop, how can we assume that they will develop towards a tolerant liberalism? Is that also part of the essential nature of the cosmos? Free trade and all. . . . Anyone who has known Germany at all intimately during recent years knows that facts go to prove the contrary.

(2) This habit of thought hinders the perception of the facts in another way. There is a second type of pacifist, who admits that if the consequences of defeat were the hegemony of Germany and the end of Europe as a collection of independent states — that the case for war would have been proved. But he does not admit that such will be the consequences of defeat; he does not seem able to perceive this obvious fact. He cannot take the argument seriously. Why? For exactly the same reason as that given in the first case. Liberty is a "good"; so, also, is the existence of Europe as a comity of independent nations. He finds it ridiculous to fight for liberty, for there can never be any real danger to liberty. The world is inevitably developing toward liberty, and liberty is thus *natural*, and grounded on the nature of things. In exactly the same way he assumes that the comity of nations is also *natural*, and cannot be

disturbed by the artificial activities of man. The matter is complicated here by (1) a habit of interpreting war by entirely *personal*
categories and (2) a misuse of facile historical metaphor. Both
these things prevent men seeing the facts as they actually are.
. . . (1) they tend to look on war as of the same nature and probably as caused by the same childish motives, as the struggles of a
number of boys in a room. Some may get more damaged than
others, but the framework of the struggle is not changed — in the
end, as at the beginning, you have a number of boys in a room.
Moreover, it is a mistake to punish one boy too much, as he may
then turn nasty, and be a nuisance in the future. "Germany would
regard defeat not as evidence of guilt . . . and would resolve to
be better prepared next time." * Here the real nature of the situation is entirely ignored, and an interpretation — in terms of the
categories appropriate only to the description of personal conduct — is substituted for it. There is no realisation of the *particular*
facts of force involved, no realisation of the *actual* danger which
victory avoids and — such being the nature of the forces concerned — probably avoids for good. (2) "Beaten nations develop
into the strongest. It was her defeat by Napoleon that created
Prussia as a military power." Generalisation depends, I suppose,
on the possibility of repetition. The amount of possible repetition
in history is very small and consequently historical generalisations
are necessarily very thin; but I think I hardly remember anything
quite so thin as this. If I put this phrase out of my head, and look
at the concrete situation at the time of the battle of Jena, and the
concrete situation now, I should probably fail to discover any common elements whatever. We need no such fantastic guidance from
history. What is needed is merely an objective examination of the
sufficiently complicated situation we have before us *to-day*. It will
not be very difficult then to perceive that this time it is not merely
that individual combatants will get more or less damaged with

* EDITOR'S NOTE. "The ordinary German would regard defeat, not as evidence
of his guilt, but as evidence of our artful diplomacy. He would resolve to be
even better prepared next time, and would follow the advice of his militarists
even more faithfully than in the past." Bertrand Russell, "The Philosophy of
Pacifism," in *Towards Ultimate Harmony* (London, 1915), p.5.

every possibility of recovery, but that the room in which they fight, the framework itself, will be permanently changed. Just as we *naturally* assume that none of the struggling boys will be killed, so we *naturally* assume that all the struggling nations will recover their old positions. But this time there is nothing *natural* about it.

⤴ THE KIND OF RUBBISH WE OPPOSE

Ce qui est certain, c'est pour en finir avec la guerre, il faut d'abord l'avoir comprise . . .

PROUDHON

At this period of the war a constant preoccupation with the pacifists may seem somewhat pointless; most of the things at issue now have been decided by fact. But this is much more than a controversy about war. A polemic has been started which will continue long after the conclusion of the peace.

The pacifists themselves clearly recognize this, and we have an abundance of prophets hastening to tell us of the *Liberal* principles on which society must be reorganized after the war. There is a certain shamelessness in the eagerness they exhibit, for a year and a-half ago, most of them proved to be false prophets indeed. It is not only the Bourbons apparently who can "learn nothing and forget nothing." I admit that the new order of society will be different from the old; the old was breaking up before; the war did not cause the decay, it merely announced the fact on a hoarding.

I was able the other day to attend one of the series of lectures by Mr. Bertrand Russell I have already referred to.* Mr. Russell drew a preliminary distinction between "desire" and impulse. Sometimes our actions are reasonable . . . i.e. we "desire" certain things and take the necessary steps to acquire them. The "reasons" are merely the homage instinct pays to intelligence. We may come to believe that these reasons were the cause of our action, but such is not the case. The true cause is the "blind" impulse.

---

* EDITOR'S NOTE. The series was published in England as *Principles of Social Reconstruction* and in the United States as *Why Men Fight.*

FURTHER SPECULATIONS

Any endeavour to understand the causes which make war possible should then be founded on an analysis of such impulses.

There is no doubt that this provides a happy method of controversy for general use by pacifists. They thus avoid the necessity for any tedious examination of the actual arguments used by their opponent, by depriving these arguments at one stroke of all validity. All the reasons are secondary, the blind impulse is the real cause. You thus get a delightfully simple picture of the true nature of the controversy. On the one hand, the bellicose, moved in reality by the "impulses of aggression and resistance to aggression," fondly imagining, however, that they are acting under the influence of reason; and, on the other hand, the wise and tolerant pacifists, seeing things by the light of their disinterested intelligence.

The worst that can be said about this method, however, is that it defeats its own avowed object. As long as you regard all the reasons put forward by your opponents as unreal, as merely the result of the "homage paid by instinct to intelligence," you are not likely to obtain any very complete understanding of the nature and causes of war. For is blind impulse the only explanation of the action of those who acquiesce in war? Is there not another possible alternative? If I examine my own state of mind about the matter, it is certainly true that such impulses do play a considerable part in it. But my attitude as a whole is *not* determined by such impulses, although it may be reinforced by them. The reasons I give are the real causes of my action.

There are two ways in which I may differ from a pacifist who asserts that A is bad because it leads to B. (1) I may deny that in fact A does lead to B; or (2) I may deny that B itself is bad. It is a difference of the latter kind that we have to deal with in controversies about the war; a difference, then, ultimately about the things we consider "good." I think B is good, you think it bad. But I do not mean that this is the last word to be said on the matter. I do not take the relativist sceptical view of ethics which would here lead us into an impasse. I do not disagree, then, with Mr. Russell in his conception of ethical values as *objective*. But

I do disagree most profoundly as to the scale or order in which particular "values" should be placed. Some are higher than others. The argument I should use about the war, then, would differ from those employed by the pacifists, principally because I regard other "values" as superior to that which they usually appeal to as the highest.

What, in more detail, is the nature of the "value" on which their arguments are based?

In Mr. Russell's lectures, the establishment of the future "principles of social reconstruction" seems always based on an appeal to the values first made prominent by Rousseau, and the romantic movement. The words "personality" and "natural growth" seem enough to settle everything. Most evils are exhibited as the result of "thwarted growth." Enmity, for example, is the result of a "thwarted joy of life." This faded Rousseauism is based on an entirely false conception of the nature of man, and of the true hierarchy of values; the hierarchy is not objective but is merely the result of an uncritical acceptance of the romantic tradition.

It is not possible here to go into any detail about the history of these values. It is sufficient to point out that there is nothing *inevitable* about them. They form part of one *ideology* amongst other possible ones. Above all, it is necessary to notice that there is no *necessary* connection between this ideology and the democratic movement. As a rule the two things are never thought of as separate. Arguments are based alternatively on the one and on the other, as if you thought that you were merely using different names for the same thing. It is this innocence — the source of so much pacifist complacency — that must be destroyed. Your ideals may be right or wrong: but they are not to be identified with democracy. It is quite possible for a democrat to deny all the ideals on which Mr. Russell's principles are based.

This appeal might then be addressed to the pacifist: Put out of your mind the illusion that those who differ from you must do so for one of the following reasons: (1) A more sordid one — a disguised attempt to defend the interests of wealth. (2) The more ideal case — reasons invented afterwards to account for actions which were really the result of blind impulse.

Your reasons are opposed by other reasons, which may also be disinterested, ethical, and *not* emotional.

It is important that you should realise this, for the polemic will continue after the war. The principles on which society will be reorganized may not be those you so confidently urge. The polemic is not one between *reason* and *impulse*. It is a polemic between two systems of value. You may win in this struggle if you clearly recognise the true character of the things at issue. Do not, however, falsely simplify matters by assuming that it is a struggle between the assailants and defenders of privilege. It is not Democracy against Privilege, but, rather,

One ideology + Democracy

against

Another ideology + Democracy

The character of the second ideology is such that it does not attach the same positive values to the abolition of minor privileges that the first does (abolition of restrictions on growth of personality, etc.). Nor does it make the same appeal to *ressentiment*. But I am now convinced that the abolition of such privileges is a necessary political measure in order that the clear character of this opposition may not be disguised.

WHY WE ARE
IN FAVOUR OF THIS WAR

So far all the arguments I have given in detail have been negative; I have said very little in favour of the war, but have endeavoured rather to meet the arguments of those who incline, for quite general reasons, to think all wars bad.

But before such arguments can be convincing, another step must be taken. Reasons which are sufficient to make us reject "pacifist philosophy" are *not* sufficient to make us accept this *particular* war. The fact, for example, that a high value should be attached to military heroism, has nothing to do with the justification of a particular event in which such heroism may be displayed. This is an absolutely different question.

There are, moreover, at this moment, a class of pacifists who do not accept "a pacifist philosophy," and whose reasons for objecting to the war are based on the nature and causes of *this* war itself. I was talking recently to a pacifist of this type, and what he said threw a good deal of light — for me, personally, at any rate, on the nature of a certain opposition to the war. He had no objection to killing; and conveyed the impression that he was quite prepared to fight himself in some more "ideal" type of struggle — one with some positive and definite aim — in a war, for example, which would bring about the final disappearance of capitalism. But he was not prepared to fight in *this* war, which, in as far as it was not an entirely unnecessary stupidity, was concerned with interests very far removed from any which had any real importance for the individual citizen, and more definitely the individual workman.

I admit that this attitude, if we *agree to certain tacit assumptions*, does seem justified. As the attitude is very real and fairly widespread it is perhaps worth while examining the nature of these assumptions. Though it may not be very conscious or formulated, I think it demonstrable that there is floating before the mind of the man who makes this objection a certain false conception of the character of human activities. What makes the objection possible and gives force to it is the conception of Progress. By that I do not mean merely the hope that capitalism will ultimately disappear. It is rather that progress is looked upon as *inevitable* in this sense — that the evils in the world are due to definite oppressions, and whenever any particular shackle has been removed, the evil it was responsible for has disappeared for ever, for human nature is on the whole, good, and a harmonious society is thus possible. As long as you hold this conception of the nature of history, you are bound, I think, to find nothing in *this war* which makes it worth while. But this is a false conception; the evil in the world is not merely due to the existence of oppression. It is part of the *nature* of things and just as man is not naturally good and has only achieved anything as the result of certain discipline, the "good" here does not preserve itself, but is also preserved by discipline. This may seem too simple to be worth emphasising, but I think this way of treating the objection justified, for it really does spring from this quite *abstract* matter, this false conception of the nature of evil in the world. It is only under the influence of this false conception that you demand an *ideal* war where great sacrifices are for great ends.

So it comes about that we are unable to name any great *positive* "good" for which we can be said to be fighting. But it is not necessary that we should; there is no harmony in the nature of things, so that from time to time great and useless sacrifices become necessary, merely that whatever precarious "good" the world has achieved may just be preserved. These sacrifices are as negative, barren, and as *necessary* as the work of those who repair sea-walls. In this war, then, we are fighting for no great *liberation* of mankind, for no great jump upward, but are merely accomplishing a work, which, if the nature of things was ultimately "good," would be useless, but which in this actual "vale of tears" becomes from time to time necessary, merely in order that bad may not get worse.

This method of stating the question avoids the subterfuges to which those who hold the optimistic conception of man are driven — of inventing imaginary positive "goods" which the war is to bring about "to end war" and the rest. But if this argument is to have any effect it must be possible to give a clear account of the definite evils that would follow our defeat.

We are fighting to avoid (1) a German Europe, (2) the inevitable reactions which would follow this inside the beaten countries.

The consequences of such a defeat seem so perfectly clear and definite to us, that we think that if we could only for once actually *focus* the attention of the pacifist on them we should convince him. But we are mistaken; to perceive things is not enough; it is necessary to attach weight to the things perceived. It is not sufficient that you shall merely *perceive* a possible German hegemony; it is necessary that you shall have a vivid realisation of what it means. It is like the distinction which writers on religion are accustomed to make, between assent to some proposition, and real *faith* — leading to action. There are many pacifists, who will assent to what you say about German hegemony — they agree verbally, but . . . it is as if you pointed out to an old lady at a garden party, that there was an escaped lion about twenty yards off — and she were to reply, "Oh, yes," and then quietly take another cucumber sandwich.

But it won't do to ignore these consequences of defeat. If you are sitting in a room carrying on a discussion with another man, on some very abstract subject, and suddenly you notice that the floor is beginning to tilt up, then you have to pay attention to the fact. In comparison with the abstract discussion it interrupts, it may be a low, material fact, but it has to be dealt with. This is exactly the position many pacifists are in. Trying to indicate to them the consequences of German hegemony is like trying to show a cat its reflection in a mirror. It isn't interested, its mind is full of other interests — it smells, for example, Mr. Blatchford.

In approaching the subject (this consequences of German hegemony) I feel at once the presence of certain difficulties. The people one wishes to convince seem instinctively inclined to *dis-*

count what one says in advance. Before going into any detail, then, it is best to deal with the reasons which prevent due weight being attached to these things.

(1) They seem disinclined to consider reasons drawn from the consequences of German hegemony, because they think that reasons we give are not the real causes of our actions. We are in favour of the war because we are moved by certain impulses of national pride and aggressiveness, and we then desire to *find* good reasons to justify our attitude. This scepticism has a good deal of force because it does describe accurately the position of many people. Many people are moved not only by the impulses mentioned above, but by a certain instinct which makes men want life at a higher pitch and intensity (the instinct that makes a man seek the excitement to be got from gambling) — and they imagine that war will provide them with this. Under these circumstances we might deceive ourselves; we should tend to think the issues at stake were much more important than we shall think them in peacetime. There is, then, something unreal about the justification we give for the war, because our action is really not dependent on the reasons we give.

I do not say that I was not moved by such impulses at the beginning of the war; but I am writing now at a period when any such bellicose impulses in us, any exuberance in this direction, have been cured by experience; I don't think I have an ounce of bellicosity left. I probably have quite as intense a *desire* for peace as any pacifist. I am fully aware of the wretched life led by those in the trenches — practically a condition of slavery — and would like to see it ended at once. It is true that if I read in a German paper some vainglorious boasting over our coming defeat, I should at once feel a very strong revival of these impulses of aggressiveness, and pride, and a desire to humiliate at all costs, the people who have written these things. But putting such moments out of court, I can honestly say that my convictions about the consequences of defeat, whether right or wrong, are founded on observation, and not on *impulses*.

(2) There is another way in which such reasons may be mis-

leading. People who can read foreign newspapers, and who take an interest in foreign policy, tend to acquire certain special interests, which they often mistake for the real interests of their country. They tend to look on these things as a kind of drama, and wish their own country to play a distinguished part. If I know the whole history of a certain disputed part of Africa, if I am fully aware of the secret designs of some other country, I have a great longing then to see my own country intervene at all costs. I then attach an undue importance to the matter for my special interest in the subject is out of all proportion to the country's real interest. It is like the passion which may be aroused in a game of chess. The pacifist who wishes to think of all these problems in terms of individual welfare rather than national glory, tends to treat all reasoning of this kind with a smile and tolerant disdain — "funny little German professors who write about welt-politik . . . these dreams of writers on foreign politics are not very real when compared with the actual interests of the workman."

The answer I make is the same as in the first case. The fears I have about German hegemony have nothing whatever to do with the concern of the man interested in foreign policy. The things at issue are realities which will affect very strongly the life of the ordinary citizen.

(3) This last objection has proved more effective than either of the other two. The usual presentment of the consequences of German hegemony as it might be given, for example, by the *Morning Post*, is soaked with false reasons, which make it seem entirely unreal to you. It is based on assumptions — Imperialist and others — which you do not share. But many false reasons can be given for true things. The two should be carefully distinguished here. I share most of your assumptions. I have no disguised reactionary motives. I am not in favour of the war, because I think all wars favour reaction. I am, on the contrary, inclined to think that this war will hasten the disappearance of the rich. I think it possible to state the reasons based on the probable reactions that would follow German hegemony in a way that should be convincing to the democrat. I shall endeavour to do this next week.

Most of the arguments used by the pacifists in their repudiation of the balance of power as a doctrine of policy really rest on the tacit assumption that this balance will take care of itself, being grounded on the nature of things. In describing the evil consequences of the policy, they forget that the alternative is not simply the same world, minus those evils; there would be much greater evils that would follow the destruction of the balance of power.

The only alternative at the present moment to the Balance of Power is a German hegemony of Europe. The only legitimate discussion of this doctrine, then, is one which tries to estimate the relative greatness of (1) the evils which accompany the attempt to maintain the balance of power — the present war, for example; and (2) the evils which would accompany a "united Europe under German military leadership." (I quote this sentence from a book on the war by a well-known German philosopher, as describing what, in his opinion, was the object for which Germany was fighting.)

In stating the matter in this way, however, I am perhaps assuming too much. The following types of pacifists would not accept this as a true account of the things at issue.

(1) Those who deny that the Balance of Power is the only alternative to the hegemony of one Power. They have visions of something better: (a) No Powers at all, (b) a harmony of Powers.

(2) Those who deny, or fail to realise, the *possibility* of such a hegemony as a result of our defeat in this war.

(3) Those who refuse to believe that a German hegemony would be necessarily evil.

(4) Those who are sceptical as to the possibility of preventing such a hegemony by war. These *fatalists* speak of the growth of

Germany as *natural*. We cannot stop it by artificial means. They even imply that it is almost sinful on our part to attempt to interfere with a *natural* force.

(5) Those who admit that a German hegemony is possible; but assert that the evils of war, and the possible evils of hegemony, belong to entirely different classes or grades of evil, as different, say, as tons and ounces. The evils of war are so great that everything else . . . honour, independence, nationality, etc. . . . becomes trivial in comparison with them.

Now while the enumeration of the actual evils of war does not, as such pacifists believe, serve to *decide* the matter, it does serve as a useful standard by which the reasons they give may be tested. Many of the reasons given by us enthusiastically as a justification for this war, suddenly appear astonishingly thin when we ask ourselves the question: "Do I really think this so important that I am willing to accept the fact that I and half my friends may be killed to prevent it?" This acts as an excellent dissolvent on any undue preoccupation with the "beautiful dream of Bagdad." I think reasons drawn from the evils of hegemony do survive the test — provided we are not under the influence of a purely pacifist ethic.

* * *

I want here to consider the *second* type of pacifist indicated above. How does it come about that they cannot believe in the *possibility* of a German hegemony? Why do they tend to think that the evils of such a hegemony are merely the inventions of hysterical journalists; and if not imaginary, at least, enormously exaggerated?

Many things in Europe which we have been accustomed to regard as fixed are now temporarily in a state of flux. When the war ends the new state in which it leaves these things will probably continue, fixed and permanent, for another half century. Now it is possible that the new state of Europe produced by the way may be a permanent German hegemony, with the enormous reaction which would follow this *inside* the beaten countries. The immense importance of the war lies in the fact that in a short space of time, when the world is, as it were, plastic, things are decided, which no efforts afterwards may be able to shift. All our future efforts will take place in a framework settled by the war.

One may illustrate this by a metaphor taken from the war itself. The line of trenches on the Western front has now remained practically unaltered for over a year. The position and shape of this line are the brute facts on which all calculations as to future military action have to be based. The apparently accidental details of its shape have to be taken into account, like the similarly accidental and irregular lines of some great natural obstacle, such as a range of mountains. They form the fixed data of the problem which has to be solved. But though now it seems fixed, there was a short period in which it was plastic; and all the accidental details of an outline which seems irregular as the course of a river are due to known causes operating inside that short period. The salient at one point, the concavity at another are perhaps the result of the events of an afternoon, when a general under-estimated the number of men required at one particular point, and overestimated the number required at another. This provides an accurate parallel for the relation of this war to the future of Europe. The relation between the three months of mobility and the year of stalemate is the same as that between the state of flux in which Europe now is and the fixed outlines the war will determine for the next fifty years.

If I assert that the moon to-night is green, and ask you to put yourself to some trouble in order to come outside and look at it, I may meet with two difficulties. In the first place, you may refuse because you say that you know that I have some interest in making this false statement; that craving always the excitement of new sensation, I am naturally credulous, or that my past history makes all my statements worthy of suspicion.

There is, however, a different type of difficulty which has its origin in the character of the *facts* indicated. All the arguments used are based on facts, ultimately connected with *Force*. Now, these people have certain habits of mind, are accustomed to think in certain ways which makes it exceedingly difficult for them to perceive the real nature of such facts; and facts, though they may be always there can only be apprehended by the appropriate organs of perception. If you look for the moon with a microscope, you are not likely to find it. If you persist in thinking of mental processes in terms of the categories appropriate only to matter, you are not likely to see these processes as they really are.

But there is no obscurity about the facts in this question; the *possibility* of hegemony is sufficiently clear. But the pacifists persist in thinking of this fact (of Force) under the influence of certain habits of mind, which make them apt to undervalue and distort it.

What are the "habits of mind" which prevent the pacifists realising this? How does it come about that they tend to disregard any description of the consequences of German hegemony? Probably for this reason — they discount all these arguments, because they are *not* really convinced that things are in a flux. They do not really believe in the possibility of any fundamental change in Europe; the change, for example, from the present state to that constituted by the hegemony of one Power. As they do not at heart believe that the effects of Force can be so irrevocable, or that such profound changes can take place, they cannot attach serious importance to any argument which postulates such a change.

At bottom, I think, their attitude is the result of the fact that they, perhaps, unconsciously, tend to think of all events of the 20th century in Europe as taking place within the framework impressed on our minds by the history of the nineteenth. This history, in a sense, hypnotises one, and makes the possibility of radical change very difficult to conceive. With many reservations it is, on the whole, true to say that in the history of the wars of the past century and a half, the protagonists remain much the same, England, France, Prussia, Austria and Russia. While the power of each of them has varied, none has ever established a permanent hegemony, or been able to destroy the others; Europe has always remained divided into independent states. The result of this is that we tend to think of these nations — the elements of this history — as the permanent and indestructible elements of all future history; the games may be different, but they will always be played with the same pieces. But we ought to get rid of this distorting effect of history on our minds. We, ourselves, have not had for centuries any desire to conquer any part of Europe, and we find it difficult to grasp the fact that other nations are really moved by this desire. This particular difficulty is considerably increased by the malign influence of school histories. These books so consistently represent our own acquisitions as the accidental and undesired results of the triumph of virtue over vice, that we remain ignorant not only of the amount of calculation and brute force that went to the making of the *colonial* empire, but also find it difficult to realise the fact, that at the present moment others may be thinking of creating a *European* empire by similar methods.

╯NORTH STAFFS
RESENTS MR. RUSSELL'S REJOINDER*

I greatly resent Mr. Russell's accusation that I entirely failed to understand his lecture. In what way exactly have I misrepresented him? He complains that I falsely suppose that he looks on the dispute as one between *Impulse* and *Reason*. " 'North Staffs' . . . begins by suggesting that I regard the bellicose as moved by *impulse* and the pacifists as moved by *reason*. . . . My whole lecture, on the contrary, was concerned to represent *both* sides as moved by impulse." Now, I entirely agree with the last sentence, but I fail to see that it in any way proves that my version of the lecture misrepresents it; it only does this if a certain assumption is made. The matter at issue can perhaps be made evident in this way. Two distinct questions should be separated, a *theoretical* and a *practical*: (1) Is war always evil? and (2) assuming that it is, how can it best be avoided? Mr. Russell always tacitly assumes the first question as settled, and deals only with the second and *practical* matter; the emphasis laid on *Impulse* is then quite legitimate. If you have already made up your mind that war is always wrong, then it becomes necessary to search out some other impulses which will counter the effect of the impulses that make for war. "If Impulse is necessary to vigorous action, then it is necessary not to weaken impulse, but to direct it to life and growth, not to death and decay, etc. . . ."

I admit all this; and if I had said (in reference to this *practical* problem) that the pacifists wished to meet impulse by Reason, I

* Bertrand Russell's replies are printed below as Appendix A.

Hulme used the pseudonym "North Staffs" (which refers to his home county, North Staffordshire) for the essays on war that he wrote while in uniform.

admit that I should have misrepresented Mr. Russell. But I was not thinking of this *practical* question. In speaking of the dispute between the pacifists and their opponents, it is clear that we must mean the *theoretical* dispute; for until this has been settled, the *practical* question is of very secondary importance. In saying that the pacifists tend to regard the dispute as one between Reason and Impulse, I do not in the least misrepresent Mr. Russell, but, on the contrary, give an accurate description of the way in which he actually treats the question.

*　　*　　*

My complaint is, then, that Mr. Russell gives many *Reasons* why wars are evils, and only deals with the *Impulses* that made men think them justifiable. He ought, on the contrary, to have dealt with the *Reasons* on both sides. He now claims, in this letter, that he has done so in various pamphlets. He refers me to *Justice in War Time*, "where he will find that I have set forth the detailed discussion which I *presupposed* in this lecture." I may say at once that I have bought this pamphlet, and find very little indeed of this "detailed discussion." What I do find is repetition after repetition of an account of the nature of the instincts, which he supposes to be the *real* cause of every justification of war.

When I say that all discussion of such impulses is irrelevant, until the Reasons which we say justify war have been dealt with — what kind of Reason do I intend? There are two types of such *Reasons*: (1) those dealing with facts; (2) those concerned with ethics. The first to *prove* that this particular war was necessary, the second to prove that the pacifists' assertion — that war is essentially evil — is not ethically justifiable.

(1) *Reasons based on the facts of the European situation.* The only discussion of the kind I can find in this pamphlet is the somewhat vaguely treated suggestion that we are responsible for German militarism, because we tried to hinder in every possible way the efforts of Germany to found a Colonial Empire of a size proportionate to her power. This seems to me a very inadequate account of our own motives. We are fighting to prevent the establish-

ment, not of a *Colonial* empire, but of a *European* hegemony, an aim which justifies any sacrifices.

(2) *Ethical reasons.* In the case of the type of Reasons just mentioned (those based on facts) there is some slight justification for his claim that the discussion he presupposed in his lecture has been given in his pamphlets. But there is no justification for the claim in the case of *ethical* reasons. There is no serious attempt to meet the ethical considerations, which are said to justify wars. He consistently refuses to admit that any such reasons can possibly exist. When I assert that the fundamental difference in this controversy about the war is an ethical one, he replies: "No doubt this is true *on the surface*. But ethical differences usually spring from differences of *impulse*. Whole philosophies . . . spring up in this way; they are the embodiment of a kind of thought which is subservient to impulse, which aims at providing a *quasi-rational ground for the indulgence of impulse.*" You see, no ethical discussion is then needed. I, poor man, imagine I am moved by ethical reasons; but Mr. Russell knows better; in reality I only want to provide myself with sham reasons for the indulgence of certain evil impulses. But this kind of discussion leads nowhere. I can retort that the ethical reasons which lead pacifists to condemn war are also quasi-rational grounds for the indulgence of impulse.

It is not very clear, however, what Mr. Russell really intends here. Does he mean merely that *my* ethics is quasi-rational, while *pacifist* ethics is objective; in other words, is he still thinking of the dispute as one between Reason and Impulse? Apparently not, for he continues: "The difference of opinion will *seem* to be ethical . . . its real basis is a difference of impulse. . . . No genuine agreement will be reached . . . so long as the differences of impulse persist." But even this is ambiguous. It may merely be meant as a *psychology* of the matter; in that case it might be accepted as correct. It might be true to say that we were led to different ethical valuations because we were moved by different impulses . . . But this, even if true, has no bearing whatever on this discussion. If it were universally agreed that war was always ethically unjustifiable, then the psychology of how some few abnormal people came to have opposed ethical views might be relevant. But this is not the situation. The opposition which pacifism has to face (on this plane of ethical discussion) comes from people who sincerely believe their own ethical valuations to be objective; they think, moreover, that the *humanitarian* ethics on which pacifism is based, is not *objective* but subjective and false — the product of certain historical conditions which can be easily traced.

If what Mr. Russell says here is to have any point, then (as a reply to my assertion that the difference is ultimately an ethical one), he must mean something more than this. When he says that systems of ethics are only quasi-rational grounds for the indulgence of impulse, he must be giving more than a psychology of their origin. He must mean that *all* systems of ethics are, in their nature, *nothing more than this*. None of them have any objective validity, they are all merely an expression of impulse. If there is nothing objective about ethics then, all purely ethical discussion is futile, "no genuine agreement will be reached so long as the difference of impulse persists." All ethical valuations are a matter of taste; this certainly provides a relevant answer to what I said about an ethical difference. But does Mr. Russell really accept this complete ethical scepticism? Has he completely changed his conception of the nature of ethics? In his "Philosophical Essays" he rejects "the widespread ethical scepticism which is based upon observations of mere differences in regard to ethical questions. . . . If X says A is good, and Y says A is bad, one of them *must be mistaken*."

I may, perhaps, make the course of this argument clearer by putting it diagrammatically. I claim that the dispute is presented by Mr. Russell as one between

> Pacifist Ethics and Warlike Impulses,

whereas it ought to be between

> Pacifist Ethics and Warlike Ethics.

Mr. Russell replies that *Warlike* ethics are merely quasi-rational grounds for indulgence of *Warlike* Impulse.

I reply that the same may be true of *Pacifist* ethics.

He then says the dispute is between

Pacifist Impulse and Warlike Impulse.

If he merely means this is psychology, then it may be true, but is irrelevant.

If meant literally it leads to complete ethical scepticism.

* * *

It seems, then, as if Mr. Russell had entirely abandoned the *ob-jective* conception of ethics; but I think it is possible to show that this is a change that might have been expected. The essay referred to above expresses agreement with a certain reaction against hedonist and utilitarian ethics. Now a *complete* reaction of this kind would accomplish two things.

(1) The establishment of the *objective* character of ethical values.

(2) The establishment of a *new* hierarchy amongst particular values.

I say "new," for I regard it as demonstrable that there is some connection between the view of the nature of value we take and the order in which we range different values, so that a change in the first is likely, *when it is thoroughly realised*, to produce a change in the second. Now the criticism I should formerly have made of Mr. Russell is that, while he had completely broken with the utilitarian tradition in the first matter, he continued it quite uncritically in the second. This is perhaps clearer when put more concretely. The utilitarian view of the nature of the good is accompanied by a hierarchy amongst the values, and an *ideology*, which follow naturally from it. If you refuse to look on any values as objective and absolute, and can only give them meaning in relation to *Life*, then you are naturally led to a pacifist ethic. I admit this entirely. Herbert Spencer's pacifism, for example, was a perfectly logical development from his conception of the nature of the "good." But Mr. Russell used to hold a very different view of the nature of ethical values. It is then somewhat surprising that the account he gives of war as an atavism is almost identical with that given by Spencer in his Ethics. It is possible, then, to look on this combination of an acceptance of all the utilitarian values with a rejection of utilitarianism itself, as unstable and bound to lead to either (1) the course apparently taken by Mr. Russell. Perhaps suspecting instinctively that the *objective* conception of ethics might lead to the establishment of values he would call reactionary, and knowing the *liberal, pacifist, progressive* values to be in this region, the things about which he felt most certain — he dropped the *objective* conception. Or (2) the abandonment of the pacifist utilitarian hierarchy of values.

I postulate here, without proof, that there is a connection between the view held about the nature of value and the order in which the values are ranged; and that consequently the conviction that certain values are *not* relative to life might lead to an ethic which was by no means necessarily pacifist. Without proof this must necessarily appear unconvincing. But for my purpose here, all that it is necessary for me to do, is to make it clear that the difference between my view of war and that taken by pacifists does (rightly or wrongly) spring from a difference about ethics — a difference about the order in which values should be placed. What I also want to make clear, later, is that this difference is extremely important in matters which have nothing to do with the war. It lies at the root of the objections we should make, for example, to all the proposals in Mr. Russell's other lectures — on education, marriage, etc. Most important of all it leads, as we see in the case of Proudhon and Sorel, to a profoundly different conception of democracy.

NORTH STAFFS
CONTINUES WHERE HE LEFT OFF

The discussion last week was left at this point: — In reply to Mr. Russell's assumption that the opposition to pacifism springs from certain *impulses*, and that even where reasons are given they are only quasi-rational grounds for the indulgence of these impulses, I attempted to show that these reasons are *not* quasi-rational, and that the difference is not only superficially but fundamentally an ethical one. When Mr. Russell condemns war for reasons based on the unquestioned acceptance of a rationalist, utilitarian ethic, I reply by *denying* the validity of this ethic. My object here is to so emphasise the reality of this difference, that no pacifist shall be unaware that it exists. They are able as a rule to ignore it, because it is mixed up and confused in the complicated mass of the other possible controversies about war — economic, political, etc. Under these conditions an agreement about (a) may be countered by a reply relevant only to (b); arguments about ethics are mixed up inextricably with arguments about whether the war will ruin us, whether it was really expedient . . . and so on.

I might as well say at once then, that the ethical discussion here provides no justification whatever for *this* war. All I urge against Mr. Russell's ethical premises might be entirely true, and yet, at the same time, this war might be the most colossal stupidity in our history. Its bearing on this subject is entirely negative. It only combats certain ethical reasons, for which all wars are condemned.

* * *

What are the two opposed ethics? Very roughly:

(1)Rationalist, humanitarian; the fundamental values are *Life* and *Personality*, and everything has reference to that. It is almost universally, but, I suppose, not essentially, connected with the optimistic conception of human nature. Mr. Russell talks of "ever widening horizons . . . shining vision of future . . . life and hope and joy." (It first became widespread in the eighteenth century, and must be sharply distinguished from Christian ethics, with which it is often identified.) As *life* is its fundamental value, it leads naturally to pacifism, and tends to regard conceptions like Honour, etc., as empty words, which cannot deceive the *emancipated*.

(2) The more heroic or tragic system of ethical values. — Values are not relative only to life, but are objective and absolute, and many of them are above life. This ethic is not, therefore, bound to condemn all sacrifice of life. In a sense it may be called *irrational*, if we give the word *rational* the narrow meaning given it by the first ethic, *i.e.* those values are rational which can be reasonably based on *life*. It is generally associated with a more pessimistic conception of the nature of man.

If the pacifists could only recognise the existence of this radical ethical difference, discussion would become much clearer; they might then recognise that if we differ from them, it is not because we are not intelligent or disinterested enough to follow their arguments. The difficulty, however, is that the rationalist ethic appears so *natural* and *inevitable* to them, they find it impossible to imagine that the other ethic can have any reality at all. They offer, instead, explanations of the ways in which men falsely come to believe in the empty words which this ethic asserts to be values. Mr. Russell talks of ". . . the blindness of inherited instinct and the sinister influence of anti-social interests . . . the lust for blood." It is, then, first of all necessary to show the reality of the "heroic" ethic.

The principal feature about this ethic is the "irrationality" of certain values (*i.e.* the assertion that certain actions, though good, may involve sacrifice of life and personality; *a sacrifice which it may be impossible to rationalise, by showing that it furthers life in remoter ways*). We can conveniently refer to such values as the

Heroic values (thus using the word in the widest possible sense). It should be noticed that for this ethic these values are as *objective*, and absolute, as independent of the subjective feelings of particular men as the laws of arithmetic.

Now the rationalist will admit that men do feel these values as superior to the more rational values; but he explains the inner necessity men may feel about the matter, by calling it an atavism — a survival from the "early stages, when a disposition to ferocity . . . was a biological advantage . . ." Such an explanation of the heroic values is on a level with Bain's explanation of maternal affection. It seems to me quite untrue. In a moment, when a man, after much weighing of motives, suddenly brushing calculations on one side . . . sees clearly that this is an *absolute* value, and must be accepted as absolute, above calculation . . . and superior to values based on *life* and *personality* . . . then, I think it wrong to say that he has been moved by some underlying atavistic impulse which has suddenly come to the surface. On the contrary, I should say that he was understanding the nature of ethics for the first time. He is discovering the facts of ethics, which are as objective as the facts of geometry, by the method of apprehension, through which alone, then, real nature is to be revealed. Even drums may not blind a man's eyes by rousing forgotten animal instincts, but rather enable him to see the real nature of ethical values by breaking up the habits which hinder his perception of such facts in a calmer rational life.

* * *

The nature of these *heroic* values is worth discussing, for such discussion throws the differences between the two ethics into the sharpest possible relief; an understanding of the nature of these values is perhaps the key to an understanding of the true (as opposed to the rationalist) ethic. Both sides seem to have instinctively realised this.

(1) The rationalists (though they could not have said why) seem to have known *instinctively* that this conception of heroism was the central *nerve* of the ethic they opposed; and have consequently

always tried to disintegrate it by ridicule. The author of "Arms and the Man" thus reminds one of the wasps described by Fabre, who sting their prey in the central ganglia in order to paralyse it, in this way acting as if they were expert entomologists, though in reality they can have no conscious knowledge of what they are doing.

(2) It is their conviction of the truth of these heroic values that has led many to instinctively reject the rationalist utilitarian ethic, without being able to state clearly the real nature of the true ethic. Many of these people might have been called reactionary. There is no necessary connection of ideas here. How does it come about that we so often find it? For this reason probably: when we almost instinctively reject any idea, say (A), without clearly knowing why, and (m, n, o . . .) are each reasons, which, *if true*, would prove that (A) was false, then we tend to think that (m, n, o . . .) are themselves true; this is a very natural process. Now many reactionary principles do accidentally involve a rejection of this rationalist ethic; and this is the explanation, I think, of the motives of many intellectual reactionaries. The conviction that the rationalist ethic is false is the profoundest conviction that they have: in comparison with this everything else seems unimportant. Above all, it seems to them necessary to *prove* the validity of this rejection — they are thus led to false reasons.

But the work of certain writers has lately made it much more possible to think clearly (and not only instinctively) about ethics, and it is now possible to completely *dissociate* the reactionary spirit, and the rejection of a rationalist humanitarian ethic.

*　　　*　　　*

There are two senses in which the heroic values may be regarded as the key to a proper understanding of ethics.

(a) It is most probably only through a realisation of these values that the sceptic about ethics comes to see what there is that is *objective* and *absolute* in the subject.

(b) Any system of ethics establishes a hierarchy of values, the lower terms of which are founded upon the higher. In this sense it may be said that most of the commoner virtues presuppose and rest upon the heroic values; just as these rest (not as a matter of individual psychology, but essentially) on the values given in religion.

* * *

(a) It must be very difficult for the writers on ethics (who seem to be more happily endowed than most of us) to realise how excessively difficult it is for the ordinary modern to realise that there is any *real* subject "Ethics" which can be at all compared with "Logic" or even with "Aesthetic." It seems almost impossible for us to look on it as anything objective; everything seems to us arbitrary and human, and we should at a certain age no more think of reading a book on ethics than we should reading one on manners or astrology. There may even seem something ridiculous about the word "Virtue." Why is this? It was not always so. The Greeks, the early Romans, and the men of the Middle Ages spoke of Virtue, as they might of Beauty, as something attractive and full of charm. To a certain extent, I suppose, because we are under the influence of a sceptical reaction against the pathetic apostrophes addressed to Virtue by the men of the eighteenth century; but much more, I think, on account of its narrow connection in our minds with sex; for this is almost the only ethical question which the ordinary undergraduate or intellectual (the only people likely to read books about ethics) is likely to have to face practically (as they have no inclination to steal or kill); and it is consequently the only part of ethics which presents a living problem, and about which he is likely to reflect much. It so happens, however, that the ethics of sex (not perhaps in reality, but as it is presented to him) contains very little that is properly ethical, but only taboo, custom, expediency, and good form. If he is irregular enough in mind to be able to set these aside, the fact that there seems here nothing really ethical, nothing obligatory, tends to make him sceptical about the whole subject. At an age when, like one George Moore, he may long "to see Elizabeth Hawkins naked," he cannot with complete honesty study the other's

Principia Ethica. With a prosperous life this may continue, until the necessity perhaps arrives, of making a decision in the region of one of the *heroic* values. Then having felt for the first time something binding, something objective to which he felt himself, to his own surprise, to his annoyance even, bound to submit, he may suddenly realise for the first time, that there is such a thing as Ethics. From that he may gradually proceed to realise that other virtues are really virtues and not merely expediency or custom. I am not describing any mere process of moral conversion or awakening in a man, who, having always known the virtues, suddenly decides to practise them. Nor, I might add, am I attempting after the manner of Kant, to derive the "Good" out of an "Ought." I am simply describing the process by which many sceptics have come to realise the true nature of ethical obligation.

(b) More important, however, than this is a more speculative assertion about the heroic values; a statement this time, not about the psychology of the process by which we come to *understand ethics,* but about ethics itself.

I think it is possible to range the ethical values in a certain order of hierarchy; and this order, though it is concerned with "feelings," is yet absolute, *not relative* to human life, and in certain respects a priori — a "logique du coeur" (those "feelings" which form part of the subject of ethics can only be studied as they occur in man, just as in the case of mathematical reasoning, yet there is nothing specifically human or relative about them). In this hierarchy the "lower" are founded, and are dependent on the "higher" values. I think that a careful examination into many values more specifically concerned with life (fidelity, for example) as we feel them in ourselves will show that they owe their meaning almost, and certainly their truth to the higher "heroic values" which are most absolute and quite independent of life. It is from these that the more specific and human ends of the other virtues draw their sanction. Virtues, like "fidelity" draw their meaning and sustenance, as it were, from these "heroic values." While humanitarian ethic then attaches ultimate value to *Life,* a true ethic can only value *Life* as a "bearer" of certain higher values, which are themselves quite independent of any relation to life.

I shall try next week to trace the practical result of this abstract difference. It should be noticed that the question is made more difficult by the fact that Mr. Russell has the habit of using all the phraseology of the *heroic* ethics, whilst denying the premisses, which can alone give substance to them.

APPENDIXES AND INDEX

BERTRAND RUSSELL'S REPLIES

The two letters included here are Bertrand Russell's replies to Hulme's criticisms in the Essays on War. *The first letter followed Hulme's third essay, "The Kind of Rubbish We Oppose"; the second letter replied to Hulme's sixth essay, "North Staffs Resents Mr. Russell's Rejoinder." Both appeared in the* Cambridge Magazine, *Vol. V, Nos. 13 and 17.*

MR. RUSSELL'S REPLY

Sir, — Your correspondent "North Staffs" has contributed to the *Magazine* a criticism of a recent lecture by me, with the courteous title, "the kind of rubbish we oppose." This criticism shows such profound misunderstanding of the lecture that I suspect "North Staffs" of being the gentleman who ostentatiously read the *Daily Express* during the greater part of the hour.

He begins by suggesting that I regard the bellicose as moved by impulse and the pacifists as moved by reason. My whole lecture on the contrary, was concerned to represent *both* sides as moved by impulse, and to show that impulse is essential to all vigorous action, good or bad. "Blind impulses," so I contended, "sometimes lead to destruction and death. But at other times they lead to the best things the world contains. Blind impulse is the source of war, but it is also the source of science and art and love. It is not the weakening of impulse that is to be desired, but the direction of impulse towards life and growth rather than towards death and decay." And again: "It is not the act of a passionless man to throw himself athwart the whole movement of the national life, to urge an outwardly hopeless cause, to incur obloquy and to resist the contagion of collective emotion. The impulse to avoid the hostility of public opinion is one of the strongest in human nature, and can only be overcome by an unusual force of direct and uncalculated impulse; it is not cold reason alone that can prompt such an act."

Having misrepresented my thesis, he continues: "there is no doubt that this provides a happy method of controversy for general use by pacifists. They thus avoid the necessity for any tedious examination of the actual arguments used by their opponents, by depriving these arguments at one stroke of all validity." If "North Staffs" has such a love of "tedious examination" as he suggests, I would refer him to *The Policy of the Entente* and *Justice in War Time* (both published by the Labour Press) where he will find that I have set forth the detailed discussion which I presupposed in the lecture.

He proceeds to suggest that the difference between him and me is one of ethical valuation. No doubt this is true on the surface. But ethical differences usually spring from differences of impulse. "Whole philosophies, whole systems of ethical valuation, spring up in this way: they are the embodiment of a kind of thought which is subservient to impulse, which aims at providing a quasi-rational ground for the indulgence of impulse." "This difference of opinion will seem to be ethical or intellectual, whereas its real basis is a difference of impulse. No genuine agreement will be reached, in such a case, so long as the differences of impulse persists." (These again are quotations from the lecture.)

I cannot imagine what led "North Staffs" to his final exhortation not to "falsely simplify matters by assuming that it is a struggle between the assailants and defenders of privilege. It is not Democracy against Privilege." There was not a syllable in my lecture to suggest to anyone who listened to it that I regarded the matter in this light. It is not democracy, but liberty, that is in danger. The persecutions of early Christians, the massacre of St. Bartholomew, the Press Gang, and Conscription for the Unmarried, have none of them been contrary to democracy. But the tyrannous power of the state, whether wielded by a monarch or by a majority, is an evil against which I will protest no matter how "negligible" may be the minority on whom it is exercised.

Yours etc.

BERTRAND RUSSELL

NORTH STAFFS' PRAISE OF WAR

In the *Cambridge Magazine* for February 26 North Staffs does something to bring to a clear issue the differences between him and me. These differences are rooted in character and disposition, and will not be dispelled by argument; but I will do my best towards helping to make them explicit.

North Staffs distinguishes two types of reasons: "(1) Those dealing with facts; (2) those concerned with ethics." I referred him to two pamphlets, one dealing with the one, the other with the other. He bought *one* of these pamphlets, and complains that it does not deal with the topics discussed in the other. This seems unreasonable.

As regards ethical reasons, he says that I "consistently refuse to admit that any such reasons can possibly exist." The reception given to Bernhardi's works in this country, and the determination to maintain that Germany is wholly responsible for the war, had led me to think that this was common ground, so far as Englishmen's explicit opinions were concerned. Does North Staffs wish to associate himself with Bernhardi in the praise of war as a good in itself? If so, he will find himself in an even smaller minority than that in which I find myself. If not, I must suppose that he wishes to praise only *defensive* wars. To this I would reply (1) that this war is less purely defensive than most of us believe; (2) that even defensive wars are less justifiable, on the grounds of their effects, than men usually suppose them to be. Both these points have been argued at length in the pamphlets referred to.

On the abstract question of ethics which North Staffs proceeds to raise, I do certainly mean to maintain that *all* ethics is subjective, and that ethical agreement can only arise through similarity of desires and impulses. It is true that I did not hold this view formerly, but I have been led to it by a number of reasons, some logical, some derived from observation. Occam's Razor, or the principle that constructions are to be substituted for inferred entities whenever possible, leads me to discard the notion of absolute good if ethics can be accounted for without it. Observation of ethical valuations leads me to think that all ethical valuations can be so accounted for, and that the claim of universality which men associate with their ethical judgments embodies merely the impulse to persecution or tyranny.

An ethical argument can only have practical efficacy in one of two ways: (1) By showing that the effects of some kind of action are different from what the opponent supposes; this is really a scientific not an ethical argument; (2) by altering the desires or impulses of the opponent, not merely his intellectual judgments. I cannot imagine any argument by which it could be shown that something is intrinsically good or intrinsically bad; for this reason, ethical valuations not embodying desires or impulses cannot have any importance.

For my part, I should wish to see in the world less cruelty, persecution, punishment, and moral reprobation than exists at present; to this end I believe that a recognition of the subjectivity of ethics might conduce. But if North Staffs likes these things, and judges them to be in themselves good, I cannot prove by argument that he is mistaken: I can only say his desires and mine are different. If his belief in the intrinsic excellence of war has some other basis, I hope he will set it forth.

BERTRAND RUSSELL

P.S. — Since writing the above I have seen North Staffs' continuation in the *Magazine* for March 4. Most of what he says in this continuation I said in my lecture on Religion on February 29. But the antithesis between heroic ethics and ethics devoted to life, which he draws, is quite baseless. An ethic is rendered heroic, not by the values which it recognises, but by the intensity of its recognition and the sacrifices it is willing to make to realise them. In that sense my ethic is as "heroic" as his; and I do not condemn *all* wars, as I stated in "The Ethics of War," and again in my lecture on war. But the things which I value are very *seldom* promoted by war. I value the kind of life which seems to me "heroic," the kind which is devoted to certain ends that are in one sense above life, but that only acquire actual existence when they are embodied in life. I find that it is not pursuit of these ends that leads to modern wars, and that modern wars are the greatest obstacle to the achievement of these ends. I wish North Staffs would tell us explicitly what are the things which he values; for so long as he keeps silence about this, the controversy remains indefinite.

POEMS AND FRAGMENTS

The first three poems printed here were found among Hulme's papers by Michael Roberts and were published as an appendix to his T. E. Hulme. *The rest appeared in the* New Age, *Vol. XXIX, No. 23 (October 6, 1921), under the title "Fragments (from the note-book of T. E. Hulme, who was killed in the war)."*

THE MAN IN THE CROW'S NEST

Strange to me sounds the wind that blows
By the masthead in the lonely night.
Maybe 'tis the sea whistling — feigning joy
To hide its fright
Like a village boy
That, shivering, past the churchyard goes.

SUSAN ANN AND IMMORTALITY

Her head hung down
Gazed at earth, finally keen,
As the rabbit at the stoat,
Till the earth was sky,
Sky that was green,
And brown clouds passed
Like chestnut leaves along the ground.

A CITY SUNSET

Alluring, earth-seducing, with high conceits
is the sunset that coquettes
at the end of westward streets.

A sudden flaring sky
troubling strangely the passer-by
with vision, alien to long streets, of Cytherea
or the smooth flesh of Lady Castlemaine . . .

A frolic of crimson
is the spreading glory of the sky
heaven's wanton
flaunting a trailed red robe
along the fretted city roofs
about the time of homeward-going crowds
— a vain maid, lingering, loth to go . . .

FRAGMENTS

Always I desire the great canvas for my lines and gestures.

———————

Old houses were scaffolding once, and workmen whistling.

The bloom of the grape has gone.

That magic momentary time.

As on a veiled stage, thin Anar
Trembles with listless arms hung limp
At the touch of the cold hand of Manar
Placed warning.

A sudden secret cove by Budley
Waveless water, cliff enclosed.
A still boudoir of the sea, which
In the noon-heat lolls in to sleep.
Velvet sand, smooth as the rounded thigh
Of the Lady of Avé, as asleep she lay.
Vibrant, noon-heat, trembling at the view.
Oh eager page! Oh velvet sand!
Tremulous faint-hearted waves creep up
Diffident — ah, how wondering!
Trembling and drawing back.
Be bold — the Abbé blesses — 'tis only feignèd sleep.
Oh smooth round thigh! . . .
A rough wind rises, dark cliffs stare down.
Sour-faced Calvin — art thou whining still?

———————

The sky is the eye of labourer earth.
Last night late in the view he stayed.
To-day, clouds pass, like motes
Across his bleared vision.

215

FURTHER SPECULATIONS

When she speaks, almost her breasts touch me.
Backward leans her head.

Solid and peaceful is Horton town
Known is all friendship and steady.
In fixed roads walks every man.

A tall woman is come to Horton town. . . .
In the midst of all men, secretly she presses my hand.
When all are looking, she seems to promise.
There is a secret garden
And a cool stream. . . .
Thus at all men she looks.
The same promise to many eyes.
Yet when she forward leans, in a room,
And by seeming accident, her breasts brush against me,
Then is the axle of the world twisted.

In the quiet land
There is a secret unknown fire.
Suddenly rocks shall melt
And the old roads mislead.

Across the familiar road
There is a deep cleft. I must stand and draw back.
In the cool land
There is a secret fire.

Her head hung down
Looked fixedly at earth,
As the rabbit at the stoat,
Till she thinks the earth is the sky.

Oh God, narrow the sky,
The old star-eaten blanket,
Till it fold me round in warmth.

Down the long desolate streets of stars.

No blanket is the sky to keep warm the little stars.

Somewhere the gods (the blanket-makers in the prairie
   of cold)
Sleep in their blankets.
["Religion is the expansive lie of temporary warmth."]

Raleigh in the dark tower prisoned
Dreamed of the blue sea and beyond
Where in strange tropic paradise
Grew musk. . . .

Here stand I on the pavement hard
From love's warm paradise debarred.

Now though the skirt be fallen,
Gone the vision of the sea.
Though braced (abominable feeling)
By the cold winds of common sense,
Still my seaman thought sails hence.
Still hears the murmur of the blue
Round the black cliffs of your shoe.

O lady, to me full of mystery
Is that blue sea beyond your knee.

The mystic sadness of the sight
Of a far town seen in the night.

Her skirt lifted as a dark mist
From the columns of amethyst.

The flounced edge of skirt, recoiling like waves off a cliff.

This to all ladies gay I say.
Away, abhorrèd lace, away.

I lie alone in the little valley, in the noon heat,
In the kingdom of little sounds.
The hot air whispers lasciviously.
The lark sings like the sound of distant unattainable brooks.

The lark crawls on the cloud
Like a flea on a white body.

———

With a courtly bow the bent tree sighed
May I present you to my friend the sun.

———

At night!
All terror's in that.
Branches of the dead tree,
Silhouetted on the hill's edge.
Dark veins diseased,
On the dead white body of the sky.
The tearing iron hook
Of pitiless Mara.
Handling soft clouds in insurrection.
Brand of the obscene gods
On their flying cattle,
Roaming the sky prairie.

———

Town sky-line.
On a summer day, in Town,
Where chimneys fret the cumuli,
Flora passing in disdain
Lifts her flounced blue gown, the sky.
So see I, her white cloud petticoat,
Clear Valenciennes, meshed by twisted cowls,
Rent by tall chimneys, torn lace, frayed and
    fissured.
Slowly died along the scented way.

———

In the city square at night, the meeting
    of the torches.
The start of the great march,
The cries, the cheers, the parting.
Marching in an order
Through the familiar streets,
Through friends for the last time seen
Marching with torches.
Over the hill summit,
The moon and the moor,
And we marching alone.

The torches are out.
On the cold hill,
The cheers of the warrior dead.
(For the first time re-seen)
Marching in an order,
To where?

The after-black lies low along the hills
Like the trailed smoke of a steamer.

Three birds flew over the red wall into the pit
  of the setting sun.
O daring, doomèd birds that pass from my sight.

Sounds fluttered, like bats in the dusk.

Sunset.
A coryphée, covetous of applause,
Loth to leave the stage,
With final diablerie, poises high her toe.
Displays scarlet lingerie of carmin'd clouds,
Amid the hostile murmur of the stalls.

Musié.
Over a void, a desert, a flat empty space,
Came in waves, like winds,
The sound of drums, in lines, sweeping like armies.
. . . . . . Dreams of soft notes
        Sail as a fleet at eve
        On a calm sea.

Far back there is a round pool,
Where trees reflected make sad memory,
Whose tense expectant surface waits
The ecstatic wave that ripples it
In sacrament of union,
The fugitive bliss that comes with the red tear
That falls from the middle-aged princess
(Sister to the princely Frog)
While she leans tranced in a dreamy curve,
As a drowsy wail in an Eastern song.

219

As a fowl in the tall grass lies
Beneath the terror of the hawk,
The tressed white light crept
Whispering with hand on mouth mysterious
Hunting the leaping shadows in straight streets
By the white houses of old Flemish towns.

————————

I walked into the wood in June
And suddenly Beauty, like a thick scented veil,
Stifled me,
Tripped me up, tight round my limbs,
Arrested me.

————————

Madman.
As I walk by the river
Those who have not yet withdrawn pass
    me.
I see past them, touch them,
And in the distance, over the water,
Far from the lights,
I see Night, that dark savage,
But I will not fear him.
Four walls are round me.
I can touch them.
If I die, I can float by.
Moan and hum and remember the sea
In heaven, Oh my spirit,
Remember the sea and its moaning.
Hum in the presence of God, it will
    sustain you.
Again I am cold, as after weeping.
And I tremble — but there is no wind.

APPENDIX C

A Bibliography of HULME'S WRITINGS

NOTE: The items preceded by an asterisk are those reprinted in this volume.

1909

"Autumn" and "A City Sunset," in *For Christmas MDCCCCVIII*, The Poets' Club, London, Women's Printing Society, Ltd. [published January 1909].

"Belated Romanticism," *New Age*, IV (February 18), 350 [letter].

"The New Philosophy," *New Age*, V (July 1), 198-199.

"Bergson and Bax," *New Age*, V (July 22), 259 [letter].

* "Searchers after Reality. I. Bax," *New Age*, V (July 29), 265-266.

* "Searchers after Reality. II. Haldane," *New Age*, V (August 19), 315-316.

"A Note on 'La Foi,'" *New Age*, V (October 28), 482-483 [letter].

*"Searchers after Reality. III. De Gaultier," *New Age*, VI (December 2), 107-108.

"A Conversion" and "The Embankment," in *The Book of the Poets' Club*, London, Christmas.

1910

"A Metaphysics Group," *New Age*, VII (June 23), 187 [letter].

1911

"A Note on the Art of Political Conversion," *The Commentator*, II (February 22), 234; (March 1), 250; (March 8), 266 [signed "Thomas Gratton"][1].

"The Art of Political Conversion," *The Commentator*, II (April 19), 357-358 [signed "Thomas Gratton"].

*"Notes on the Bologna Congress," *New Age*, VIII (April 27), 607-608.

"Bergsonism in Paris," *New Age*, IX (June 22), 189-190 [letter].

"On Progress and Democracy," *The Commentator*, III (August 2), 165-166; (August 9), 179-180 [signed "Thomas Gratton"].

"Bax on Bergson," *New Age*, IX (August 3), 328-330.

Review of *L'Attitude du Lyrisme Contemporain*, by Tancrède de Visan, *New Age*, IX (August 24), 400-401.

"A Metaphysics Group," *New Age*, IX (October 12), 575 [letter signed by Hulme, John Stuart Hay, and E. Belfort Bax].

* "Notes on Bergson, I," *New Age*, IX (October 19), 587-588.

* "Notes on Bergson, II," *New Age*, IX (October 26), 610-611.

---

[1] The pseudonyms "Thomas Gratton" and "T. K. White" are identified as Hulme's in Alun Jones, *The Life and Opinions of T. E. Hulme* (London, 1960), p. 152.

"Bergson Lecturing," *New Age*, X (November 2), 15-16 [signed "Thomas Gratton"].

"Mr. Balfour, Bergson and Politics," *New Age*, X (November 9), 38-40; [signed "T.E.H."].

"Bergsonism," *New Age*, X (November 9), 46-47 [letter signed "T.E.H."].

"A Personal Impression of Bergson," *Saturday Westminister Gazette* (Weekly Edition) vol. XXXVIII, no. 5771, p. 11 [signed "T. K. White"].

* "Notes on Bergsonism, III," *New Age*, X (November 23), 79-82.

"Bergsonism," *New Age*, X (November 23), 94 [letter signed "T.E.H."].

* "Notes on Bergson, IV," *New Age*, X (November 30), 110-112.

1912

"The Complete Poetical Works of T. E. Hulme," *New Age*, X (January 23), 307 [includes "Autumn," "Mana Aboda," "Conversion," "Above the Dock," "Embankment"].

"Notes on Bergson," *New Age*, X (February 8), 359 [letter].

* "Notes on Bergson, V," *New Age*, X (February 22), 401-403.

"A Tory Philosophy," *The Commentator*, IV (April 3), 294-295; (April 10), 310; (May 1), 362; (May 8), 380; (May 15), 388-389 [signed "Thomas Gratton"].

"Bergson in English," *Cambridge Magazine*, I (April 27), 265 [letter].

"Bergson in English," *Cambridge Magazine*, I (May 18), 353 [letter].

"The Complete Poetical Works of T. E. Hulme," in Ezra Pound, *Ripostes*, London: Stephen Swift and Co., Ltd. [same poems as in *New Age* above].

1913

* "Mr. Epstein and the Critics," *New Age*, XIV (December 25), 251-253.

Henri Bergson, *Introduction to Metaphysics*, Authorized translation by T. E. Hulme. London: Macmillan & Co., Ltd.

1914

* "Modern Art. I. The Grafton Group," *New Age*, XIV (January 15), 341-342.

* "Modern Art. II. A Preface Note and Neo-Realism," *New Age*, XIV (February 12), 467-469.

* "Modern Art. III. The London Group," *New Age*, XIV (March 26), 661-662.

"Contemporary Drawings," *New Age*, XIV (April 2), 688.

"Contemporary Drawings," *New Age*, XIV (April 16), 753.

"Contemporary Drawings," *New Age*, XIV (April 30), 821.

"German Chronicle," *Poetry and Drama*, II (June), 221-228.

* "Modern Art. IV. Mr. David Bomberg's Show," *New Age*, XV (July 9), 230-232.

1915

"The Translator's Preface to Sorel's 'Reflections on Violence,'" *New Age*, XVII (October 28), 569-570.

"War Notes by North Staffs," *New Age*, XVIII (November 11), 29-30; (November 18), 53-55; (November 25), 77; (December 2), 101-102; (December 9), 125-126; (December 16), 149-151; (December 23), 173-174; (December 30), 197-199.

"A Notebook by T. E. H.," *New Age*, XVIII (December 2), 112-113; (December 9), 137-138; (December 16), 158-160; (December 23), 186-188.

1916

"War Notes by North Staffs," *New Age*, XVIII (January 6), 222-223; (January 13), 246-247; (January 20), 269-270; (January 27), 293-294; (February 3), 317-318; (February 10), 341-342; (February 17), 365-366; (February 24), 389-391; (March 2), 413-414.

"A Notebook by T. E. H.," *New Age*, XVIII (January 6), 234-235; (January 27), 305-307; (February 10), 353-354.

* "On Liberty," *Cambridge Magazine*, V (January 22), 221.

* "Inevitability Inapplicable," *Cambridge Magazine*, V (January 29), 242-243.

* "The Kind of Rubbish We Oppose," *Cambridge Magazine*, V (February 5), 266-267.

* "Why We Are in Favour of this War," *Cambridge Magazine*, V (February 12), 304-305.

* "The Framework of Europe," *Cambridge Magazine*, V (February 19), 329-330.

* "North Staffs Resents Mr. Russell's Rejoinder," *Cambridge Magazine*, V (February 26), 352-354.

* "North Staffs Continues Where He Left Off," *Cambridge Magazine*, V (March 4), 376-377.

Georges Sorel, *Reflections on Violence*, Translated with a bibliography by T. E. Hulme. London: George Allen & Unwin, Ltd. [Hulme's introduction is omitted from the 1925 edition.]

1920

"Readers and Writers," by "R. H. C." [A. R. Orage], *New Age*, XXVII (August 26), 259 [article containing quotations from Hulme's manuscripts which do not appear elsewhere].

1921

* "Fragments (from the note-book of T. E. Hulme)," *New Age*, XIX (October 6), 275-276.

FURTHER SPECULATIONS

1922

"The Note-Books of T. E. Hulme," ed. Herbert Read, *New Age*, XXX
(January 19), 148-149; (January 26), 167-168; (February 9), 193-194;
(February 16), 207-208 ["Cinders," slightly different in content and order
from the *Speculations* version].

"The Note-Books of T. E. Hulme," ed. Herbert Read, *New Age*, XXX
(March 30), 287-288; (April 6), 301-302; (April 13), 310-312 ["Bergson's
Theory of Art," as in *Speculations*].

1924

Speculations, ed. Herbert Read. London: Kegan Paul, Trench, Trubner
& Co., Ltd.

1925

* "Notes on Language and Style," ed. Herbert Read, *Criterion*, III (July),
485-497.

1929

* *Notes on Language and Style*, ed. Herbert Read. Seattle: University of
Washington Chapbook, No. 25 (copyright Glenn Hughes).

1938

* "Three Poems," "A Lecture on Modern Poetry," and "Notes on Language
and Style," Appendixes to Michael Roberts, *T. E. Hulme*. London:
Faber & Faber, Ltd.

1960

"The Poetical Works of T. E. Hulme," "A Tory Philosophy," "A Personal
Impression of Bergson," and letters to Edward Marsh and Miss A. M.
Pattinson, in Alun R. Jones, *The Life and Opinions of T. E. Hulme*,
London: Victor Gollancz Ltd.

APPENDIX D

A Selected Bibliography of
CRITICISM ON HULME

Browning, W. R. F. "T. E. Hulme," *Church Quarterly Review*, CXLV (October 1947), 59–65.

Coffman, Stanley K., Jr. *Imagism: A Chapter for the History of Modern Poetry*. Norman, Okla.: University of Oklahoma Press, 1951.

Collin, W. E. "Beyond Humanism: Some Notes on T. E. Hulme," *Sewanee Review*, XXXVIII (July 1930), 332–339.

Daiches, David. *Poetry and the Modern World*. Chicago: University of Chicago Press, 1940.

Daniells, J. R. "T. S. Eliot and His Relation to T. E. Hulme," *University of Toronto Quarterly*, II (April 1933), 380–396.

Davis, Robert Gorham. "The New Criticism and the Democratic Tradition," *American Scholar*, XIX (Winter 1949–50), 9–19.

Hendry, J. F. "Hulme as Horatio," *Life and Letters Today*, XXXV (December 1942), 136–147.

Hughes, Glenn. *Imagism and the Imagists*. Stanford University, Calif.: Stanford University Press, 1931.

Krieger, Murray. "The Ambiguous Anti-Romanticism of T. E. Hulme," *ELH*, XX (December 1953), 300–314.

Nelson, Francis W. "Valet to the Absolute: A Study of the Philosophy of T. E. Hulme," *The Municipal University of Wichita Bulletin*, Vol. XXV, No. 4 (October 1950).

Nott, Kathleen. *The Emperor's Clothes*. Bloomington, Ind.: University of Indiana Press, 1954.

Read, Herbert. *The True Voice of Feeling*. London: Faber & Faber, Ltd., 1952.

Richards, I. A. *The Philosophy of Rhetoric*. Oxford University Press, 1936.

Riding, Laura. *Contemporaries and Snobs*. London: Jonathan Cape, 1928.

Roberts, Michael. *T. E. Hulme*. London: Faber & Faber, Ltd., 1938.

Savage, D. S. *The Personal Principle*. London: Routledge, 1944.

Stallman, Robert Wooster. "The New Criticism and the Southern Critics," in Allen Tate, ed. *A Southern Vanguard*, pp. 28–51. New York: Prentice-Hall, 1947.

Tate, Allen. "Poetry and the Absolute," *Sewanee Review*, XXXV (January 1927), 41–52.

Wecter, Dixon. "Hulme and the Tragic View," *Southern Review*, V (1939), 141–152.

NOTE. References to material that is primarily biographical will be found on p. ix, footnote 4. There is also a biographical sketch in Michael Roberts' *T. E. Hulme*.

INDEX

227

A NOTE ABOUT THE EDITOR

SAM HYNES was born in Chicago, Illinois, in 1924, and has studied at the University of Minnesota (B.A., 1947) and Columbia University (M.A., 1948; Ph.D., 1956). Mr. Hynes, who was a Fulbright Fellow in 1953-1954 and a Guggenheim Fellow in 1959-60, is now Associate Professor of English at Swarthmore College. He is the author of *The Pattern of Hardy's Poetry* (1961).

PB-0005924-SB
507-16